D1645940

SACRED SPACE

The Prayer Book 2020

from the website www.sacredspace.ie

Prayer from the Irish Jesuits

Messenger Publications,
37 Lower Leeson Street, Dublin D02 W938
www.messenger.ie

Published under arrangement with Loyola Press, Chicago, IL, USA.

Cover art credit: Liam O'Connell SJ

Printed by Hussar Books

ISBN: 978 1 78812 093 7

Contents

Sacred Space Prayer

Bless all who worship you, almighty God,
from the rising of the sun to its setting:
from your goodness enrich us,
by your love inspire us,
by your Spirit guide us,
by your power protect us,
in your mercy receive us,
now and always.

Preface

In 1999 an Irish Jesuit named Alan McGuckian had the simple—but at the time radical—idea of bringing daily prayer to the Internet. No one imagined that his experimental project would grow into a global community with volunteers translating the prayer experience into seventeen different languages.

Millions of people, from numerous Christian traditions, visit *www.sacredspace.ie* each year, and what they find is an invitation to step away from their busy routines for a few minutes each day to concentrate on what is really important in their lives. Sacred Space offers its visitors the opportunity to grow in prayerful awareness of their friendship with God.

Besides the daily prayer experience, Sacred Space also offers Living Space, with commentaries on the Scripture readings for each day's Catholic Mass. The Chapel of Intentions allows people to add their own prayers, while Pray with the Pope joins the community to the international Apostleship of Prayer. In addition, Sacred Space provides Lenten and Advent retreats, often in partnership with Pray as You Go, an audio prayer service from the British Jesuits.

The contents of this printed edition, first produced in 2004, are taken directly from our Internet site. Despite the increased use of Sacred Space on mobile devices, many people want a book they can hold and carry, and this book has proven especially helpful for prayer groups.

In 2014 the Irish Jesuits entered into an apostolic agreement with the Chicago-Detroit Jesuits, and Sacred Space now operates in partnership with Loyola Press.

I am delighted to bring you the *Sacred Space* book, and I pray that your prayer life will flourish with its help.

Yours in Christ,

Paul Brian Campbell, SJ

Introduction to *Sacred Space*, 2020

Saint Ignatius of Loyola, founder of the Society of Jesus, is famously known for wanting to find God in all things. *Is that even possible?* you might ask. He believed it was, but only as a gift from God and only as the fruit of our paying attention to our experience. Ignatius developed an optimistic spiritual practice that assumed the presence of God at every moment of our existence. While we tend to think of God's presence as a "sometimes thing," Ignatius came to believe that our perception of God's presence as a sometimes occurrence is a major spiritual hindrance. Ignatius believed that God is always creating this universe, always keeping it in existence, always working to bring about God's purpose in creation, and always trying to move us to join God in the great adventure of bringing about what Jesus called the kingdom of God.

In order to experience this ever-present God, we need to develop a regular spiritual practice, a practice Ignatius had learned from his experience as a relatively untutored layman. Ignatius began to teach people and to write down the spiritual practices that helped him move toward uniting himself with God's purposes and thus toward finding God in all things. *Spiritual Exercises* is Ignatius's manual for those who want to follow his example of helping others get in touch with our ever-present God. God wants a close personal relationship with each of us, and he wants each of us to join him in the great work of bringing about a world where peace and justice prevail. Over the almost five centuries since the time of Ignatius, Jesuits and many others have found through these spiritual practices the answer to their own deepest desires.

Over the centuries, the Spiritual Exercises have been adapted in many ways. Jesuits originally followed Ignatius's own practice of giving the Exercises to individuals for thirty days. But they also used the methods of prayer suggested in the Exercises in their preaching, missions, and talks to larger groups. Eventually, houses were set aside for the giving of the Exercises to individuals and large groups. One of the adaptations suggested by Ignatius himself was to make the Exercises in daily life under the direction of someone trained in giving them. In this format, an individual maintained his or her regular daily life and work but promised to devote time every day to the spiritual practices suggested by Ignatius and to see the spiritual director once a week. In the past fifty years, this adaptation has seen a worldwide resurgence and has touched many lives. It has also been used with groups to great advantage. In modern times, the giving of the Spiritual Exercises has become something of a cottage industry in many countries.

Enter the age of the Internet. Could this new tool be used to help large numbers of people move toward finding God in all things? The answer is a resounding *yes*! Many websites, in multiple languages, try to help people become more aware of God's presence in their lives, using practices stemming from the Spiritual Exercises. One example is the book you have in your hands. In 1999 the Irish Jesuits began offering daily prompts for prayer based on Ignatius's Exercises on the website Sacred Space (*www.sacredspace.ie*). The English edition was soon translated into other languages, and the site now features twenty-one languages that span the globe.

In my work as a spiritual director and in my travels, I have come across many, many people from various walks of life who use the daily prompts for prayer provided through Sacred Space. People find the site and the daily suggestions to be user-friendly, inviting, and—in keeping with Ignatian spirituality—optimistic. The suggestions help them pay attention to their experience, notice intimations of God's presence in that experience, and engage in honest conversations with God.

For each week, there is an overarching suggested theme and a method for spending time with God every day. One of the methods is to turn to the Scripture and reflections suggested for each day of the week. Each day's text is taken from the Gospel reading for Mass that day. Thus, someone who follows Sacred Space every day will, in the course of a year, work prayerfully through all four Gospels. No wonder that so many have been enthralled by this site!

In spite of the digital age, many of us still like the feel of a book in our hands. The book *Sacred Space*, which you now hold in your hands, was designed for the likes of us. I am very happy to introduce the book and even happier that Loyola Press, a Jesuit institution, is now the publisher. Ignatian spiritual practice has brought me closer to God, for which I am immensely grateful. Through Ignatius's spiritual practices I have experienced God's desire for my friendship, and I figure, if God wants *my* friendship, he wants *everyone's* friendship. If you take this book seriously and engage in the relationship with God that it suggests, you will, I'm sure, find as much joy in God's friendship as I have. Try it—you'll like it.

William A. Barry, SJ

How to Use This Book

During each week of the Liturgical year, begin by reading the section entitled "Something to think and pray about each day this week." Then proceed through "The Presence of God," "Freedom," and "Consciousness" steps to prepare yourself to hear the word of God in your heart. In the next step, "The Word," turn to the Scripture reading for each day of the week. Inspiration points are provided in case you need them. Then return to the "Conversation" and "Conclusion" steps. Use this process every day of the year.

December 1—December 7, 2019

Something to think and pray about each day this week:

In a way, it is we who have to make the Gospels meaningful, because their meaning is not meant to be contained in the covers of a book, however well read. The Scriptures function fully as revelation when we reveal the love of Christ in what we say and do. The Bible, without readers who love, is just a book on the shelf. . . .

The Scriptures testify to a love called for whether we're simply passing strangers on the sidewalk, living next to neighbors, attending to the needs of a friend, or involved in an ugly dispute with someone we passionately dislike. The span of time, whether seven seconds or seventy times or seven years, makes no difference. Love is eternal; it is unconstrained by time.

—Kyle C. Cupp, *Living by Faith, Dwelling in Doubt*

The Presence of God

"Be still, and know that I am God." Lord, your words lead us to the calmness and greatness of your presence.

Freedom

I am free. When I look at these words in writing, they seem to create in me a feeling of awe. Yes, a wonderful feeling of freedom. Thank you, God.

Consciousness

At this moment, Lord, I turn my thoughts to you.
I will leave aside my chores and preoccupations.
I will take rest and refreshment in your presence, Lord.

The Word

The word of God comes down to us through the Scriptures. May the Holy Spirit enlighten my mind and my heart to respond to the Gospel teachings. (Please turn to the Scripture on the following pages. Inspiration points are there, should you need them. When you are ready, return here to continue.)

Conversation

Begin to talk with Jesus about the Scripture you have just read. What part of it strikes a chord in you? Perhaps the words of a friend—or some story you have heard recently—will slowly rise to the surface of your consciousness. If so, does the story throw light on what the Scripture passage may be trying to say to you?

Conclusion

Glory be to the Father, and to the Son, and to the Holy Spirit,
As it was in the beginning, is now and ever shall be,
World without end. Amen.

Sunday 1st December
First Sunday of Advent
Matthew 24:37–44

For as the days of Noah were, so will be the coming of the Son of Man. For as in those days before the flood they were eating and drinking, marrying and giving in marriage, until the day Noah entered the ark, and they knew nothing until the flood came and swept them all away, so too will be the coming of the Son of Man. Then two will be in the field; one will be taken and one will be left. Two women will be grinding meal together; one will be taken and one will be left. Keep awake therefore, for you do not know on what day your Lord is coming. But understand this: if the owner of the house had known in what part of the night the thief was coming, he would have stayed awake and would not have let his house be broken into. Therefore you also must be ready, for the Son of Man is coming at an unexpected hour.

- As we begin our new church year in Advent, we are reminded that we are to be ready and looking forward to the Lord's appearance. This call can come upon us suddenly. However, a person who is watchful and full of hope will be quick to recognize the Lord when he appears. Even in day-to-day life, Jesus comes to us through people, situations, even our own prayer. Today, pray expecting to see him.

- Jesus desires our friendship when he calls us and offers his friendship. And this offer continues throughout life. How can you develop your friendship with Jesus here and now?

Monday 2nd December
Matthew 8:5–11

When Jesus entered Capernaum, a centurion came to him, appealing to him and saying, "Lord, my servant is lying at home paralyzed, in terrible distress." And he said to him, "I will come and cure him." The centurion answered, "Lord, I am not worthy to have you come under my roof; but only speak the word, and my servant will be healed. For I also am a man under authority, with soldiers under me; and I say to one, 'Go,' and he goes, and to another, 'Come,' and he comes, and to my slave, 'Do this,' and the slave does it." When Jesus heard him, he was amazed and said to those who followed him, "Truly I tell you, in no one in Israel have I found such faith. I tell you, many will come from east and west and will eat with Abraham and Isaac and Jacob in the kingdom of heaven."

- The centurion interceded with Jesus on behalf of his servant, not himself. Who do I want to intercede for today?

- "Lord, I am not worthy." Do I ever feel that way? Do I ever feel that I am getting more than I deserve? We live in a culture of entitlement, thinking we deserve to get everything on offer. How about me?

Tuesday 3rd December
Saint Francis Xavier, Priest
Luke 10:21–24

At that same hour Jesus rejoiced in the Holy Spirit and said, "I thank you, Father, Lord of heaven and earth, because you have hidden these things from the wise and the intelligent and have revealed them to infants; yes, Father, for such was your gracious will. All things have been handed over to me by my Father; and no one knows who the Son is except the Father, or who the Father is except the Son and anyone to whom the Son chooses to reveal him." Then turning to the disciples, Jesus said to them privately, "Blessed are the eyes that see what you see! For I tell you that many prophets and kings desired to see what you see, but did not see it, and to hear what you hear, but did not hear it."

- Christian joy is a deep reality. It is different from being lighthearted or in a good mood. Its fundamental constituent is peace. As in Jesus, so in us, it comes from the Holy Spirit. What is my own experience today?

- Children trust their parents and, because of that trust, listen to what their parents say. Jesus trusted and listened to the Father. Can I imitate that trust in my prayer today?

Wednesday 4th December
Matthew 15:29–37

After Jesus had left that place, he passed along the Sea of Galilee, and he went up the mountain, where he sat down. Great crowds came to him, bringing with them the lame, the maimed, the blind, the mute, and many others. They put them at his feet, and he cured them, so that the crowd was amazed when they saw the mute speaking, the maimed whole, the lame walking, and the blind seeing. And they praised the God of Israel. Then Jesus called his disciples to him and said, "I have compassion for the crowd, because they have been with me now for three days and have nothing to eat; and I do not want to send them away hungry, for they might faint on the way." The disciples said to him, "Where are we to get enough bread in the desert to feed so great a crowd?" Jesus asked them, "How many loaves have you?" They said, "Seven, and a few small fish." Then ordering the crowd to sit down on the ground, he took the seven loaves and the fish; and after giving thanks he broke them and gave them to the disciples, and the disciples gave them to the crowds. And all of them ate and were filled; and they took up the broken pieces left over, seven baskets full.

- The people who came to Jesus were broken people. This is still true. It is why I am here, listening to him. Where is my life broken; where do I need his healing power? It is important to get in touch with that place in my life.

- Jesus feeds us well with the miraculous food, which is his Word. There is more than enough to satisfy our hunger completely. We listen and chew and digest, and we feel the peace it brings.

Thursday 5th December
Matthew 7:21, 24–27

"Not everyone who says to me, 'Lord, Lord,' will enter the kingdom of heaven, but only the one who does the will of my Father in heaven. . . . Everyone then who hears these words of mine and acts on them will be like a wise man who built his house on rock. The rain fell, the floods came, and the winds blew and beat on that house, but it did not fall, because it had been founded on rock. And everyone who hears these words of mine and does not act on them will be like a foolish man who built his house on sand. The rain fell, and the floods came, and the winds blew and beat against that house, and it fell—and great was its fall!"

- We establish our belief by acting on it. Jesus knew that only those who followed God through action would build for their own faith a strong foundation. What action will I take today to live out my faith and help it grow stronger?

- Lord, Francis Xavier experienced the rains of misfortune and floods of disaster as he worked to spread your word. When I am threatened by disasters that seek to smother me and overwhelm my faith in you, keep me firm—keep me rooted in you, my rock!

Friday 6th December
Matthew 9:27–31

As Jesus went on from there, two blind men followed him, crying loudly, "Have mercy on us, Son of David!" When he entered the house, the blind men came to him; and Jesus said to them, "Do you believe that I am able to do this?" They said to him, "Yes, Lord." Then he touched their eyes and said, "According to your faith let it be done to you." And their eyes were opened. Then Jesus sternly ordered them, "See that no one knows of this." But they went away and spread the news about him throughout that district.

- The blind men were not afraid to be heard—they cried out for you loudly. May I be unafraid to voice my needs, whether in private prayer to you, Lord, or within my faith community when I need your assistance through their gifts.
- Lord, I name for you a specific need today; I know you are able to help me. Please touch my life where it needs restoration.

Saturday 7th December
Saint Ambrose, Bishop and Doctor of the Church
Matthew 9:35—10:1, 5a, 6–8

Then Jesus went about all the cities and villages, teaching in their synagogues, and proclaiming the Good News of the kingdom, and curing every disease and every sickness. When he saw the crowds, he had compassion for them, because they were harassed and helpless, like sheep without a shepherd. Then he said to his disciples, "The harvest is plentiful, but the laborers are few; therefore ask the Lord of the harvest to send out laborers into his harvest." Then Jesus summoned his twelve disciples and gave them authority over unclean spirits, to cast them out, and to cure every disease and every sickness. . . . These twelve Jesus sent out with the following instructions: . . . "Go . . . to the lost sheep of the house of Israel. As you go, proclaim the Good News, 'The kingdom of heaven has come near.' Cure the sick, raise the dead, cleanse the lepers, cast out demons. You received without payment; give without payment."

- Jesus had compassion on the people who were harassed and helpless. What about me? Do I feel the need of his help in some part of my life?

- He tells us to pray to send laborers into his harvest. So, let's do it! Am I free to help the mission in some way?

The Second Week of Advent
December 8—December 14, 2019

Something to think and pray about each day this week:

What I know is that God makes stories. In his genius and mercy, he takes our triumphs and our failures and weaves beautiful tapestries that are full of irony. The reverse of the fabric may look messy with its tangled threads—the events of our lives—and maybe this is the side we dwell on when we doubt. But the right side of the tapestry displays a magnificent story, and this is the side that God sees.

—Pope Francis and Friends, *Sharing the Wisdom of Time*

The Presence of God

"Come to me, all you who are weary and are carrying heavy burdens, and I will give you rest." Here I am, Lord. I come to seek your presence. I long for your healing power.

Freedom

"In these days, God taught me as a schoolteacher teaches a pupil" (Saint Ignatius).

I remind myself that there are things God has to teach me yet, and I ask for the grace to hear those things and let them change me.

Consciousness

Help me, Lord, to be more conscious of your presence. Teach me to recognize your presence in others.

Fill my heart with gratitude for the times your love has been shown to me through the care of others.

The Word

God speaks to each of us individually. I listen attentively to hear what he is saying to me. Read the text a few times, then listen. (Please turn to the Scripture on the following pages. Inspiration points are there, should you need them. When you are ready, return here to continue.)

Conversation

Conversation requires talking and listening.

As I talk to Jesus, may I also learn to be still and listen.

I picture the gentleness in his eyes and the smile full of love as he gazes on me.

I can be totally honest with Jesus as I tell him of my worries and my cares. I will open my heart to him as I tell him of my fears and my doubts.

I will ask him to help me place myself fully in his care and to abandon myself to him, knowing that he always wants what is best for me.

Conclusion

I thank God for these moments we have spent together and for any insights I have been given concerning the text.

Sunday 8th December
Second Sunday of Advent
Matthew 3:1–12

In those days John the Baptist appeared in the wilderness of Judea, proclaiming, "Repent, for the kingdom of heaven has come near." This is the one of whom the prophet Isaiah spoke when he said, "The voice of one crying out in the wilderness: Prepare the way of the Lord, make his paths straight." Now John wore clothing of camel's hair with a leather belt around his waist, and his food was locusts and wild honey. Then the people of Jerusalem and all Judea were going out to him, and all the region along the Jordan, and they were baptized by him in the river Jordan, confessing their sins. But when he saw many Pharisees and Sadducees coming for baptism, he said to them, "You brood of vipers! Who warned you to flee from the wrath to come? Bear fruit worthy of repentance. Do not presume to say to yourselves, 'We have Abraham as our ancestor'; for I tell you, God is able from these stones to raise up children to Abraham. Even now the ax is lying at the root of the trees; every tree therefore that does not bear good fruit is cut down and thrown into the fire. I baptize you with water for repentance, but one who is more powerful than I is coming after me; I am not worthy to carry his sandals. He will baptize you with the Holy Spirit and fire. His winnowing fork is in his hand, and he will clear his threshing floor and will gather his wheat into the granary; but the chaff he will burn with unquenchable fire."

- The Chosen People lived in expectation. They were waiting for the day when God's envoy or agent would appear on earth and set the affairs of the world to rights—vindicating those "just ones" who had remained faithful to the Lord and to his message conveyed by the prophets. This final Messiah would represent the Lord in person. It would be the Coming of the Lord, the Day of the Lord, the End Time. The people were to purify themselves in readiness. One kind of purification was the cleansing by water: baptism. During these days of Advent, I can live in expectation of the Christ child's coming and meditate on my own baptism.

- John the Baptist warns that a deeper purification is to come, at the hands of the "one . . . coming after me": purification by fire. We remember what had been said long before—that no human can look on the face of God and live: "you cannot see my face; for no one shall see me and live" (Exodus 33:20). The brightness and holiness of God could burn up any impurity in sight. People are to put their lives in order while there is still time and not simply rely on the promise to Abraham or on fidelity to any man-made set of laws. In our own lives, we can never know when, in the plan of God, huge changes may be in the offing.

Monday 9th December
The Immaculate Conception of the Blessed Virgin Mary
Luke 1:26–38

In the sixth month the angel Gabriel was sent by God to a town in Galilee called Nazareth, to a virgin engaged to a man whose name was Joseph, of the house of David. The virgin's name was Mary. And he came to her and said, "Greetings, favored one! The Lord is with you." But she was much perplexed by his words and pondered what sort of greeting this might be. The angel said to her, "Do not be afraid, Mary, for you have found favor with God. And now, you will conceive in your womb and bear a son, and you will name him Jesus. He will be great, and will be called the Son of the Most High, and the Lord God will give to him the throne of his ancestor David. He will reign over the house of Jacob forever, and of his kingdom there will be no end." Mary said to the angel, "How can this be, since I am a virgin?" The angel said to her, "The Holy Spirit will come upon you, and the power of the Most High will overshadow you; therefore the child to be born will be holy; he will be called Son of God. And now, your relative Elizabeth in her old age has also conceived a son; and this is the sixth month for her who was said to be barren. For nothing will be impossible with God." Then Mary said, "Here am I, the servant of the Lord; let it be with me according to your word." Then the angel departed from her.

• Scripture leaves us in no doubt about God being a long-range planner; he can determine a whole series of events to come to maturity in his own good time. In fact, he has done this for the benefit of us all, planning, even before the beginning of the world, for us to become sisters and brothers of Jesus. Today, I thank God for planning to bring me into the family.

- For the grand plan to come to completion, the cooperation of Mary was needed. How is my cooperation needed in what God is doing in my community today? Where do I see God's invitation to me?

Tuesday 10th December
Matthew 18:12–14

"What do you think? If a shepherd has a hundred sheep, and one of them has gone astray, does he not leave the ninety-nine on the mountains and go in search of the one that went astray? And if he finds it, truly I tell you, he rejoices over it more than over the ninety-nine that never went astray. So it is not the will of your Father in heaven that one of these little ones should be lost."

- In God's view, there are no dispensable people—no people God is willing to lose, even with all the people who are already in the kingdom. Who are the people—or the type of people—I tend not to think about much? Who are the people I would not miss if they were out of the picture? Lord, develop in me a compassionate heart.

- Jesus speaks of the sheep going astray. It's in the sheep's nature to get lost without a shepherd to guide them. So, when Jesus refers to us going astray, he speaks of our tendency to go the wrong way without guidance. We need the shepherd, and the shepherd cares for us willingly. Thank you, Lord, for understanding my struggles and wrong turns, my need for help. I receive your help with thanksgiving.

Wednesday 11th December
Matthew 11:28–30

[Jesus said,] "Come to me, all you that are weary and are carrying heavy burdens, and I will give you rest. Take my yoke upon you, and learn from me; for I am gentle and humble in heart, and you will find rest for your souls. For my yoke is easy, and my burden is light."

- The reign of the coming savior king will bring not only security and welcome to any persons who feel lost and abandoned. Jesus' kingdom also promises relief and support to those who simply feel that life has become too much for them. Jesus understands each of us better than we understand ourselves. His heart, gentle and humble, goes out to us. Name, in this prayer time, what relief or support you need today.

- One day Jesus will invite his band of first followers to come apart to a quiet place and to rest a while. They will feel at ease in his presence and be rejuvenated. This rest—a sense of having been accepted—banishes weariness and renews our energy. No surprise here: the Lord happens to be the energy center of the universe, the creator—the one who names the stars. Rely on that energy for yourself today.

Thursday 12th December
Our Lady of Guadalupe
Luke 1:26–38

In the sixth month the angel Gabriel was sent by God to a town in Galilee called Nazareth, to a virgin engaged to a man whose name was Joseph, of the house of David. The virgin's name was Mary. And he came to her and said, "Greetings, favored one! The Lord is with you." But she was much perplexed by his words and pondered what sort of greeting this might be. The angel said to her, "Do not be afraid, Mary, for you have found favor with God. And now, you will conceive in your womb and bear a son, and you will name him Jesus. He will be great, and will be called the Son of the Most High, and the Lord God will give to him the throne of his ancestor David. He will reign over the house of Jacob forever, and of his kingdom there will be no end." Mary said to the angel, "How can this be, since I am a virgin?" The angel said to her, "The Holy Spirit will come upon you, and the power of the Most High will overshadow you; therefore the child to be born will be holy; he will be called Son of God. And now, your relative Elizabeth in her old age has also conceived a son; and this is the sixth month for her who was said to be barren. For nothing will be impossible with God." Then Mary said, "Here am I, the servant of the Lord; let it be with me according to your word." Then the angel departed from her.

- How does Mary react in a crisis? She hears God's messenger but wonders, Can it be true? And how does it square with my virginity? She knows that she is free to say "Yes" or "No," and her response is from a full heart.

- Lord, this is not an easy prayer to make. You prayed it yourself in Gethsemane in a sweat of blood: "Not my will but yours be done." Help me make it the pattern of my life. What issues of surrender and trust does it raise for me?

Friday 13th December
Saint Lucy, Virgin and Martyr
Matthew 11:16–19

Jesus spoke to the crowds, "But to what will I compare this generation? It is like children sitting in the marketplaces and calling to one another, 'We played the flute for you, and you did not dance; we wailed, and you did not mourn.' For John came neither eating nor drinking, and they say, 'He has a demon'; the Son of Man came eating and drinking, and they say, 'Look, a glutton and a drunkard, a friend of tax collectors and sinners!' Yet wisdom is vindicated by her deeds."

- God has always wanted to shower his people with gifts. But when the offer was made (through the mouth of his messengers, the prophets), the people often turned their backs. It seemed that they always wanted something different, and they tended to complain to God more than give thanks. This pattern is present throughout the Old Testament. What is my history of response to God's gifts?

- Jesus points out that people are never satisfied; they nearly always find something wrong with the person or the message presented to them. They faulted John the Baptist for being so strange and austere; they faulted Jesus for eating and drinking with all sorts of people. Can I think of anyone whose message I've rejected because he or she did not fit my idea of a person of God?

Saturday 14th December
Saint John of the Cross, Priest and Doctor of the Church
Matthew 17:9a, 10–13

As they were coming down the mountain, Jesus ordered them, "Tell no one about the vision until after the Son of Man has been raised from the dead." . . . And the disciples asked him, "Why, then, do the scribes say that Elijah must come first?" He replied, "Elijah is indeed coming and will restore all things; but I tell you that Elijah has already come, and they did not recognize him, but they did to him whatever they pleased. So also the Son of Man is about to suffer at their hands." Then the disciples understood that he was speaking to them about John the Baptist.

- The Jewish faith looked forward to the "last days," or end times when the Lord would come in glory and finally wrap up the affairs of this world. And a conviction had arisen that the end times would be signaled by a forerunner: the figure of the larger-than-life prophet Elijah would make a renewed appearance. There is continuity between the prophets of old and the coming of Jesus. Why not revisit some Old Testament writing of the prophets, such as Isaiah or Jeremiah?

- Jesus reveals that John the Baptist is the forerunner. Some of Jesus' disciples had first followed John—until John pointed them to Jesus. God often uses others to point us to Jesus. Who were "forerunners" for me?

December 15—December 21, 2019

Something to think and pray about each day this week:

Preparation may be on your mind as Christmas approaches. Gifts, chores, baking, and travel all remind us of this theme. As we prepare our homes and our menus, are we also preparing our hearts to encounter Christ, however we may meet him? Pause today and look for our ever-present Savior and friend.

—Margaret Felice, *2019: A Book of Grace-Filled Days*

The Presence of God

"I am standing at the door, knocking," says the Lord. What a wonderful privilege that the Lord of all creation desires to come to me. I welcome his presence.

Freedom

Leave me here freely all alone. / In cell where never sunlight shone / should no one ever speak to me. / This golden silence makes me free.

—Part of a poem written by a prisoner at
Dachau concentration camp

Consciousness

How am I really feeling? Lighthearted? Heavy-hearted? I may be very much at peace, happy to be here. Equally, I may be frustrated, worried, or angry.

I acknowledge how I really am. It is the real me whom the Lord loves.

The Word

I take my time to read the word of God slowly, a few times, allowing myself to dwell on anything that strikes me. (Please turn to the Scripture on the following pages. Inspiration points are there, should you need them. When you are ready, return here to continue.)

Conversation

Do I notice myself reacting as I pray with the word of God? Do I feel challenged, comforted, angry? Imagining Jesus sitting or standing by me, I speak out my feelings, as one trusted friend to another.

Conclusion

Glory be to the Father, and to the Son, and to the Holy Spirit,
As it was in the beginning, is now and ever shall be,
World without end. Amen.

Sunday 15th December
Third Sunday of Advent
Matthew 11:2–11

When John heard in prison what the Messiah was doing, he sent word by his disciples and said to him, "Are you the one who is to come, or are we to wait for another?" Jesus answered them, "Go and tell John what you hear and see: the blind receive their sight, the lame walk, the lepers are cleansed, the deaf hear, the dead are raised, and the poor have Good News brought to them. And blessed is anyone who takes no offence at me." As they went away, Jesus began to speak to the crowds about John: "What did you go out into the wilderness to look at? A reed shaken by the wind? What then did you go out to see? Someone dressed in soft robes? Look, those who wear soft robes are in royal palaces. What then did you go out to see? A prophet? Yes, I tell you, and more than a prophet. This is the one about whom it is written, 'See, I am sending my messenger ahead of you, who will prepare your way before you.' Truly I tell you, among those born of women no one has arisen greater than John the Baptist; yet the least in the kingdom of heaven is greater than he.

• Two strands run through the Scriptures regarding people's expectations about the Messiah. In one strand the dominant idea is that the Messiah will focus on chastisement and correction—where corruption has grown, he will lay an ax to the root of the tree, or he will come armed with a winnowing fan to separate the noxious elements from the good. Although not imposing a regime of penance as such, John the Baptist insisted on high moral standards, and so he might seem to veer toward the stricter view.

• John is unsure, apparently, about the approach taken by Jesus, so he is making inquiries. And Jesus' answer recalls that other strand, where the dominant idea is building up people wherever they are in need of healing. All the miracles listed here are in line with the prophetic vision of Isaiah, in which strength and salvation are brought to the people. What is my dominant view of the Messiah?

Monday 16th December
Matthew 21:23–27

When Jesus entered the temple, the chief priests and the elders of the people came to him as he was teaching, and said, "By what authority are you doing these things, and who gave you this authority?" Jesus said to them, "I will also ask you one question; if you tell me the answer, then I will also tell you by what authority I do these things. Did the baptism of John come from heaven, or was it of human origin?" And they argued with one another, "If we say, 'From heaven,' he will say to us, 'Why then did you not believe him?' But if we say, 'Of human origin,' we are afraid of the crowd; for all regard John as a prophet." So they answered Jesus, "We do not know." And he said to them, "Neither will I tell you by what authority I am doing these things."

- In Jewish circles, if someone claimed power and authority, he would be asked about the warranty for his claim: Did he belong to the priestly tribe of Levi? Did his claim have the backing of the tradition of the ancestors? Could he prove his claim through the direct intervention of God, such as miracle? The chief priests and elders were extremely concerned about where Jesus got his authority. How do I see authority in my life of faith? What have I been taught to recognize as God's authority?

- This exchange between Jesus and the elders and chief priests indirectly bolsters the stature of John the Baptist. Most of Jesus' questioners had not accepted John's teaching even though it had caused a dramatic response of repentance in many people of the region. The elders are afraid to choose one way or another regarding John—they cannot deny his impact, yet he—as now, with Jesus—seems to be acting outside their approved sources of authority. Lord Jesus, help me discern true authority in my life, authority that comes from you.

Tuesday 17th December
Matthew 1:1–17

An account of the genealogy of Jesus the Messiah, the son of David, the son of Abraham. Abraham was the father of Isaac, and Isaac the father of Jacob, and Jacob the father of Judah and his brothers, and Judah the father of Perez and Zerah by Tamar, and Perez the father of Hezron, and Hezron the father of Aram, and Aram the father of Aminadab, and Aminadab the father of Nahshon, and Nahshon the father of Salmon, and Salmon the father of Boaz by Rahab, and Boaz the father of Obed by Ruth, and Obed the father of Jesse, and Jesse the father of King David. And David was the father of Solomon by the wife of Uriah, and Solomon the father of Rehoboam, and Rehoboam the father of Abijah, and Abijah the father of Asaph, and Asaph the father of Jehoshaphat, and Jehoshaphat the father of Joram, and Joram the father of Uzziah, and Uzziah the father of Jotham, and Jotham the father of Ahaz, and Ahaz the father of Hezekiah, and Hezekiah the father of Manasseh, and Manasseh the father of Amos, and Amos the father of Josiah, and Josiah the father of Jechoniah and his brothers, at the time of the deportation to Babylon. And after the deportation to Babylon: Jechoniah was the father of Salathiel, and Salathiel the father of Zerubbabel, and Zerubbabel the father of Abiud, and Abiud the father of Eliakim, and Eliakim the father of Azor, and Azor the father of Zadok, and Zadok the father of Achim, and Achim the father of Eliud, and Eliud the father of Eleazar, and Eleazar the father of Matthan, and Matthan the father of Jacob, and Jacob the father of Joseph the husband of Mary, of whom Jesus was born, who is called the Messiah. So all the generations from Abraham to David are fourteen generations; and from David to the deportation to Babylon, fourteen generations; and from the deportation to Babylon to the Messiah, fourteen generations.

- In the eight days of the immediate run up to Christmas, the focus is on the characters who were alive when Jesus came, beginning here with Mary and Joseph, cast as the end-product, as it were, of generation after generation. God had long begun the groundwork for the coming of his Son, preparing a people who would be ready to receive him when he arrived. Each of us, in our own way, has been prepared for Jesus' arrival.

- The chronicle here presents the grand span of God's plan, akin to a video clip of the main developments, run through at top speed. The epochs or eras or ages or eons belonging to the named individuals are grouped in doubles of seven (a pure number long used to indicate the sacred). Included in the lineup are various "extras" to underline the universalism of God's plan: women, foreigners, sinners. This is a meditation on the slow-growth miracle of God's providence: sowing seeds that would one day come to maturity. We, too, can always do a parallel meditation on the milestones of salvation history occurring in our own lives.

Wednesday 18th December
Matthew 1:18–25

Now the birth of Jesus the Messiah took place in this way. When his mother Mary had been engaged to Joseph, but before they lived together, she was found to be with child from the Holy Spirit. Her husband Joseph, being a righteous man and unwilling to expose her to public disgrace, planned to dismiss her quietly. But just when he had resolved to do this, an angel of the Lord appeared to him in a dream and said, "Joseph, son of David, do not be afraid to take Mary as your wife, for the child conceived in her is from the Holy Spirit. She will bear a son, and you are to name him Jesus, for he will save his people from their sins." All this took place to fulfill what had been spoken by the Lord through the prophet: "Look, the virgin shall conceive and bear a son, and they shall name him Emmanuel," which means, 'God is with us.'" When Joseph awoke from sleep, he did as the angel of the Lord commanded him; he took her as his wife, but had no marital relations with her until she had borne a son; and he named him Jesus.

- Saint Joseph had a very important part in the birth of Christ. Our salvation depends on Mary's obedience to the will of God. It also depends on Joseph's. In the continuing story of Jesus, through the Church, our obedience is crucial, too.

- It all happened to fulfill what the prophets had foretold. God knows everything, plans everything. It is all for our good, and we can accept it all in peace.

Thursday 19th December
Luke 1:5–25

In the days of King Herod of Judea, there was a priest named Zechariah, who belonged to the priestly order of Abijah. His wife was a descendant of Aaron, and her name was Elizabeth. Both of them were righteous before God, living blamelessly according to all the commandments and regulations of the Lord. But they had no children, because Elizabeth was barren, and both were getting on in years. Once when he was serving as priest before God and his section was on duty, he was chosen by lot, according to the custom of the priesthood, to enter the sanctuary of the Lord and offer incense. Now at the time of the incense offering, the whole assembly of the people was praying outside. Then there appeared to him an angel of the Lord, standing at the right side of the altar of incense. When Zechariah saw him, he was terrified; and fear overwhelmed him. But the angel said to him, "Do not be afraid, Zechariah, for your prayer has been heard. Your wife Elizabeth will bear you a son, and you will name him John. You will have joy and gladness, and many will rejoice at his birth, for he will be great in the sight of the Lord. He must never drink wine or strong drink; even before his birth he will be filled with the Holy Spirit. He will turn many of the people of Israel to the Lord their God. With the spirit and power of Elijah he will go before him, to turn the hearts of parents to their children, and the disobedient to the wisdom of the righteous, to make ready a people prepared for the Lord." Zechariah said to the angel, "How will I know that this is so? For I am an old man, and my wife is getting on in years." The angel replied, "I am Gabriel. I stand in the presence of God, and I have been sent to speak to you and to bring you this Good News. But now, because you did not believe my words, which will be fulfilled in their time, you will become mute, unable to speak, until the day these things occur." Meanwhile the people were waiting for Zechariah, and wondered at his delay in the sanctuary. When he did come out, he could not speak to them, and they realized that he had seen a vision in the sanctuary. He kept motioning to them and remained unable to speak. When his time of service was ended, he went to his home. After those days his wife Elizabeth conceived, and for five months she remained in seclusion. She said, "This is what the Lord has done for me when he looked favorably on me and took away the disgrace I have endured among my people."

- Zechariah and Elizabeth belonged among the Lord's own "little ones" of the earth, among the God-fearing masses. Each of them, judged by the depth of their belief, could be rated as being one in a thousand, while, to the external view, each was unknown and just like a thousand others. In a similar way, you and I may appear to be anonymous faces in a vast crowd; yet, God is speaking to us and has something for us to do. What has God said to me lately?

- Their child was being sent to prepare the way, in a role akin to that always expected of the prophet Elijah, for God's final intervention in the last days of this age. Even the name ("God has shown favor") being invoked for the child spoke of God's intention. Certainly, God's ways are not our ways, and the very people who have always tried to remain fully loyal to the Lord are sometimes going to find themselves called to even deeper faith—involving an ever more privileged closeness to God.

Friday 20th December
Luke 1:26–38

In the sixth month the angel Gabriel was sent by God to a town in Galilee called Nazareth, to a virgin engaged to a man whose name was Joseph, of the house of David. The virgin's name was Mary. And he came to her and said, "Greetings, favored one! The Lord is with you." But she was much perplexed by his words and pondered what sort of greeting this might be. The angel said to her, "Do not be afraid, Mary, for you have found favor with God. And now, you will conceive in your womb and bear a son, and you will name him Jesus. He will be great, and will be called the Son of the Most High, and the Lord God will give to him the throne of his ancestor David. He will reign over the house of Jacob forever, and of his kingdom there will be no end." Mary said to the angel, "How can this be, since I am a virgin?" The angel said to her, "The Holy Spirit will come upon you, and the power of the Most High will overshadow you; therefore the child to be born will be holy; he will be called Son of God. And now, your relative Elizabeth in her old age has also conceived a son; and this is the sixth month for her who was said to be barren. For nothing will be impossible with God." Then Mary said, "Here am I, the servant of the Lord; let it be with me according to your word." Then the angel departed from her.

- See how specific the details are in this account. Gabriel was sent to a certain town and a certain person. The angel had a certain message for Mary. If I consider that God also seeks me specifically, for specific purposes, how do I feel myself responding to that? Excited? Afraid? Hesitant?

- Mary's life was intricately connected with the larger community. Her son's life would enrich and also complicate that connection. Today I meditate on how my life—and my responses to God—have an impact on others.

Saturday 21st December
Luke 1:39–45

In those days Mary set out and went with haste to a Judean town in the hill country, where she entered the house of Zechariah and greeted Elizabeth. When Elizabeth heard Mary's greeting, the child leaped in her womb. And Elizabeth was filled with the Holy Spirit and exclaimed with a loud cry, "Blessed are you among women, and blessed is the fruit of your womb. And why has this happened to me, that the mother of my Lord comes to me? For as soon as I heard the sound of your greeting, the child in my womb leaped for joy. And blessed is she who believed that there would be a fulfillment of what was spoken to her by the Lord."

- Birth, the gift of life from God, was always sacred to the people of Israel; and the mothers had a special place through sacred history, as the bearers of life. Mary and Elizabeth outdo one another in giving thanks. But this particular case is special, unique. Jesus, the child Mary is carrying, is recognized by the child in Elizabeth's womb. John leaps in recognition of the one whom both mothers revere as Lord (John himself being of miraculous origin from an elderly mother). Imagine yourself in this scene, watching the two women greet each other. How does it feel to witness this interaction and to understand the great secrets Mary and Elizabeth carry?

- Beyond what is happening to each mother, earthshaking events are beginning. The Lord (long awaited) has finally come to visit his people, to be victorious over enemies, to exult with joy over those who are his own. What praise can you compose and offer to God for this marvelous salvation?

The Fourth Week of Advent/Christmas
December 22—December 28, 2019

Something to think and pray about each day this week:

God never stops coming to us. No matter how receptive we are, God is always ready with the graces that will free us. For many, Christmas can be a difficult season in which family tensions or other hardships bubble up. If there is something holding you back from the spirit of Christmas, know that God is there, ready to free you of that stress, sadness, or worry.

—Margaret Felice, *2019: A Book of Grace-Filled Days*

The Presence of God

"Be still, and know that I am God!" Lord, may your spirit guide me to seek your loving presence more and more for it is there I find rest and refreshment from this busy world.

Freedom

By God's grace I was born to live in freedom. Free to enjoy the pleasures he created for me. Dear Lord, grant that I may live as you intended, with complete confidence in your loving care.

Consciousness

How am I today?
Where am I with God? With others?
Do I have something to be grateful for? Then I give thanks.
Is there something I am sorry for? Then I ask forgiveness.

The Word

God speaks to each of us individually. I need to listen, to hear what he is saying to me. Read the text a few times, then listen. (Please turn to the Scripture on the following pages. Inspiration points are there, should you need them. When you are ready, return here to continue.)

Conversation

How has God's word moved me? Has it left me cold?
Has it consoled me or moved me to act in a new way?
I imagine Jesus standing or sitting beside me.
I turn and share my feelings with him.

Conclusion

I thank God for these moments we have spent together and for any insights I have been given concerning the text.

Sunday 22nd December
Fourth Sunday of Advent
Matthew 1:18–24

Now the birth of Jesus the Messiah took place in this way. When his mother Mary had been engaged to Joseph, but before they lived together, she was found to be with child from the Holy Spirit. Her husband Joseph, being a righteous man and unwilling to expose her to public disgrace, planned to dismiss her quietly. But just when he had resolved to do this, an angel of the Lord appeared to him in a dream and said, "Joseph, son of David, do not be afraid to take Mary as your wife, for the child conceived in her is from the Holy Spirit. She will bear a son, and you are to name him Jesus, for he will save his people from their sins." All this took place to fulfill what had been spoken by the Lord through the prophet: "Look, the virgin shall conceive and bear a son, and they shall name him Emmanuel," which means, "God is with us." When Joseph awoke from sleep, he did as the angel of the Lord commanded him; he took her as his wife.

• Hearing the words to Joseph about Mary's child, we would first think of a special child, in the sense of "made over" to the Lord, as Samuel or Samson was. But reading between the lines, taking into account the scriptural allusions, we find that this child is much more. His coming ushers in a whole new (although promised) heaven- and earth-shaking epoch in the relationship between God and his people. The child will save his people from their sins—but not only from individual sins. They will be saved from the sins of the people, which includes the oppression into which their sins have brought them.

• It's the same for us: we are saved from individual sins but also from sins that are communal and systemic. I consider the communal sins in my city and my country and thank God today for our salvation brought through Jesus.

Monday 23rd December
Luke 1:57–66

Now the time came for Elizabeth to give birth, and she bore a son. Her neighbors and relatives heard that the Lord had shown his great mercy to her, and they rejoiced with her. On the eighth day they came to circumcise the child, and they were going to name him Zechariah after his father. But his mother said, "No; he is to be called John." They said to her, "None of your relatives has this name." Then they began motioning to his father to find out what name he wanted to give him. He asked for a writing tablet and wrote, "His name is John." And all of them were amazed. Immediately his mouth was opened and his tongue freed, and he began to speak, praising God. Fear came over all their neighbors, and all these things were talked about throughout the entire hill country of Judea. All who heard them pondered them and said, "What then will this child become?" For, indeed, the hand of the Lord was with him.

- The name (John) of this child-to-come tells us, in its original meaning, that God has shown special favor. The Lord is shaping a new future for humanity, and the newborn's call will be to announce to all that this is just what is happening. Zechariah and Elizabeth have been blessed with this new life in their declining years. And through the miracle of the unexpected birth and of the binding and loosing of Zechariah's tongue, the people realize that God is taking a very direct hand in events. They know that they are on the threshold of mystery.

- Each and every new life arriving is a reason for rejoicing. Any new life (including one's own) is sent to earth by God for some purpose unique to itself—and always merits deep thankfulness and celebration.

Tuesday 24th December

Luke 1:67–79

Then his father Zechariah was filled with the Holy Spirit and spoke this prophecy: "Blessed be the Lord God of Israel, for he has looked favorably on his people and redeemed them. He has raised up a mighty savior for us in the house of his servant David, as he spoke through the mouth of his holy prophets from of old, that we would be saved from our enemies and from the hand of all who hate us. Thus he has shown the mercy promised to our ancestors, and has remembered his holy covenant, the oath that he swore to our ancestor Abraham, to grant us that we, being rescued from the hands of our enemies, might serve him without fear, in holiness and righteousness before him all our days. And you, child, will be called the prophet of the Most High; for you will go before the Lord to prepare his ways, to give knowledge of salvation to his people by the forgiveness of their sins. By the tender mercy of our God, the dawn from on high will break upon us, to give light to those who sit in darkness and in the shadow of death, to guide our feet into the way of peace."

- Having long steeped himself in the ancient prophecies, Zechariah is sharp enough to know that things would not be taking such a sudden, miraculous turn unless God's people were on the brink of a new age. This has to be another age of peace, prosperity, and honor, like that one promised before, when King David proved strong enough to repel all enemies. Now must be the cusp of a new dawn, of the sunburst of God's power, when the Lord from on high will make himself intimately present to his people, dispelling the darkness of sin and death.

- And the herald to announce God's approach will be none other than this newborn child, John. We might all pray that, in our own lives, we would be as clear-sighted as Zechariah in reading the signs of the times—in picking up the hints of what God has in store for us.

Wednesday 25th December
The Nativity of the Lord
Luke 2:15–20

When the angels had left them and gone into heaven, the shepherds said to one another, "Let us go now to Bethlehem and see this thing that has taken place, which the Lord has made known to us." So they went with haste and found Mary and Joseph, and the child lying in the manger. When they saw this, they made known what had been told them about this child; and all who heard it were amazed at what the shepherds told them. But Mary treasured all these words and pondered them in her heart. The shepherds returned, glorifying and praising God for all they had heard and seen, as it had been told them.

- We are told that because of a decree from the Emperor in Rome, Mary and Joseph find themselves in Bethlehem. The Emperor Augustus prided himself on being the bringer of peace to the known world. But in Bethlehem we pay homage to the newly born real Prince of Peace, Jesus, who is bringing the fullness of peace and salvation to his people. His is a peace that will ultimately include security from enemies, prosperity, wholeness, and well-being. I pray today for peace in my community.

- This peace is not to be found in palaces but among the little people of the earth—God's own—such as travelers like Mary and Joseph, and the shepherds. I thank God for the peace offered me this day and every day because of Jesus' coming.

Thursday 26th December
Saint Stephen, The First Martyr
Matthew 10:17–22

"Beware of them, for they will hand you over to councils and flog you in their synagogues; and you will be dragged before governors and kings because of me, as a testimony to them and the Gentiles. When they hand you over, do not worry about how you are to speak or what you are to say; for what you are to say will be given to you at that time; for it is not you who speak, but the Spirit of your Father speaking through you. Brother will betray brother to death, and a father his child, and children will rise against parents and have them put to death; and you will be hated by all because of my name. But the one who endures to the end will be saved."

• At the first Christmas, we are told, heaven descended to earth and earth ascended to heaven. Jesus joined our life on earth, and through his life, death, and eventual rising, the way was opened for his followers among earth's people to join the life of heaven. On December 25 we commemorate the arrival of Jesus on earth, and on the very next day, December 26, we commemorate that follower of Jesus—Stephen—as the first to arrive in heaven through martyrdom.

• Jesus freely gave up heaven's glory to join our life on earth. And the Christian, in turn, often must give up earth's privileges, even (in martyrdom) the freedom to live, to be worthy of joining the life of heaven. Martyrdom happened to Stephen, and we cannot rule out its happening to any of us. In such a predicament, we will need courage, not just to know how to react in words, but also to go through the ordeal. However, Jesus assures us that his Spirit—the Spirit who now takes his place on earth—will be with us to give us strength.

Friday 27th December
Saint John, Apostle and Evangelist
John 20:1a, 2–8

Early on the first day of the week, while it was still dark, Mary Magdalene came to the tomb and saw that the stone had been removed from the tomb. . . . So she ran and went to Simon Peter and the other disciple, the one whom Jesus loved, and said to them, "They have taken the Lord out of the tomb, and we do not know where they have laid him." Then Peter and the other disciple set out and went toward the tomb. The two were running together, but the other disciple outran Peter and reached the tomb first. He bent down to look in and saw the linen wrappings lying there, but he did not go in. Then Simon Peter came, following him, and went into the tomb. He saw the linen wrappings lying there, and the cloth that had been on Jesus' head, not lying with the linen wrappings but rolled up in a place by itself. Then the other disciple, who reached the tomb first, also went in, and he saw and believed.

• It may be unfair to say that one person is better at believing than another, but today's Gospel incident gives us a portrait of two followers of Jesus. You might say that the strong point of Peter was action and the strong point of John (today's saint) was believing. How do I imagine myself reacting if I had gone to the empty tomb?

• Peter is always generously pushing himself to the front of things, while John is willing to hold back and ponder. Their contrasting styles are obvious when they reach the tomb left empty by the risen Jesus. Peter bustles in and busies himself; John takes time to reflect and then to be awed. In the words of one Gospel petitioner, we ask, "Lord, I believe. Help my unbelief." And the praying itself will always set the stage for believing.

Saturday 28th December
The Holy Innocents, Martyrs
Matthew 2:13–18

Now after they had left, an angel of the Lord appeared to Joseph in a dream and said, "Get up, take the child and his mother, and flee to Egypt, and remain there until I tell you; for Herod is about to search for the child, to destroy him." Then Joseph got up, took the child and his mother by night, and went to Egypt, and remained there until the death of Herod. This was to fulfill what had been spoken by the Lord through the prophet, "Out of Egypt I have called my son." When Herod saw that he had been tricked by the wise men, he was infuriated, and he sent and killed all the children in and around Bethlehem who were two years old or under, according to the time that he had learned from the wise men. Then was fulfilled what had been spoken through the prophet Jeremiah: "A voice was heard in Ramah, wailing and loud lamentation, Rachel weeping for her children; she refused to be consoled, because they are no more."

- Having recounted the angel saluting Mary's child as the long-promised "God with us," Matthew in his Gospel loses no time in picturing the newborn Jesus as representing, even in the events of his earliest days, the mixed historical fortunes of God's chosen people (who often saw themselves as, collectively, God's favorite firstborn). The Holy Family must flee to Egypt, an ironic destination given that the Jewish people had spent generations there in slavery. Is it so unusual for God to take us back to a place of wounding so that we can heal and begin again? Has this ever happened for you?

- The Chosen People still had further trials to come through, with mothers mourning because they were separated from their children by death or exile. Jesus' people journeyed through much trouble, and so would he. So will we, as we follow God's path and learn how to trust and follow while the road falls and rises. Prepare me, Lord for my own journey ahead.

First Week of Christmas
December 29, 2019—January 4, 2020

Something to think and pray about each day this week:

Beginnings and endings may be on your mind today. We say goodbye to what came before and embark on something new, with God always a part of every beginning and end. We can enter into the unknown with hope and courage because we know that the Word is in all times and places. And we meet God anew with each new endeavor. As T. S. Eliot writes in "Little Gidding," "And the end of all our exploring / will be to arrive where we started / and know the place for the first time."

—Margaret Felice, *2019: A Book of Grace-Filled Days*

The Presence of God

As I sit here, the beating of my heart,
the ebb and flow of my breathing, the movements of my mind
are all signs of God's ongoing creation of me.
I pause for a moment and become aware
of this presence of God within me.

Freedom

Everything has the potential to draw from me a fuller love and life.
Yet my desires are often fixed, caught, on illusions of fulfillment.
I ask that God, through my freedom, may orchestrate my desires in a
vibrant loving melody rich in harmony.

Consciousness

I ask, how am I within myself today? Am I particularly tired, stressed,
or off-form? If any of these characteristics apply, can I try to let go of the
concerns that disturb me?

The Word

I read the word of God slowly, a few times over, and I listen to what God
is saying to me. (Please turn to the Scripture on the following pages.
Inspiration points are there, should you need them. When you are ready,
return here to continue.)

Conversation

I begin to talk with Jesus about the Scripture I have just read. What part
of it strikes a chord in me? Perhaps the words of a friend or a story I have
heard recently will slowly rise to the surface of my consciousness. If so,
does the story throw light on what the Scripture passage may be trying
to say to me?

Conclusion

Glory be to the Father, and to the Son, and to the Holy Spirit,
As it was in the beginning, is now and ever shall be,
World without end. Amen.

Sunday 29th December
The Holy Family of Jesus, Mary, and Joseph
Matthew 2:13–15, 19–23

Now after they had left, an angel of the Lord appeared to Joseph in a dream and said, "Get up, take the child and his mother, and flee to Egypt, and remain there until I tell you; for Herod is about to search for the child, to destroy him." Then Joseph got up, took the child and his mother by night, and went to Egypt, and remained there until the death of Herod. This was to fulfill what had been spoken by the Lord through the prophet, "Out of Egypt I have called my son." . . . When Herod died, an angel of the Lord suddenly appeared in a dream to Joseph in Egypt and said, "Get up, take the child and his mother, and go to the land of Israel, for those who were seeking the child's life are dead." Then Joseph got up, took the child and his mother, and went to the land of Israel. But when he heard that Archelaus was ruling over Judea in place of his father Herod, he was afraid to go there. And after being warned in a dream, he went away to the district of Galilee. There he made his home in a town called Nazareth, so that what had been spoken through the prophets might be fulfilled, "He will be called a Nazorean."

- According to this narrative, Jesus, Mary, and Joseph—like tens of millions of people today—went through a period of being displaced persons. Joseph was the one taking instructions on how to respond as events unfolded. We could say that each move was a leap in the dark, but of course none of the messages was anything like the first utterly unique and earth-shattering announcement that the Spirit of God had intervened in Mary's life. One might say that Joseph, at this annunciation, had more right than Zechariah not to know what to make of it all and to be dumb-struck. I pray for faith when I must make a leap in the dark.

- Perhaps we could call Joseph the patron saint of trust. He was kept in the dark till the last moment and then faithfully followed whatever direction he was given. Some of us will readily admit that, in a rapidly changing society, we never know what's around the corner. Joseph's willingness to fly blind under heaven's bidding provides a model for us.

Monday 30th December
Luke 2:36–38

There was also a prophet, Anna the daughter of Phanuel, of the tribe of Asher. She was of a great age, having lived with her husband for seven years after her marriage, then as a widow to the age of eighty-four. She never left the temple but worshipped there with fasting and prayer night and day. At that moment she came, and began to praise God and to speak about the child to all who were looking for the redemption of Jerusalem.

- Anna never left the temple but worshipped there with fasting and prayer night and day! Imagine! We can't all be quite as focused as that, but we do all want to put God first in our lives—truly first. How can I show my devotion today?

- Anna's life had dealt her the early loss of marriage through her husband's death. She chose to spend the remainder of her energy and love in God's service. This is not a path for everyone, but we can learn from Anna that new life can be created after the destruction of the life we had before. What losses have I suffered? Have certain parts of my life ended? If so, do I see yet the new life that waits for me? I pray to be open to the next chapter, whatever it is.

Tuesday 31st December
John 1:1–18

In the beginning was the Word, and the Word was with God, and the Word was God. He was in the beginning with God. All things came into being through him, and without him not one thing came into being. What has come into being in him was life, and the life was the light of all people. The light shines in the darkness, and the darkness did not overcome it. There was a man sent from God, whose name was John. He came as a witness to testify to the light, so that all might believe through him. He himself was not the light, but he came to testify to the light. The true light, which enlightens everyone, was coming into the world. He was in the world, and the world came into being through him; yet the world did not know him. He came to what was his own, and his own people did not accept him. But to all who received him, who believed in his name, he gave power to become children of God, who were born, not of blood or of the will of the flesh or of the will of man, but of God. And the Word became flesh and lived among us, and we have seen his glory, the glory as of a father's only son, full of grace and truth. (John testified to him and cried out, "This was he of whom I said, 'He who comes after me ranks ahead of me because he was before me.'") From his fullness we have all received, grace upon grace. The law indeed was given through Moses; grace and truth came through Jesus Christ. No one has ever seen God. It is God the only Son, who is close to the Father's heart, who has made him known.

- The crib gives us one perspective on Jesus: on a human scale, easy to imagine and love. The fourth Gospel gives us a cosmic perspective: Jesus as the power and intelligence with which God created and sustains the world, existing before time and space. Jesus is the Logos, the word, the source of life, which is the light of all people.

- Because Jesus is both human and divine—the vulnerable infant as well as the source of all creation—we can bring him the entire scale of our experience. What "human" issues do you face today: illness, relationship problems, lack of resources? And what "divine" issues might you bring: faith in God's unending love; hope in the growth and understanding you do not yet see?

Wednesday 1st January
Solemnity of Mary, the Holy Mother of God
Luke 2:16–21

So they went with haste and found Mary and Joseph, and the child lying in the manger. When they saw this, they made known what had been told them about this child; and all who heard it were amazed at what the shepherds told them. But Mary treasured all these words and pondered them in her heart. The shepherds returned, glorifying and praising God for all they had heard and seen, as it had been told them. After eight days had passed, it was time to circumcise the child; and he was called Jesus, the name given by the angel before he was conceived in the womb.

- We begin the year, as we begin our lives, under the protection of a mother. Today we celebrate the most passionate and enduring of all human relationships, that of mother and child. As Mary looked at her baby and gave him her breast, she knew that there was a dimension here beyond her knowing. Whatever parent-child questions or problems you may have, you also have Mary's companionship.

- Christians thought about it for three centuries before the Council of Ephesus, when they dared to consecrate the title *qeotokos*, "Mother of God." Like Mary, I treasure the words spoken about Jesus, and I ponder them in my heart.

Thursday 2nd January
Saints Basil the Great and Gregory Nazianzen, Bishops and Doctors of the Church
John 1:19–28

This is the testimony given by John when the Jews sent priests and Levites from Jerusalem to ask him, "Who are you?" He confessed and did not deny it, but confessed, "I am not the Messiah." And they asked him, "What then? Are you Elijah?" He said, "I am not." "Are you the prophet?" He answered, "No." Then they said to him, "Who are you? Let us have an answer for those who sent us. What do you say about yourself?" He said, "I am the voice of one crying out in the wilderness, 'Make straight the way of the Lord,'" as the prophet Isaiah said. Now they had been sent from the Pharisees. They asked him, "Why then are you baptizing if you are neither the Messiah, nor Elijah, nor the prophet?" John answered them, "I baptize with water. Among you stands one whom you do not know, the one who is coming after me; I am not worthy to untie the thong of his sandal." This took place in Bethany across the Jordan where John was baptizing.

- St. John Paul II, writing on the need for ecumenism, stated that the Church must breathe with her two lungs. He was recognizing that the Church has an Eastern as well as a Western tradition and needs both if it is to be whole and healthy. Saints Basil and Gregory, whom we honor today, represent the Eastern tradition and remind us to pray for the unity of all Christians. What do you know about these men and their legacy? Have you ever visited an Eastern church?

- John the Baptist deflects attention from himself onto Christ. John's role is to make straight the way of the Lord and then to step aside. John represents what all Christians are called to be: witnesses to Christ, heralds of the Good News. Do you see yourself as a witness and a herald?

Friday 3rd January
John 1:29–34

The next day he saw Jesus coming toward him and declared, "Here is the Lamb of God who takes away the sin of the world! This is he of whom I said, 'After me comes a man who ranks ahead of me because he was before me.' I myself did not know him; but I came baptizing with water for this reason, that he might be revealed to Israel." And John testified, "I saw the Spirit descending from heaven like a dove, and it remained on him. I myself did not know him, but the one who sent me to baptize with water said to me, 'He on whom you see the Spirit descend and remain is the one who baptizes with the Holy Spirit.' And I myself have seen and have testified that this is the Son of God."

• Artists frequently depict John the Baptist with one arm outstretched, pointing to Jesus. This image accurately reminds us of John's part in the Gospel story. It also illustrates his self-understanding. John can identify who Jesus is, but only Jesus takes away the sin of the world and baptizes with the Holy Spirit. In my prayer today, I meditate on the gift of the Holy Spirit.

• John recognizes signs of God's favor upon Jesus. It's hard to imagine that John would have seen the Spirit descend on Jesus if he had not been following God's path for him. Because John was in communion with God, he was given understanding of the signs. I pray that my on-going communion with Jesus the Lord and God the Father will open my eyes to wisdom.

Saturday 4th January
Saint Elizabeth Ann Seton, Religious
John 1:35–42

The next day John again was standing with two of his disciples, and as he watched Jesus walk by, he exclaimed, "Look, here is the Lamb of God!" The two disciples heard him say this, and they followed Jesus. When Jesus turned and saw them following, he said to them, "What are you looking for?" They said to him, "Rabbi" (which translated means Teacher), "where are you staying?" He said to them, "'Come and see." They came and saw where he was staying, and they remained with him that day. It was about four o'clock in the afternoon. One of the two who heard John speak and followed him was Andrew, Simon Peter's brother. He first found his brother Simon and said to him, "We have found the Messiah" (which is translated Anointed). He brought Simon to Jesus, who looked at him and said, "'You are Simon son of John. You are to be called Cephas" (which is translated Peter).

- John pointed his disciples to Jesus. He recognized that Jesus' ministry would supersede his own. Wise teachers know when it is time for their students or mentees to leave them and go to the next stage of their growth. Today, I remember those who have mentored me. How did they help me see when it was time to move on? Or I think of those I have mentored or am mentoring. Can I let them go when it is time? Can I rejoice when a new teacher comes to their evolving spiritual needs?

- The disciples understood that if they were to follow Jesus, that meant being with him, not just listening to his teaching. It was not unusual for teachers to keep their disciples close to them so that learning happened in the context of daily living. How do I stay close to Jesus? What mentors help me learn through daily example?

The Epiphany of Our Lord/The Second Week of Christmas
January 5—January 12, 2020

Something to think and pray about each day this week:

Life is often a desert; it is difficult to walk in life, but if we trust in God it can become beautiful and wide as a highway. Never lose hope, continue to believe, always, in spite of everything. When we are before a child, although we have many problems and many difficulties, a smile comes to us from within, because we see hope in front of us: a child is hope. And in this way, we must be able to discern in life the way of hope which leads us to find God, God who became a child for us. He will make us smile; he will give us everything.

—Pope Francis, *On Hope*

The Presence of God

Dear Jesus, I come to you today longing for your presence. I desire to love you as you love me. May nothing ever separate me from you.

Freedom

Lord, grant me the grace to be free from the excesses of this life. Let me not get caught up with the desire for wealth. Keep my heart and mind free to love and serve you.

Consciousness

Where do I sense hope, encouragement, and growth in my life? By looking back over the past few months, I may be able to see which activities and occasions have produced rich fruit. If I do notice such areas, I will determine to give those areas both time and space in the future.

The Word

God speaks to each of us individually. I listen attentively to hear what he is saying to me. Read the text a few times, then listen. (Please turn to the Scripture on the following pages. Inspiration points are there, should you need them. When you are ready, return here to continue.)

Conversation

What is stirring in me as I pray? Am I consoled, troubled, left cold? I imagine Jesus standing or sitting at my side, and I share my feelings with him.

Conclusion

Glory be to the Father, and to the Son, and to the Holy Spirit,
As it was in the beginning, is now and ever shall be,
World without end. Amen.

Sunday 5th January
The Epiphany of the Lord
Matthew 2:1–12

In the time of King Herod, after Jesus was born in Bethlehem of Judea, wise men from the East came to Jerusalem, asking, "Where is the child who has been born king of the Jews? For we observed his star at its rising, and have come to pay him homage." When King Herod heard this, he was frightened, and all Jerusalem with him; and calling together all the chief priests and scribes of the people, he inquired of them where the Messiah was to be born. They told him, "In Bethlehem of Judea; for so it has been written by the prophet: 'And you, Bethlehem, in the land of Judah, are by no means least among the rulers of Judah; for from you shall come a ruler who is to shepherd my people Israel.'" Then Herod secretly called for the wise men and learned from them the exact time when the star had appeared. Then he sent them to Bethlehem, saying, "Go and search diligently for the child; and when you have found him, bring me word so that I may also go and pay him homage." When they had heard the king, they set out; and there, ahead of them, went the star that they had seen at its rising, until it stopped over the place where the child was. When they saw that the star had stopped, they were overwhelmed with joy. On entering the house, they saw the child with Mary his mother; and they knelt down and paid him homage. Then, opening their treasure chests, they offered him gifts of gold, frankincense, and myrrh. And having been warned in a dream not to return to Herod, they left for their own country by another road.

- The wise men saw the star and steadily followed it. The people of Jerusalem did not. What star am I being called to follow this year? What gifts from my treasure chest will I offer Jesus in service of his mission? Lord, send me out each day to be a bearer of your love to all I encounter.

- Life is sometimes full of questions, seeking, and searching. I pray that I may always seek the truth and that I might recognize it when God puts it in my path.

Monday 6th January
Matthew 4:12–17, 23–25

Now when Jesus heard that John had been arrested, he withdrew to Galilee. He left Nazareth and made his home in Capernaum by the sea, in the territory of Zebulun and Naphtali, so that what had been spoken through the prophet Isaiah might be fulfilled: "Land of Zebulun, land of Naphtali, on the road by the sea, across the Jordan, Galilee of the Gentiles—the people who sat in darkness have seen a great light, and for those who sat in the region and shadow of death light has dawned." From that time Jesus began to proclaim, "Repent, for the kingdom of heaven has come near." . . . Jesus went throughout Galilee, teaching in their synagogues and proclaiming the Good News of the kingdom and curing every disease and every sickness among the people. So his fame spread throughout all Syria, and they brought to him all the sick, those who were afflicted with various diseases and pains, demoniacs, epileptics, and paralytics, and he cured them. And great crowds followed him from Galilee, the Decapolis, Jerusalem, Judea, and from beyond the Jordan.

• In this Gospel story, we hear how Jesus devoted himself tirelessly to proclaiming the Good News of God's love and providence. You might ask yourself what that Good News means for you in practice today. Jesus also spends a lot of time healing people of the wounds from their past, and he sets people free from their demons.

• If you want to pray about this, quiet your mind for a short while and hear Jesus saying to you, "Come and see" several times. Then be with Jesus and the Good News he has for you and with how he wants to heal the wounds from your past, so that you might be free to ponder his love for you.

Tuesday 7th January
Mark 6:34–44

As he went ashore, he saw a great crowd; and he had compassion for them, because they were like sheep without a shepherd; and he began to teach them many things. When it grew late, his disciples came to him and said, "This is a deserted place, and the hour is now very late; send them away so that they may go into the surrounding country and villages and buy something for themselves to eat." But he answered them, "You give them something to eat." They said to him, "Are we to go and buy two hundred denarii worth of bread, and give it to them to eat?" And he said to them, "How many loaves have you? Go and see." When they had found out, they said, "Five, and two fish." Then he ordered them to get all the people to sit down in groups on the green grass. So they sat down in groups of hundreds and of fifties. Taking the five loaves and the two fish, he looked up to heaven, and blessed and broke the loaves, and gave them to his disciples to set before the people; and he divided the two fish among them all. And all ate and were filled; and they took up twelve baskets full of broken pieces and of the fish. Those who had eaten the loaves numbered five thousand men.

• Jesus allowed the disciples to see the people's need and bring up the question of their hunger. What need does he wait for me to recognize in those around me? What hunger might I bring to his attention so that he can show me what to do?

• Jesus began with the food at hand, and then multiplied it. So often, we already have the beginning of an answered prayer. We look outside ourselves for the answer and yet the seed of it is already in front of us. Lord, help me see the resources I already have.

Wednesday 8th January
Mark 6:45–52

Immediately he made his disciples get into the boat and go on ahead to the other side, to Bethsaida, while he dismissed the crowd. After saying farewell to them, he went up on the mountain to pray. When evening came, the boat was out on the sea, and he was alone on the land. When he saw that they were straining at the oars against an adverse wind, he came towards them early in the morning, walking on the sea. He intended to pass them by. But when they saw him walking on the sea, they thought it was a ghost and cried out; for they all saw him and were terrified. But immediately he spoke to them and said, "Take heart, it is I; do not be afraid." Then he got into the boat with them and the wind ceased. And they were utterly astounded, for they did not understand about the loaves, but their hearts were hardened.

• This is a story about peace of soul. At the end of a long day beset by crowds, Jesus does not sleep but climbs a mountain to pray on his own. That bond with his Father was the source of his strength. We enjoy the same bond, the Holy Spirit in us. Today I thank the Holy Spirit for this ever-present help.

- This Gospel passage is also a story about panic. With the waves breaking over the boat, the disciples cannot believe that the Lord has seen them and is approaching. I hear him say to me: Come.

Thursday 9th January
Luke 4:14–22a

Then Jesus, filled with the power of the Spirit, returned to Galilee, and a report about him spread through all the surrounding country. He began to teach in their synagogues and was praised by everyone. When he came to Nazareth, where he had been brought up, he went to the synagogue on the sabbath day, as was his custom. He stood up to read, and the scroll of the prophet Isaiah was given to him. He unrolled the scroll and found the place where it was written: "The Spirit of the Lord is upon me, because he has anointed me to bring Good News to the poor. He has sent me to proclaim release to the captives and recovery of sight to the blind, to let the oppressed go free, to proclaim the year of the Lord's favor." And he rolled up the scroll, gave it back to the attendant, and sat down. The eyes of all in the synagogue were fixed on him. Then he began to say to them, "Today this scripture has been fulfilled in your hearing." All spoke well of him and were amazed at the gracious words that came from his mouth. They said, "Is not this Joseph's son?"

- The details of this passage tell us much about the ordinary life of Jesus. It was his custom to go to the synagogue on the Sabbath; though he took issue with details of the Law proclaimed there, he chose to join with his community in the worship of God. Though he wrote nothing (as far as we know), he read the Scriptures and was chosen to read to the assembly. He read standing, and then sat down—the posture for serious teaching. The eyes of all were fixed on him. It is a moment of grace and promise, as he brings the Good News to his own people.

- In imagination I join the synagogue congregation, and I hear this charismatic young man speaking the prophecy of Isaiah as his own mission statement. As I listen, I sense with excitement that he is reaching out to me to join him. Lord, let me be part of that unending mission, to bring Good News, vision, and freedom to those who need them.

Friday 10th January
Luke 5:12–16

Once, when he was in one of the cities, there was a man covered with leprosy. When he saw Jesus, he bowed with his face to the ground and begged him, "Lord, if you choose, you can make me clean." Then Jesus stretched out his hand, touched him, and said, "I do choose. Be made clean." Immediately the leprosy left him. And he ordered him to tell no one. "Go," he said, "and show yourself to the priest, and, as Moses commanded, make an offering for your cleansing, for a testimony to them." But now more than ever the word about Jesus spread abroad; many crowds would gather to hear him and to be cured of their diseases. But he would withdraw to deserted places and pray.

- The demands made on Jesus were great, the expectations many. Still, he was able to keep his focus, to maintain his relationship with God. As I give this time to prayer, I am doing as he did. Lord, let me never be too busy to give time to you, to us.

- Are there places I might go or conditions I might create to withdraw to a deserted place? What do I need to turn off, metaphorically or literally?

Saturday 11th January
John 3:22–30

After this Jesus and his disciples went into the Judean countryside, and he spent some time there with them and baptized. John also was baptizing at Aenon near Salim because water was abundant there; and people kept coming and were being baptized—John, of course, had not yet been thrown into prison. Now a discussion about purification arose between John's disciples and a Jew. They came to John and said to him, "Rabbi, the one who was with you across the Jordan, to whom you testified, here he is baptizing, and all are going to him." John answered, "No one can receive anything except what has been given from heaven. You yourselves are my witnesses that I said, 'I am not the Messiah, but I have been sent ahead of him.' He who has the bride is the bridegroom. The friend of the bridegroom, who stands and hears him, rejoices greatly at the bridegroom's voice. For this reason my joy has been fulfilled. He must increase, but I must decrease."

- My question as I grow older is not "Am I qualified enough to show Jesus to people?" More and more it is "Am I weak enough?" Do I accept my failures and the wounds of life as more important than my strengths in witnessing to Jesus? I am a wounded healer. Like my fellow human beings, I am searching and struggling.

- Loving Father, you wake me from sleep today and call me into life and service. You want something of your goodness to shine through my frailty and brokenness. Bless this day!

The Baptism of the Lord / First Week in Ordinary Time
January 12—January 18

Something to think and pray about each day this week:

Life is often a desert; it is difficult to walk in life, but if we trust in God it can become beautiful and wide as a highway. Never lose hope, continue to believe, always, in spite of everything. When we are before a child, although we have many problems and many difficulties, a smile comes to us from within, because we see hope in front of us: a child is hope. And in this way, we must be able to discern in life the way of hope which leads us to find God, God who became a child for us. He will make us smile; he will give us everything.

—Pope Francis, *On Hope*

The Presence of God
"Be still, and know that I am God!" Lord, your words lead us to the calmness and greatness of your presence.

Freedom
If God were trying to tell me something, would I know?
If God were reassuring me or challenging me, would I notice?
I ask for the grace to be free of my own preoccupations
and open to what God may be saying to me.

Consciousness
In the presence of my loving Creator, I look honestly at my feelings over the past day: the highs, the lows, and the level ground. Can I see where the Lord has been present?

The Word
In this expectant state of mind, please turn to the text for the day with confidence. Believe that the Holy Spirit is present and may reveal whatever the passage has to say to you. Read reflectively, listening with a third ear to what may be going on in your heart. (Please turn to the Scripture on the following pages. Inspiration points are there, should you need them. When you are ready, return here to continue.)

Conversation
Remembering that I am still in God's presence,
I imagine Jesus standing or sitting beside me,
and I say whatever is on my mind, whatever is in my heart,
speaking as one friend to another.

Conclusion
Glory be to the Father, and to the Son, and to the Holy Spirit,
As it was in the beginning, is now and ever shall be,
World without end. Amen.

Sunday 12th January
The Baptism of the Lord
Matthew 3:13–17

Then Jesus came from Galilee to John at the Jordan, to be baptized by him. John would have prevented him, saying, "I need to be baptized by you, and do you come to me?" But Jesus answered him, "Let it be so now; for it is proper for us in this way to fulfill all righteousness." Then he consented. And when Jesus had been baptized, just as he came up from the water, suddenly the heavens were opened to him and he saw the Spirit of God descending like a dove and alighting on him. And a voice from heaven said, "This is my Son, the Beloved, with whom I am well pleased."

- This is one of the three times that the Father speaks to us in the Gospel story. Here it is to acknowledge that Jesus is his beloved, the one he loves with a passion. During the first millennium this came to be the way Christians saw themselves, especially as they realized the meaning of Jesus' words, "As the Father has loved me, so I have loved you; abide in my love" (John 15:9).

- If you would like to ponder this prayerfully, quiet yourself for a short while by relaxing your body. Then listen to the Father call you his beloved a few times, and when you have savored his words, tell him how you feel about this.

Monday 13th January
First Week in Ordinary Time
Mark 1:14–20

Now after John was arrested, Jesus came to Galilee, proclaiming the Good News of God, and saying, "The time is fulfilled, and the kingdom of God has come near; repent, and believe in the Good News." As Jesus passed along the Sea of Galilee, he saw Simon and his brother Andrew casting a net into the sea—for they were fishermen. And Jesus said to them, "Follow me and I will make you fish for people." And immediately they left their nets and followed him. As he went a little farther, he saw James son of Zebedee and his brother John, who were in their boat mending the nets. Immediately he called them; and they left their father Zebedee in the boat with the hired men, and followed him.

- Two things make it difficult to hear how Jesus invites each of us to be with him as his companions and to share in his work. One is our limitations and consequent feeling of insignificance. The second is how exalted Jesus is as God, even though the same Jesus walked our earth.

- If you wish to pray with this reality, be with Jesus in a quiet place and let him call you by name. Let him call you, first to be with him as his friend, and then to share in his work.

Tuesday 14th January
Mark 1:21–28

When the sabbath came, Jesus entered the synagogue and taught. They were astounded at his teaching, for he taught them as one having authority, and not as the scribes. Just then there was in their synagogue a man with an unclean spirit, and he cried out, "What have you to do with us, Jesus of Nazareth? Have you come to destroy us? I know who you are, the Holy One of God." But Jesus rebuked him, saying, "Be silent, and come out of him!" And the unclean spirit, convulsing him and crying with a loud voice, came out of him. They were all amazed, and they kept on asking one another, What is this? A new teaching—with authority! He commands even the unclean spirits, and they obey him. At once his fame began to spread throughout the surrounding region of Galilee.

- Jesus not only preached the Good News in what he said but more so by what he did. Today's Gospel story shows us a person who spoke with courage and wisdom that struck the ordinary people with its ring of authority.

- For a few moments of prayer, allow yourself to notice and admire what so impressed people about Jesus.

Wednesday 15th January
Mark 1:29–39

As soon as they left the synagogue, they entered the house of Simon and Andrew, with James and John. Now Simon's mother-in-law was in bed with a fever, and they told him about her at once. He came and took her by the hand and lifted her up. Then the fever left her, and she began to serve them. That evening, at sunset, they brought to him all who were sick or possessed with demons. And the whole city was gathered around the door. And he cured many who were sick with various diseases, and cast out many demons; and he would not permit the demons to speak, because they knew him. In the morning, while it was still very dark, he got up and went out to a deserted place, and there he prayed. And Simon and his companions hunted for him. When they found him, they said to him, "Everyone is searching for you." He answered, "Let us go on to the neighboring towns, so that I may proclaim the message there also; for that is what I came out to do." And he went throughout Galilee, proclaiming the message in their synagogues and casting out demons.

- The Gospel stories tell us that, as well as healing, casting out demons, and preaching, Jesus was in the habit of going off to a quiet place to pray. He felt a need to be in touch with the fact that he was the Father's beloved. He must have found the lack of human affirmation very wearing.

- In prayer, perhaps you might speak to Jesus about your shared experience of this lack of human acceptance and appreciation. Let him tell you how much he appreciates you as a companion and as one who shares his work. Notice and express how much you resist as well as relish what he says to you.

Thursday 16th January
Mark 1:40–45

A leper came to him begging him, and kneeling he said to him, "If you choose, you can make me clean." Moved with pity, Jesus stretched out his hand and touched him, and said to him, "I do choose. Be made clean!" Immediately the leprosy left him, and he was made clean. After sternly warning him he sent him away at once, saying to him, "See that you say nothing to anyone; but go, show yourself to the priest, and offer for your cleansing what Moses commanded, as a testimony to them." But he went out and began to proclaim it freely, and to spread the word, so that Jesus could no longer go into a town openly, but stayed out in the country; and people came to him from every quarter.

- The most painful wounds we carry from the past are more wounds of spirit than of body. Of these spiritual wounds, the one that causes us most pain is the belief that we are insignificant. In this Gospel story we hear in Jesus' words to the leper his concern to heal this wound we carry with us from the past.

- In your prayer today tell Jesus of some way you were hurt or wounded by something people said or did to you. Listen to how sensitive and responsive he is when he is "moved with pity" or compassion for you. Tell him how you feel about him being like this.

Friday 17th January
Mark 2:1–12

When he returned to Capernaum after some days, it was reported that he was at home. So many gathered around that there was no longer room for them, not even in front of the door; and he was speaking the word to them. Then some people came, bringing to him a paralyzed man, carried by four of them. And when they could not bring him to Jesus because of the crowd, they removed the roof above him; and after having dug through it, they let down the mat on which the paralytic lay. When Jesus saw their faith, he said to the paralytic, "Son, your sins are forgiven." Now some of the scribes were sitting there, questioning in their hearts, "Why does this fellow speak in this way? It is blasphemy! Who can forgive sins but God alone?" At once Jesus perceived in his spirit that they were discussing these questions among themselves; and he said to them, "Why do you raise such questions in your hearts? Which is easier, to say to the paralytic, 'Your sins are forgiven,' or to say, 'Stand up and take your mat and walk'? But so that you may know that the Son of Man has authority on earth to forgive sins"—he said to the paralytic—"I say to you, stand up, take your mat and go to your home." And he stood up, and immediately took the mat and went out before all of them; so that they were all amazed and glorified God, saying, "We have never seen anything like this!"

- One of Jesus' most life-giving actions in Gospel texts like today's is forgiving our sins. In doing this he encourages us to forgive not only others but also ourselves. If we do, we learn to live at peace with the reality that we are limited human beings and make mistakes or are sometimes neglectful in the way we relate to God or others.

- Bring to Jesus one of your past failures—one for which you find it hard to forgive yourself. In light of today's Scripture reading, listen to

Jesus' desire to forgive you and also his desire that you forgive yourself. If you find Jesus' capacity to forgive attractive, tell him so.

Saturday 18th January
Mark 2:13–17

Jesus went out again beside the sea; the whole crowd gathered around him, and he taught them. As he was walking along, he saw Levi son of Alphaeus sitting at the tax booth, and he said to him, "Follow me." And he got up and followed him. And as he sat at dinner in Levi's house, many tax collectors and sinners were also sitting with Jesus and his disciples—for there were many who followed him. When the scribes of the Pharisees saw that he was eating with sinners and tax collectors, they said to his disciples, "Why does he eat with tax collectors and sinners?" When Jesus heard this, he said to them, "Those who are well have no need of a physician, but those who are sick; I have come to call not the righteous but sinners."

- Jesus is at home with the very weak and wayward side of humanity and wants us to be at home with it in ourselves. If we do not accept ourselves, then we tend to become preoccupied with what is inadequate, lacking, and negative about our lives.

- In prayer, you might tell Jesus about something that you do not like about yourself. Given how comfortable Jesus is in relating to this side of you, can you let him put this fault in perspective, helping you see it as a small part of the very good person he finds you to be?

January 19—January 25

Something to think and pray about each day this week:

During high school we were told—warned really—that when we left the school grounds in our uniforms, when we wore them at Friendly's restaurant after school or while on a field trip, we were representing Cathedral High School, that how we behaved while wearing these uniforms represented the larger group of students. Which makes me wonder: what about the clothes I don't wear, but still hold on to; what do they say about me?

In Colossians, we're told to clothe ourselves with love, over everything else, over whatever styles we're wearing, over whatever ways we're seeking to define or distinguish ourselves. Like a less itchy and less tangible version of a school uniform, this love unites us. And the way we wear that love represents the larger group of Christians. It is up to each of us to make it unique in the way we live out that love—the spiritual version of wearing goofy socks and homemade jewelry—but this love must have at its core the same basic pieces. "They will know we are Christians by our Love," we are told. But only if we wear it well.

—Kerry Weber, *Mercy in the City*

The Presence of God
"I am standing at the door, knocking" says the Lord. What a wonderful privilege that the Lord of all creation desires to come to me. I welcome his presence.

Freedom
I will ask God's help
to be free from my own preoccupations,
to be open to God in this time of prayer,
to come to know, love, and serve God more.

Consciousness
In God's loving presence I unwind the past day,
starting from now and looking back, moment by moment.
I gather in all the goodness and light, in gratitude.
I attend to the shadows and what they say to me,
seeking healing, courage, forgiveness.

The Word
Now I turn to the Scripture set out for me this day. I read slowly over the words and see if any sentence or sentiment appeals to me. (Please turn to the Scripture on the following pages. Inspiration points are there, should you need them. When you are ready, return here to continue.)

Conversation
Sometimes I wonder what I might say if I were to meet you in person, Lord.
I think I might say, "Thank you" because you are always there for me.

Conclusion
I thank God for these moments we have spent together and for any insights I have been given concerning the text.

Sunday 19th January
Second Sunday in Ordinary Time
John 1:29–34

The next day he saw Jesus coming toward him and declared, "Here is the Lamb of God who takes away the sin of the world! This is he of whom I said, 'After me comes a man who ranks ahead of me because he was before me.' I myself did not know him; but I came baptizing with water for this reason, that he might be revealed to Israel." And John testified, "I saw the Spirit descending from heaven like a dove, and it remained on him. I myself did not know him, but the one who sent me to baptize with water said to me, 'He on whom you see the Spirit descend and remain is the one who baptizes with the Holy Spirit.' And I myself have seen and have testified that this is the Son of God."

• "Lamb of God" evokes Old Testament passages: of the Passover lamb, and of the suffering servant in Isaiah, led like a lamb to the slaughter, bearing our sins.

• Lord, whenever I hear of some atrocious barbarism and of the injustice and pain people suffer through others' wickedness, I remember that this is the world you entered, the burden you took on yourself. You had a strong back to carry the evil that is in the world. Remind me to rely on your strength and compassion.

Monday 20th January
Mark 2:18–22

Now John's disciples and the Pharisees were fasting; and people came and said to Jesus, "Why do John's disciples and the disciples of the Pharisees fast, but your disciples do not fast?" Jesus said to them, "The wedding guests cannot fast while the bridegroom is with them, can they? As long as they have the bridegroom with them, they cannot fast. The days will come when the bridegroom is taken away from them, and then they will fast on that day. No one sews a piece of unshrunk cloth on an old cloak; otherwise, the patch pulls away from it, the new from the old, and a worse tear is made. And no one puts new wine into old wineskins; otherwise, the wine will burst the skins, and the wine is lost, and so are the skins; but one puts new wine into fresh wineskins."

- In today's Gospel story, Jesus portrays your life with him as a wedding celebration. During the first millennium of Christianity, this became the context in which Christians saw their lives.

- In a few moments of reflective prayer, see if you can be with Jesus as one he loves with a passion or as his beloved disciple. When you have dwelt for some time with this reality, tell Jesus what you like about this way of viewing your relationship with him and tell him also how you resist it.

Tuesday 21st January
Mark 2:23–28

One sabbath Jesus was going through the grainfields; and as they made their way his disciples began to pluck heads of grain. The Pharisees said to him, "Look, why are they doing what is not lawful on the sabbath?" And he said to them, "Have you never read what David did when he and his companions were hungry and in need of food? He entered the house of God, when Abiathar was high priest, and ate the bread of the Presence, which it is not lawful for any but the priests to eat, and he gave some to his companions." Then he said to them, "The sabbath was made for humankind, and not humankind for the sabbath; so the Son of Man is lord even of the sabbath."

- The Sabbath was meant to be a day of rest, when people would be free to think of God, to give thanks for God's gifts, and to take care of health and well-being. But some religious authorities gradually encroached on the Sabbath with so many regulations that it risked no longer serving its purpose.

- Jesus is portrayed as one who sees life as a celebration, to be enjoyed. In your prayer with this Gospel story, sit with its portrait of Jesus as a more easeful and joyful person than we have often portrayed him. After contemplating this portrait of Jesus, tell him how you feel about him being this way, the ways you savor it or resist it.

Wednesday 22nd January
Mark 3:1–6

[Jesus] entered the synagogue, and a man was there who had a withered hand. They watched him to see whether he would cure him on the sabbath, so that they might accuse him. And he said to the man who had the withered hand, "Come forward." Then he said to them, "Is it lawful to do good or to do harm on the sabbath, to save life or to kill?" But they were silent. He looked around at them with anger; he was grieved at their hardness of heart and said to the man, "Stretch out your hand." He stretched it out, and his hand was restored. The Pharisees went out and immediately conspired with the Herodians against him, how to destroy him.

• Jesus had to deal with a lot of opposition to his plans to create a more caring and just environment for people to live in. Where do you find the need for more care and justice in your world?

• If you wish to encounter this aspect of Jesus, you might listen to him express his care for you in an area of your life in which you experience conflict with others. Dwell with Jesus' sensitivity and compassion for you, rather than any advice he might offer you. You might let him say to you, "I know exactly how you feel for I have found myself in the same kind of situation."

Thursday 23rd January
Mark 3:7–12

Jesus departed with his disciples to the sea, and a great multitude from Galilee followed him; hearing all that he was doing, they came to him in great numbers from Judea, Jerusalem, Idumea, beyond the Jordan, and the region around Tyre and Sidon. He told his disciples to have a boat ready for him because of the crowd, so that they would not crush him; for he had cured many, so that all who had diseases pressed upon him to touch him. Whenever the unclean spirits saw him, they fell down before him and shouted, "You are the Son of God!" But he sternly ordered them not to make him known.

• When we hear a story like this and experience how hectic Jesus' life was, we may feel that our lives are very uneventful by comparison. At such times it is important to realize that Jesus is present and speaks to us in the *inner* eventfulness of our lives, loving each of us individually, and in his presence we can be fully who we are.

• Linger with Jesus as he highlights for you what he most appreciates about your life.

Friday 24th January
Saint Francis de Sales, Bishop and Doctor of the Church
Mark 3:13–19

[Jesus] went up the mountain and called to him those whom he wanted, and they came to him. And he appointed twelve, whom he also named apostles, to be with him, and to be sent out to proclaim the message, and to have authority to cast out demons. So he appointed the twelve: Simon (to whom he gave the name Peter); James son of Zebedee and John the brother of James (to whom he gave the name Boanerges, that is, Sons of Thunder); and Andrew, and Philip, and Bartholomew, and Matthew, and Thomas, and James son of Alphaeus, and Thaddaeus, and Simon the Cananaean, and Judas Iscariot, who betrayed him. Then he went home.

- Like the apostles, each of us is called by name into a profoundly personal relationship with Jesus. When we allow him to look on us in this way, we get a sense of our deepest significance and personal worth.

- Spend some moments in prayer or in conversation with Jesus about the relationship he wants with you. Meditate on thought: In the Gospel stories, Jesus prefers to relate to people one-on-one.

Saturday 25th January
The Conversion of Saint Paul the Apostle
Mark 16:15–18

And he said to them, "Go into all the world and proclaim the Good News to the whole creation. The one who believes and is baptized will be saved; but the one who does not believe will be condemned. And these signs will accompany those who believe: by using my name they will cast out demons; they will speak in new tongues; they will pick up snakes in their hands, and if they drink any deadly thing, it will not hurt them; they will lay their hands on the sick, and they will recover."

- In this story we hear the central truth that Jesus preaches and sends us out to proclaim. He calls it the "Good News" of God's love; some have called it God's dream for us.

- If you wish to bring this truth to prayer, you might consider whether the Good News is about something God wants you to do for him or largely about what God wants to do for you. "We learn to love by being loved" (Jean Vanier).

January 26—February 1

Something to think and pray about each day this week:

One of the most effective means of learning to see ourselves as we really are and to cultivate a sense of humility is to develop a profound sense of gratitude. The moment we conclude that we are responsible for who we are, what we have done, and what we possess, then we are in big trouble. When we recognize that God is the source of all the blessing our lives, we respond with an attitude of gratitude. A profound sense of gratitude reminds us of the source of all good gifts. It reminds us of the responsibility we have to share those blessings with others.

—Joe Paprocki, *7 Keys to Spiritual Wellness*

The Presence of God
At any time of the day or night we can call on Jesus.
He is always waiting, listening for our call.
What a wonderful blessing.
No phone needed, no emails, just a whisper.

Freedom
If God were trying to tell me something, would I know?
If God were reassuring me or challenging me, would I notice?
I ask for the grace to be free of my own preoccupations
and open to what God may be saying to me.

Consciousness
Help me, Lord, become more conscious of your presence. Teach me to recognize your presence in others. Fill my heart with gratitude for the times your love has been shown to me through the care of others.

The Word
In this expectant state of mind, please turn to the text for the day with confidence. Believe that the Holy Spirit is present and may reveal whatever the passage has to say to you. Read reflectively, listening with a third ear to what may be going on in your heart. (Please turn to the Scripture on the following pages. Inspiration points are there, should you need them. When you are ready, return here to continue.)

Conversation
Conversation requires talking and listening.
As I talk to Jesus, may I also learn to pause and listen.
I picture the gentleness in his eyes and the love in his smile.
I can be totally honest with Jesus as I tell him my worries and cares.
I will open my heart to Jesus as I tell him my fears and doubts.
I will ask him to help me place myself fully in his care, knowing that he always desires good for me.

Conclusion
I thank God for these moments we have spent together and for any insights I have been given concerning the text.

Sunday 26th January
Third Sunday in Ordinary Time
Matthew 4:12–23

Now when Jesus heard that John had been arrested, he withdrew to Galilee. He left Nazareth and made his home in Capernaum by the sea, in the territory of Zebulun and Naphtali, so that what had been spoken through the prophet Isaiah might be fulfilled: "Land of Zebulun, land of Naphtali, / on the road by the sea, across the Jordan, / Galilee of the Gentiles—the people who sat in darkness / have seen a great light, and for those who sat in the region and shadow of death light has dawned." From that time Jesus began to proclaim, "Repent, for the kingdom of heaven has come near." As he walked by the Sea of Galilee, he saw two brothers, Simon, who is called Peter, and Andrew his brother, casting a net into the sea—for they were fishermen. And he said to them, "Follow me, and I will make you fish for people." Immediately they left their nets and followed him. As he went from there, he saw two other brothers, James son of Zebedee and his brother John, in the boat with their father Zebedee, mending their nets, and he called them. Immediately they left the boat and their father, and followed him. Jesus went throughout Galilee, teaching in their synagogues and proclaiming the Good News of the kingdom and curing every disease and every sickness among the people.

• Here we see the big picture of the extent and depth of what Jesus comes to do. He wants us to repent or to undergo a complete change in the way we see and value everything. We are also told of how Jesus effects this by attracting people so that they leave everything in order to be with him and enter his vision of them.

• If you wish to engage in the profound nature of Jesus' love and dream for you, ponder any aspect of this love that appeals to you. Talk to Jesus about this and especially how you are moved by his love and his desire that you be with him as friend and companion worker.

Monday 27th January
Mark 3:22–30

And the scribes who came down from Jerusalem said, "He has Beelzebul, and by the ruler of the demons he casts out demons." And he called them to him, and spoke to them in parables, "How can Satan cast out Satan?

If a kingdom is divided against itself, that kingdom cannot stand. And if a house is divided against itself, that house will not be able to stand. And if Satan has risen up against himself and is divided, he cannot stand, but his end has come. But no one can enter a strong man's house and plunder his property without first tying up the strong man; then indeed the house can be plundered. Truly I tell you, people will be forgiven for their sins and whatever blasphemies they utter; but whoever blasphemes against the Holy Spirit can never have forgiveness, but is guilty of an eternal sin"— for they had said, "He has an unclean spirit."

- How easy it is to accuse one you do not understand or like of being evil. The scribes could not understand Jesus; therefore, he must be working by the power of Beelzebul. This is not as extreme as it sounds. When was the last time I suggested that someone—perhaps a public figure I really dislike—was horrible, stupid, or out to hurt others?

- Jesus speaks to the scribes in a no-nonsense, logical way. They are, after all, the attorneys of that day; they need a rational explanation. In my life, too, Lord, you speak to me in ways that make sense to me, in ways I can hear you. Thank you.

Tuesday 28th January
Saint Thomas Aquinas, Priest and Doctor of the Church
Mark 3:31–35

Then his mother and his brothers came; and standing outside, they sent to him and called him. A crowd was sitting around him; and they said to him, "Your mother and your brothers and sisters are outside, asking for you." And he replied, "Who are my mother and my brothers?" And looking at those who sat around him, he said, "Here are my mother and my brothers! Whoever does the will of God is my brother and sister and mother."

- The crowd around Jesus, according to the norms of the time, thought of family as the chief place where a person would experience an intimate relationship. But Jesus finds it primarily in the union that God wants with us.

- Try to engage Jesus in conversation about the relationship you have with him. You might spend time with his words: "I do not call you servants any longer, because the servant does not know what the master is doing; but I have called you friends, because I have made known to you everything that I have heard from my Father." (John 15:15).

Wednesday 29th January
Mark 4:1–20

Again he began to teach beside the sea. Such a very large crowd gathered around him that he got into a boat on the sea and sat there, while the whole crowd was beside the sea on the land. He began to teach them many things in parables, and in his teaching he said to them: "Listen! A sower went out to sow. And as he sowed, some seed fell on the path, and the birds came and ate it up. Other seed fell on rocky ground, where it did not have much soil, and it sprang up quickly, since it had no depth of soil. And when the sun rose, it was scorched; and since it had no root, it withered away. Other seed fell among thorns, and the thorns grew up and choked it, and it yielded no grain. Other seed fell into good soil and brought forth grain, growing up and increasing and yielding thirty and sixty and a hundredfold." And he said, "Let anyone with ears to hear listen!" When he was alone, those who were around him along with the twelve asked him about the parables. And he said to them, "To you has been given the secret of the kingdom of God, but for those outside, everything comes in parables; in order that 'they may indeed look, but not perceive, and may indeed listen, but not understand so that they may not turn again and be forgiven.'" And he said to them, "Do you not understand this parable? Then how will you understand all the parables? The sower sows the word. These are the ones on the path where the word is sown: when they hear, Satan immediately comes and takes away the word that is sown in them. And these are the ones sown on rocky ground: when they hear the word, they immediately receive it with joy. But they have no root, and endure only for a while; then, when trouble or persecution arises on account of the word, immediately they fall away. And others are those sown among the thorns: these are the ones who hear the word, but the cares of the world, and the lure of wealth, and the desire for other things come in and choke the word, and it yields nothing. And these are the ones sown on the good soil: they hear the word and accept it and bear fruit, thirty and sixty and a hundredfold."

- The word *parable* comes from two Greek words meaning "to throw" and "alongside"—that is, to talk about one thing in terms of another. A parable will reveal its meaning to those "with ears to hear" but conceal it from those with closed minds and resistant hearts. Today Mark offers us the familiar Parable of the Sower, followed by an explanation of its meaning. As an experiment, try to forget you ever heard the explanation and listen to the parable as if for the first time. (Note that the parable begins and ends with the word "listen.") What do you make of it? What does it mean for you?

- In Mark's explanation, the seed is the "word." Do you recall other biblical references to the "word"? In what contexts do they occur? Remember Isaiah: "For as the rain and the snow come down from heaven, and do not return there until they have watered the earth, . . . so shall my word be that goes out from my mouth; it shall not return to me empty" (Isaiah 55:10–11). Both Isaiah and Mark associate the word with fruitfulness. How do you see this mystery at work in your own life? In the world around you?

Thursday 30th January
Mark 4:21–25

[Jesus] said to them, "Is a lamp brought in to be put under the bushel basket, or under the bed, and not on the lampstand? For there is nothing hidden, except to be disclosed; nor is anything secret, except to come to light. Let anyone with ears to hear listen!" And he said to them, "Pay attention to what you hear; the measure you give will be the measure you get, and still more will be given you. For to those who have, more will be given; and from those who have nothing, even what they have will be taken away."

- Jesus tells us that Good News is to be shared. Pope Francis, speaking to people who were concerned about the shortage of priests, spoke of people who lived authentically Christian lives as being preachers of the Good News in today's world.

- Perhaps you can spend some moments of prayer reflecting on your memories of someone who embodied Good News without ever explicitly preaching it.

Friday 31st January
Saint John Bosco, Priest
Mark 4:26–34

[Jesus said to the crowd,] "The kingdom of God is as if someone would scatter seed on the ground, and would sleep and rise night and day, and the seed would sprout and grow, he does not know how. The earth produces of itself, first the stalk, then the head, then the full grain in the head. But when the grain is ripe, at once he goes in with his sickle, because the harvest has come." He also said, "With what can we compare the kingdom of God, or what parable will we use for it? It is like a mustard seed, which, when sown upon the ground, is the smallest of all the seeds on earth; yet when it is sown it grows up and becomes the greatest of all shrubs, and puts forth large branches, so that the birds of the air can make nests in its shade." With many such parables he spoke the word to them, as they were able to hear it; he did not speak to them except in parables, but he explained everything in private to his disciples.

• These parables indicate how unobtrusive and unnoticeable our growth in the Christian life can be. Jesus continues to remind us that we must pay attention to signs of God's love and activity in our lives, in the lives of family and friends, and in the larger world.

• I might think of my life as God's garden project. I give God permission to keep working on me—because God will not force growth when I'm not ready or willing.

Saturday 1st February
Mark 4:35–41

On that day, when evening had come, Jesus said to the disciples, "Let us go across to the other side." And leaving the crowd behind, they took him with them in the boat, just as he was. Other boats were with him. A great windstorm arose, and the waves beat into the boat, so that the boat was already being swamped. But he was in the stern, asleep on the cushion; and they woke him up and said to him, "Teacher, do you not care that we are perishing?" He woke up and rebuked the wind, and said to the sea, "Peace! Be still!" Then the wind ceased, and there was a dead calm. He said to them, "Why are you afraid? Have you still no faith?" And they were filled with great awe and said to one another, "Who then is this, that even the wind and the sea obey him?"

- Today's Gospel story highlights the stormy journey our faith must make today. How easily our sense of Jesus' love and presence is drowned out by a multiplicity of voices. As a result, this lessening or loss of faith gives way to fear. At such times, Jesus may be asleep in the boat, but his love never leaves us.

- For your prayer, talk to Jesus about how you feel when he seems to be asleep. Look for ways in which he is awake and active in the way you accept, appreciate, and care for those who people your day.

Fourth Week in Ordinary Time
February 2—February 8

Something to think and pray about each day this week:

Ignatius says that people often make decisions backward. They say, "I want to do this. Now how can I do this and somehow praise, reverence, and serve God? How can I work the means around to the end?" Ignatius says that we should instead start with the end. The end is being a disciple of Jesus: "What does it mean for me to love as Jesus loved?" The most challenging line in all of Scripture is "Love one another as I have loved you." What could be more challenging? That makes the Golden Rule look like a piece of cake. This love of altruism and self-sacrifice is our goal. Ignatius wants us to reflect first on why we are here and what the purpose of our life is. Then in that context, we choose the best means to get there.

—Gerald M. Fagin, SJ, *Discovering Your Dream*

The Presence of God

As I sit here, the beating of my heart,
the ebb and flow of my breathing, the movements of my mind
are all signs of God's ongoing creation of me.
I pause for a moment and become aware
of this presence of God within me.

Freedom

It is so easy to get caught up
with the trappings of wealth in this life.
Grant, O Lord, that I may be free
from greed and selfishness.
Remind me that the best things in life are free:
Love, laughter, caring, and sharing.

Consciousness

Knowing that God loves me unconditionally, I can afford to be honest
about how I am.
How has the day been, and how do I feel now? I share my feelings openly
with the Lord.

The Word

Lord Jesus, you became human to communicate with me.
You walked and worked on this earth.
You endured the heat and struggled with the cold.
All your time on this earth was spent in caring for humanity.
You healed the sick, you raised the dead.
Most important of all, you saved me from death.
(Please turn to the Scripture on the following pages. Inspiration points
are there, should you need them. When you are ready, return here to
continue.)

Conversation

Sometimes I wonder what I might say if I were to meet you in person, Lord.
I think I might say, "Thank you" because you are always there for me.

Conclusion

I thank God for these moments we have spent together and for any insights I have been given concerning the text.

Sunday 2nd February
The Presentation of the Lord
Luke 2:22–40

When the time came for their purification according to the law of Moses, they brought him up to Jerusalem to present him to the Lord (as it is written in the law of the Lord, "Every firstborn male shall be designated as holy to the Lord"), and they offered a sacrifice according to what is stated in the law of the Lord, "a pair of turtledoves or two young pigeons." Now there was a man in Jerusalem whose name was Simeon; this man was righteous and devout, looking forward to the consolation of Israel, and the Holy Spirit rested on him. It had been revealed to him by the Holy Spirit that he would not see death before he had seen the Lord's Messiah. Guided by the Spirit, Simeon came into the temple; and when the parents brought in the child Jesus, to do for him what was customary under the law, Simeon took him in his arms and praised God, saying, "Master, now you are dismissing your servant in peace, / according to your word; / for my eyes have seen your salvation, / which you have prepared in the presence of all peoples, / a light for revelation to the Gentiles / and for glory to your people Israel." And the child's father and mother were amazed at what was being said about him. Then Simeon blessed them and said to his mother Mary, "This child is destined for the falling and the rising of many in Israel, and to be a sign that will be opposed so that the inner thoughts of many will be revealed—and a sword will pierce your own soul too." There was also a prophet, Anna the daughter of Phanuel, of the tribe of Asher. She was of a great age, having lived with her husband for seven years after her marriage, then as a widow to the age of eighty-four. She never left the temple but worshiped there with fasting and prayer night and day. At that moment she came, and began to praise God and to speak about the child to all who were looking for the redemption of Jerusalem. When they had finished everything required by the law of the Lord, they returned to Galilee, to their own town of Nazareth. The child grew and became strong, filled with wisdom; and the favor of God was upon him.

- I stand nearby and share the joy of Simeon and Anna, marveling at what they say about this forty-day-old child of a poor and observant

Jewish family. How do I feel for his parents when I hear what the future holds for them?

• After all these miraculous events, Mary, Jesus, and Joseph went home. Life carried on. Can I accept that, between the exciting or miraculous events in my life, there are years of ordinary living and doing and being? I thank God for everyday graces.

Monday 3rd February
Mark 5:1–20

They came to the other side of the sea, to the country of the Gerasenes. And when he had stepped out of the boat, immediately a man out of the tombs with an unclean spirit met him. He lived among the tombs; and no one could restrain him any more, even with a chain; for he had often been restrained with shackles and chains, but the chains he wrenched apart, and the shackles he broke in pieces; and no one had the strength to subdue him. Night and day among the tombs and on the mountains he was always howling and bruising himself with stones. When he saw Jesus from a distance, he ran and bowed down before him; and he shouted at the top of his voice, "What have you to do with me, Jesus, Son of the Most High God? I adjure you by God, do not torment me." For he had said to him, "Come out of the man, you unclean spirit!" Then Jesus asked him, "What is your name?" He replied, "My name is Legion; for we are many." He begged him earnestly not to send them out of the country. Now there on the hillside a great herd of swine was feeding; and the unclean spirits begged him, "Send us into the swine; let us enter them." So he gave them permission. And the unclean spirits came out and entered the swine; and the herd, numbering about two thousand, rushed down the steep bank into the sea, and were drowned in the sea. The swineherds ran off and told it in the city and in the country. Then people came to see what it was that had happened. They came to Jesus and saw the demoniac sitting there, clothed and in his right mind, the very man who had had the legion; and they were afraid. Those who had seen what had happened to the demoniac and to the swine reported it. Then they began to beg Jesus to leave their neighborhood. As he was getting into the boat, the man who had been possessed by demons begged him that he might be with him. But Jesus refused, and said to him, "Go home to your friends, and tell them how much the Lord has done for you, and what mercy he has shown you." And he went away and began to proclaim in the Decapolis how much Jesus had done for him; and everyone was amazed.

- In your time of prayer with Jesus, pay attention to how he acknowledges and cares for the man possessed by demons in today's Gospel story. What is your reaction to this?

- The man delivered of demons wanted to go with Jesus, but Jesus sent him home to his friends, to tell others what had happened to him. We begin telling the Good News right where we are. How do Jesus' instructions to this man translate into your situation?

Tuesday 4th February
Mark 5:21–43

When Jesus had crossed again in the boat to the other side, a great crowd gathered round him; and he was by the sea. Then one of the leaders of the synagogue named Jairus came and, when he saw him, fell at his feet and begged him repeatedly, "My little daughter is at the point of death. Come and lay your hands on her, so that she may be made well, and live." So he went with him. And a large crowd followed him and pressed in on him. Now there was a woman who had been suffering from hemorrhages for twelve years. She had endured much under many physicians, and had spent all that she had; and she was no better, but rather grew worse. She had heard about Jesus, and came up behind him in the crowd and touched his cloak, for she said, "If I but touch his clothes, I will be made well." Immediately her hemorrhage stopped; and she felt in her body that she was healed of her disease. Immediately aware that power had gone forth from him, Jesus turned about in the crowd and said, "Who touched my clothes?" And his disciples said to him, "You see the crowd pressing in on you; how can you say, 'Who touched me?'" He looked all around to see who had done it. But the woman, knowing what had happened to her, came in fear and trembling, fell down before him, and told him the whole truth. He said to her, "Daughter, your faith has made you well; go in peace, and be healed of your disease." While he was still speaking, some people came from the leader's house to say, "Your daughter is dead. Why trouble the teacher any further?" But overhearing what they said,

Jesus said to the leader of the synagogue, "Do not fear, only believe." He allowed no one to follow him except Peter, James, and John, the brother of James. When they came to the house of the leader of the synagogue, he saw a commotion, people weeping and wailing loudly. When he had entered, he said to them, "Why do you make a commotion and weep? The child is not dead but sleeping." And they laughed at him. Then he put them all outside, and took the child's father and mother and those who were with him, and went in where the child was. He took her by the hand and said to her, "Talitha cum," which means, "Little girl, get up!" And immediately the girl got up and began to walk about (she was twelve years of age). At this they were overcome with amazement. He strictly ordered them that no one should know this, and told them to give her something to eat.

- You might allow yourself to identify with Jairus or his wife (or even with their daughter) or with the distressed woman—inserting yourself into the world's suffering but also experiencing the world's hope. Throughout, keep your focus on Jesus, becoming aware of his deep compassion as well as of his healing power.

- Jesus is tender to the two women, calling one "Daughter!" and the other "Little girl" (literally, "Little lamb"). In my need I, too, can turn to him and find healing. Then I can in turn become a tender and healing presence to those around me.

Wednesday 5th February
Saint Agatha, Virgin and Martyr
Mark 6:1–6

He left that place and came to his hometown, and his disciples followed him. On the sabbath he began to teach in the synagogue, and many who heard him were astounded. They said, "Where did this man get all this? What is this wisdom that has been given to him? What deeds of power are being done by his hands! Is not this the carpenter, the son of Mary and brother of James and Joses and Judas and Simon, and are not his sisters here with us?" And they took offense at him. Then Jesus said to them, "Prophets are not without honor, except in their hometown, and among their own kin, and in their own house." And he could do no deed of power there, except that he laid his hands on a few sick people and cured them. And he was amazed at their unbelief. Then he went about among the villages teaching.

- As part of his tour of the towns and villages of Galilee, teaching and healing, Jesus visits Nazareth—this time, remarkably, with companions. We recall that at his baptism in the River Jordan by John, God the Father had declared Jesus, a working man in his thirties, to be his beloved Son: Jesus is true man and true God!

- I sit in the simple synagogue with the local people, join them in reciting the psalms, and then watch Jesus unroll the scroll, read from the Scriptures, and interpret them with great personal authority. What impression does Jesus make on me? On his own people? Do I feel for him?

Thursday 6th February
Saint Paul Mikki and Companions, Martyrs
Mark 6:7–13

He called the twelve and began to send them out two by two, and gave them authority over the unclean spirits. He ordered them to take nothing for their journey except a staff; no bread, no bag, no money in their belts; but to wear sandals and not to put on two tunics. He said to them, "Wherever you enter a house, stay there until you leave the place. If any place will not welcome you and they refuse to hear you, as you leave, shake off the dust that is on your feet as a testimony against them." So they went out and proclaimed that all should repent. They cast out many demons, and anointed with oil many who were sick and cured them.

- The story of human salvation is getting under way. The group is centered on Jesus, they are to carry his message to an unprepared world; they are being sent out on mission. They have to let go of their securities: a fixed abode, workplace, possessions, money. They must trust that Jesus knows what he is doing; they also need the goodwill of those they visit. In return, Jesus shares with them his authority over evil and his power to heal. Is that a fair exchange?

- Jesus' trust in us is breathtaking. I, too, am being sent out each day to bring Good News to those I engage with. Jesus, make me aware that you are with me wherever I go.

Friday 7th February
Mark 6:14–29

King Herod heard of it, for Jesus' name had become known. Some were saying, "John the baptizer has been raised from the dead; and for this reason these powers are at work in him." But others said, "It is Elijah." And others said, "It is a prophet, like one of the prophets of old." But when Herod heard of it, he said, "John, whom I beheaded, has been raised." For Herod himself had sent men who arrested John, bound him, and put him in prison on account of Herodias, his brother Philip's wife, because Herod had married her. For John had been telling Herod, "It is not lawful for you to have your brother's wife." And Herodias had a grudge against him, and wanted to kill him. But she could not, for Herod feared John, knowing that he was a righteous and holy man, and he protected him. When he heard him, he was greatly perplexed; and yet he liked to listen to him. But an opportunity came when Herod on his birthday gave a banquet for his courtiers and officers and for the leaders of Galilee. When his daughter Herodias came in and danced, she pleased Herod and his guests; and the king said to the girl, "Ask me for whatever you wish, and I will give it." And he solemnly swore to her, "Whatever you ask me, I will give you, even half of my kingdom." She went out and said to her mother, "What should I ask for?" She replied, "The head of John the baptizer." Immediately she rushed back to the king and requested, "I want you to give me at once the head of John the Baptist on a platter." The king was deeply grieved; yet out of regard for his oaths and for the guests, he did not want to refuse her. Immediately the king sent a soldier of the guard with orders to bring John's head. He went and beheaded him in the prison, brought his head on a platter, and gave it to the girl. Then the girl gave it to her mother. When his disciples heard about it, they came and took his body, and laid it in a tomb.

- The one redeeming feature in this appalling story is John's fearless stand for marital fidelity, even challenging the Tetrarch of Galilee, Herod Antipas. May we have the courage to remain steadfast to God's ways in the face of opposition.

- What he was hearing about Jesus disturbed Herod. In less than two years, he would be complicit in the death of Jesus, when Pilate would try to evade responsibility Jesus' execution by having Herod, the ruler of Galilee, try him. How would you describe Herod, based on this story?

Saturday 8th February
Mark 6:30–34

The apostles gathered around Jesus, and told him all that they had done and taught. He said to them, "Come away to a deserted place all by yourselves and rest a while." For many were coming and going, and they had no leisure even to eat. And they went away in the boat to a deserted place by themselves. Now many saw them going and recognized them, and they hurried there on foot from all the towns and arrived ahead of them. As he went ashore, he saw a great crowd; and he had compassion for them, because they were like sheep without a shepherd; and he began to teach them many things.

- "Come away . . ." Every time you make time to pray, hear and cherish Jesus' invitation to spend quiet time in his company. The apostles had come back to Jesus after being sent out by him on their mission of teaching and healing. They were eager to share their stories.

- Jesus too needed time out, to recover from the shock of John the Baptist's death; by this point, he probably knew that he would meet a similar fate. Yet he put aside his own needs to care for the people.

February 9—February 15

Something to think and pray about each day this week:

In an essay about the crushing loss of a friendship, novelist Jacquelyn Mitchard crafted a brilliant phrase. To describe how she'd neglected other relationships during the ill-fated friendship, Mitchard wrote that she had given "the very best strawberries" of her personal life only to that one particular friend.

I was skimming a magazine in the waiting room at my kids' orthodontist when I first read those words: the very best strawberries. The phrase ran through me like a chill; I didn't want to forget it. It made me consider my own relationships. Was I hanging onto any friendships that were lopsided or unhealthy, as Mitchard later discerned that one to be? Were there any friends I was taking for granted? What were my "best strawberries," anyway? Listening well? Surprising a friend with a meal? Sending an encouraging note? The gift of my time?

After reading the essay, I resolved to make sure to nurture my healthy friendships.

—Jennifer Grant, *Wholehearted Living*

The Presence of God

"Come to me, all you who are weary and are carrying heavy burdens, and I will give you rest." Here I am, Lord. I come to seek your presence. I long for your healing power.

Freedom

God is not foreign to my freedom. The Spirit breathes life into my most intimate desires, gently nudging me toward all that is good. I ask for the grace to let myself be enfolded by the Spirit.

Consciousness

I remind myself that I am in the presence of the Lord. I will take refuge in his loving heart. He is my strength in times of weakness. He is my comforter in times of sorrow.

The Word

I take my time to read the word of God slowly, a few times, allowing myself to dwell on anything that strikes me. (Please turn to the Scripture on the following pages. Inspiration points are there, should you need them. When you are ready, return here to continue.)

Conversation

Jesus, you always welcomed little children when you walked on this earth. Teach me to have a childlike trust in you. Teach me to live in the knowledge that you will never abandon me.

Conclusion

Glory be to the Father, and to the Son, and to the Holy Spirit,
As it was in the beginning, is now and ever shall be,
World without end. Amen.

Sunday 9th February
Fifth Sunday in Ordinary Time
Matthew 5:13–16

"You are the salt of the earth; but if salt has lost its taste, how can its saltiness be restored? It is no longer good for anything, but is thrown out and trampled under foot. You are the light of the world. A city built on a hill cannot be hid. No one after lighting a lamp puts it under the bushel basket, but on the lampstand, and it gives light to all in the house. In the same way, let your light shine before others, so that they may see your good works and give glory to your Father in heaven."

- Salt purifies, seasons, and preserves. Jesus wants us, by our gospel-centered lives, to be a distinctive seasoning in our communities.

- I am to let the message of Jesus shine out through my words and actions. Goodness lights up both the giver and the recipient. I stand up for the just rights of God's "little ones." I work for a world of kindness, peace, and love.

Monday 10th February
Saint Scholastica, Virgin
Mark 6:53–56

When Jesus and the disciples had crossed over, they came to land at Gennesaret and moored the boat. When they got out of the boat, people at once recognized him, and rushed about that whole region and began to bring the sick on mats to wherever they heard he was. And wherever he went, into villages or cities or farms, they laid the sick in the marketplaces, and begged him that they might touch even the fringe of his cloak; and all who touched it were healed.

- How the people of Gennesaret must have rejoiced over Jesus' visit. It was such a wondrous time of healing. They welcomed him as a healer. How do I welcome Jesus? How do I see him—as healer, friend, advocate?

- I imagine Jesus playing his part in rowing the boat and then mooring it. I watch as the word spreads that he has arrived. People rush about; they grab this chance to have their friends healed. Where am I in the scene? Am I helping others to reach him, or am I perhaps waiting for someone to bring me to Jesus? Can I let Jesus touch me?

Tuesday 11th February
Mark 7:1–13

Now when the Pharisees and some of the scribes who had come from Jerusalem gathered around him, they noticed that some of his disciples were eating with defiled hands, that is, without washing them. (For the Pharisees, and all the Jews, do not eat unless they thoroughly wash their hands, thus observing the tradition of the elders; and they do not eat anything from the market unless they wash it; and there are also many other traditions that they observe, the washing of cups, pots, and bronze kettles.) So the Pharisees and the scribes asked him, "Why do your disciples not live according to the tradition of the elders, but eat with defiled hands?" He said to them, "Isaiah prophesied rightly about you hypocrites, as it is written, 'This people honors me with their lips, but their hearts are far from me; in vain do they worship me, teaching human precepts as doctrines.' You abandon the commandment of God and hold to human tradition." Then he said to them, "You have a fine way of rejecting the commandment of God in order to keep your tradition! For Moses said, 'Honor your father and your mother'; and, 'Whoever speaks evil of father or mother must surely die.' But you say that if anyone tells father or mother, 'Whatever support you might have had from me is Corban' (that is, an offering to God)—then you no longer permit doing anything for a father or mother, thus making void the word of God through your tradition that you have handed on. And you do many things like this."

- The Pharisees multiplied religious laws and rituals to such an extent that it was impossible to know them all, much less observe them. Jesus accuses them of putting petty regulations above the law of God, the law of love and compassion.

- Am I, like the Pharisees, inclined to be judgmental and censorious at times? For a son to declare something to be "Corban," an offering devoted to God, when his parents are in need, is in direct conflict with the commandment of God to honor father and mother.

Wednesday 12th February

Mark 7:14–23

Then he called the crowd again and said to them, "Listen to me, all of you, and understand: there is nothing outside a person that by going in can defile, but the things that come out are what defile." When he had left the crowd and entered the house, his disciples asked him about the parable. He said to them, "Then do you also fail to understand? Do you not see that whatever goes into a person from outside cannot defile, since it enters, not the heart but the stomach, and goes out into the sewer?" (Thus he declared all foods clean.) And he said, "It is what comes out of a person that defiles. For it is from within, from the human heart, that evil intentions come: fornication, theft, murder, adultery, avarice, wickedness, deceit, licentiousness, envy, slander, pride, folly. All these evil things come from within, and they defile a person."

- For Jesus, the battlefield between good and evil is the human heart, and my heart is included! How clean is my heart?

- We can be grasping, we can spoil things for others, and leave our smudge on them. We can make things difficult for others, humiliate them, reduce them to tears. Lord, you list twelve "evil intentions" that defile a person. Reveal to me the one I need to address right now!

Thursday 13th February

Mark 7:24–30

From there Jesus set out and went away to the region of Tyre. He entered a house and did not want anyone to know he was there. Yet he could not escape notice, but a woman whose little daughter had an unclean spirit immediately heard about him, and she came and bowed down at his feet. Now the woman was a Gentile, of Syrophoenician origin. She begged him to cast the demon out of her daughter. He said to her, "Let the children be fed first, for it is not fair to take the children's food and throw it to the dogs." But she answered him, "Sir, even the dogs under the table eat the children's crumbs." Then he said to her, "For saying that, you may go—the demon has left your daughter." So she went home, found the child lying on the bed, and the demon gone.

- The prayer of the woman was not answered immediately. Her persistence shows Jesus how serious she was. Jesus, forgive me for my trivial requests. Help me listen to my prayers that I might learn what is really closest to my heart.

- This is a brave and determined woman! She risks her self-respect and dignity to save her sick daughter. She is the only woman in this Gospel to win an argument with Jesus. She gets him to change his mind about the scope of his ministry. Lord, may I have courage to do what I can so that the gifts women bring to the church may be more fully appreciated.

Friday 14th February
Saints Cyril, Monk, and Methodius, Bishop
Mark 7:31–37

Then he returned from the region of Tyre, and went by way of Sidon towards the Sea of Galilee, in the region of the Decapolis. They brought to him a deaf man who had an impediment in his speech; and they begged him to lay his hand on him. He took him aside in private, away from the crowd, and put his fingers into his ears, and he spat and touched his tongue. Then looking up to heaven, he sighed and said to him, "Ephphatha," that is, Be opened. And immediately his ears were opened, his tongue was released, and he spoke plainly. Then Jesus ordered them to tell no one; but the more he ordered them, the more zealously they proclaimed it. They were astounded beyond measure, saying, "He has done everything well; he even makes the deaf to hear and the mute to speak."

- Do I share in the astonishment of the onlookers? The people see in this miracle the fulfillment of the Jewish expectation that the Messiah would make the deaf hear and the dumb speak.

- Jesus does not see his healing powers as proofs of his divinity, but rather as signs that the God of mercy and goodness is close to us. He heals because he is moved with compassion. When we are compassionate to others, we, too, bring God's mercy close to them.

Saturday 15th February

Mark 8:1–10

In those days when there was again a great crowd without anything to eat, he called his disciples and said to them, "I have compassion for the crowd, because they have been with me now for three days and have nothing to eat. If I send them away hungry to their homes, they will faint on the way—and some of them have come from a great distance." His disciples replied, "How can one feed these people with bread here in the desert?" He asked them, "How many loaves do you have?" They said, "Seven." Then he ordered the crowd to sit down on the ground; and he took the seven loaves, and after giving thanks he broke them and gave them to his disciples to distribute; and they distributed them to the crowd. They had also a few small fish; and after blessing them, he ordered that these too should be distributed. They ate and were filled; and they took up the broken pieces left over, seven baskets full. Now there were about four thousand people. And he sent them away. And immediately he got into the boat with his disciples and went to the district of Dalmanutha.

- Jesus had already fed five thousand people. They had followed him when they saw him set out to have a quiet break on a deserted part of the lake shore (Mark 6:32–44). What do you imagine about the crowd that surrounds him now? Have they heard of the miraculous feeding? Are many of them ill as well as hungry? Can you imagine the spectrum of belief represented in that crowd?

- Jesus loved to share meals with everybody. Do I recognize his familiar ritual—"he took bread, gave thanks, broke, and gave"—with its Eucharistic overtones?

February 16—February 22

Something to think and pray about each day this week:

The Camino always challenged me: What would happen that day? Whom would I meet? Would I find openness in myself and others? Would I find life and consolation? For Ignatius it was about being sensitive to the divine, speaking in and through the ordinary events of the day. For me, it was often only after the event, reflecting back on it, that I could clearly see God working to take care of me, challenging me and leading me in very concrete ways. Being a pilgrim strips away protective insulation and accentuates the sense of trusting dependency, stepping out into the unknown. Every day is an act of trust, believing that all will be resolved on the road.

—Brendan McManus, SJ, *Redemption Road*

The Presence of God
What is present to me is what has a hold on my becoming.
I reflect on the presence of God always there in love,
amidst the many things that have a hold on me.
I pause and pray that I may let God
affect my becoming in this precise moment.

Freedom
By God's grace I was born to live in freedom. Free to enjoy the pleasures
he created for me. Dear Lord, grant that I may live as you intended, with
complete confidence in your loving care.

Consciousness
I exist in a web of relationships: links to nature, people, God.
I trace out these links, giving thanks for the life that flows through them.
Some links are twisted or broken; I may feel regret, anger, disappointment.
I pray for the gift of acceptance and forgiveness.

The Word
God speaks to each of us individually. I listen attentively to hear what he
is saying to me. Read the text a few times, then listen. (Please turn to the
Scripture on the following pages. Inspiration points are there, should you
need them. When you are ready, return here to continue.)

Conversation
I begin to talk with Jesus about the Scripture I have just read. What part
of it strikes a chord in me? Perhaps the words of a friend—or some story
I have heard recently—will rise to the surface in my consciousness. If so,
does the story throw light on what the Scripture passage may be saying
to me?

Conclusion
Glory be to the Father, and to the Son, and to the Holy Spirit,
As it was in the beginning, is now and ever shall be,
World without end. Amen.

Sunday 16th February
Sixth Sunday in Ordinary Time
Matthew 5:20–22a, 27–28, 33–34a, 37

"For I tell you, unless your righteousness exceeds that of the scribes and Pharisees, you will never enter the kingdom of heaven. You have heard that it was said to those of ancient times, 'You shall not murder'; and 'whoever murders shall be liable to judgment.' But I say to you that if you are angry with a brother or sister, you will be liable to judgment; and if you insult a brother or sister, you will be liable to the council; and if you say, 'You fool,' you will be liable to the hell of fire. You have heard that it was said, 'You shall not commit adultery.' But I say to you that everyone who looks at a woman with lust has already committed adultery with her in his heart. Again, you have heard that it was said to those of ancient times, 'You shall not swear falsely, but carry out the vows you have made to the Lord.' But I say to you, Do not swear at all . . . . Let your word be 'Yes, Yes' or 'No, No'; anything more than this comes from the evil one."

• These words are from the Sermon on the Mount. For the scribes and Pharisees, virtue was largely measured by external observance of the law. For Jesus, real virtue is in the heart. He expects honorable, respectful relationships between people. A Christian must be honest and trustworthy, a person of his word.

• What part of today's Scripture touches me—and in what way? I pray over any phrases that inspire me or challenge me. I pray over any phrases that give me joy or that elicit some resistance within me.

Monday 17th February
Mark 8:11–13

The Pharisees came and began to argue with him, asking him for a sign from heaven, to test him. And he sighed deeply in his spirit and said, "Why does this generation ask for a sign? Truly I tell you, no sign will be given to this generation." And he left them, and getting into the boat again, he went across to the other side.

• All the wonders that Jesus is doing are the "sign from heaven" that the Pharisees are demanding. But their hearts are closed. If a new sign came, they would look for yet another. Jesus realizes he can't satisfy the demanding, grasping search for evidence.

- Lord, what about me? Am I always looking for something more from you? You reveal yourself as being totally on my side, through your Passion and Resurrection. Let me accept these great signs. Let me trust that you are on my side even when smaller things do not go well.

Tuesday 18th February
Mark 8:14–21

Now the disciples had forgotten to bring any bread; and they had only one loaf with them in the boat. And he cautioned them, saying, "Watch out—beware of the yeast of the Pharisees and the yeast of Herod." They said to one another, "It is because we have no bread." And becoming aware of it, Jesus said to them, "Why are you talking about having no bread? Do you still not perceive or understand? Are your hearts hardened? Do you have eyes, and fail to see? Do you have ears, and fail to hear? And do you not remember? When I broke the five loaves for the five thousand, how many baskets full of broken pieces did you collect?" They said to him, "Twelve." "And the seven for the four thousand, how many baskets full of broken pieces did you collect?" And they said to him, "Seven." Then he said to them, "Do you not yet understand?"

- Jesus is frustrated with the disciples. Why?
- Jesus reminds the disciples of the signs they have already seen from him. What signs in my own life do I need to remember when my faith is weak?

Wednesday 19th February
Mark 8:22–26

They came to Bethsaida. Some people brought a blind man to him and begged him to touch him. He took the blind man by the hand and led him out of the village; and when he had put saliva on his eyes and laid his hands on him, he asked him, "Can you see anything?" And the man looked up and said, "I can see people, but they look like trees, walking." Then Jesus laid his hands on his eyes again; and he looked intently and his sight was restored, and he saw everything clearly. Then he sent him away to his home, saying, "Do not even go into the village."

- Jesus took the blind man out of the village and, having healed him, told him not to return there. This time of prayer for me is a time of stepping apart, of being alone with Jesus. Are there some concerns I have from which I can step away for a while? Are there some things about which I worry that I might leave in the hands of the Lord?

- This miracle is unusual in that it is gradual. Mark uses it to highlight the blindness embedded in our minds and heart, which can hinder God's working in us. I reflect on my own slow struggle to believe fully in Jesus, and I ask his help. Lord, may I see people as you see them— each a sister or brother for whom you died.

Thursday 20th February
Mark 8:27–33

Jesus went on with his disciples to the villages of Caesarea Philippi; and on the way he asked his disciples, "Who do people say that I am?" And they answered him, "John the Baptist; and others, Elijah; and still others, one of the prophets." He asked them, "But who do you say that I am?" Peter answered him, "You are the Messiah." And he sternly ordered them not to tell anyone about him. Then he began to teach them that the Son of Man must undergo great suffering, and be rejected by the elders, the chief priests, and the scribes, and be killed, and after three days rise again. He said all this quite openly. And Peter took him aside and began to rebuke him. But turning and looking at his disciples, he rebuked Peter and said, "Get behind me, Satan! For you are setting your mind not on divine things but on human things."

- We can sympathize with Peter because who among us can bear the thought of our best friend being tortured and killed? But Jesus tells Peter that God's plans are so much bigger than he imagines. Someone has said that God's dreams come to us several sizes too large! It takes us time to grow into them.

- What about my inner growth: have I stopped growing at some point, so that God cannot do more creative work with me? Lord, let me be open to your unrestricted dreams for me, even though they involve change and pain and, ultimately, death. This is the way to eternal joy.

Friday 21st February
Mark 8:34—9:1

He called the crowd with his disciples, and said to them, "If any want to become my followers, let them deny themselves and take up their cross and follow me. For those who want to save their life will lose it, and those who lose their life for my sake, and for the sake of the gospel, will save it. For what will it profit them to gain the whole world and forfeit their life? Indeed, what can they give in return for their life? Those who are ashamed of me and of my words in this adulterous and sinful generation, of them the Son of Man will also be ashamed when he comes in the glory of his Father with the holy angels." And he said to them, "Truly I tell you, there are some standing here who will not taste death until they see that the kingdom of God has come with power."

- I note that "the multitude"—all of us—are called to be faithful to the values of Jesus: self-denial, justice, compassionate goodness to others, rather than to the values of the world: greed, self-indulgence, celebrity. This is how I am to attain true life.
- When Mark was writing (AD 64), Christians were being persecuted for the sake of the gospel. In our day, how many more Christians are being put to death for their loyalty to Christ! I pray for God to strengthen them.

Saturday 22nd February
The Chair of Saint Peter the Apostle
Matthew 16:13–19

Now when Jesus came into the district of Caesarea Philippi, he asked his disciples, "Who do people say that the Son of Man is?" And they said, "Some say John the Baptist, but others Elijah, and still others Jeremiah or one of the prophets." He said to them, "But who do you say that I am?" Simon Peter answered, "You are the Messiah, the Son of the living God." And Jesus answered him, "Blessed are you, Simon son of Jonah! For flesh and blood has not revealed this to you, but my Father in heaven. And I tell you, you are Peter, and on this rock I will build my church, and the gates of Hades will not prevail against it. I will give you the keys of the kingdom of heaven, and whatever you bind on earth will be bound in heaven, and whatever you loose on earth will be loosed in heaven."

- Today's celebration of the Chair or primacy of Saint Peter, the original ancestor of our Christian family, marks the establishment of an organized Christian community under the leadership of Simon (now uniquely renamed Rock) and his successors.

- Do I believe and affirm with love Peter's declaration of faith in Jesus, not just as Messiah but as the Son of God?

Seventh Week in Ordinary Time
February 23—February 29

Something to think and pray about each day this week:

Love continually flows back and forth between God and me because that is the nature of love—it is reciprocal. Such love begins with God, and in freedom I am invited to accept this love to make my corresponding loving response. Each day I desire to know with ever-increasing joy that I am loved unconditionally. My response to this deepening interior knowledge of the heart is to love God in return through my praise, reverence, and service.

—Casey Beaumier, SJ, *A Purposeful Path*

The Presence of God

"Be still, and know that I am God!" Lord, your words lead us to the calmness and greatness of your presence.

Freedom

"In these days, God taught me as a schoolteacher teaches a pupil" (Saint Ignatius). I remind myself that there are things God has to teach me yet, and I ask for the grace to hear them and let them change me.

Consciousness

How am I really feeling? Lighthearted? Heavyhearted? I may be very much at peace, happy to be here.
Equally, I may be frustrated, worried, or angry.
I acknowledge how I really am. It is the real me whom the Lord loves.

The Word

God speaks to each of us individually. I listen attentively to hear what he is saying to me. Read the text a few times, then listen. (Please turn to the Scripture on the following pages. Inspiration points are there, should you need them. When you are ready, return here to continue.)

Conversation

Do I notice myself reacting as I pray with the word of God? Do I feel challenged, comforted, angry? Imagining Jesus sitting or standing by me, I speak out my feelings, as one trusted friend to another.

Conclusion

I thank God for these moments we have spent together and for any insights I have been given concerning the text.

Sunday 23rd February
Seventh Sunday in Ordinary Time
Matthew 5:38–48

"You have heard that it was said, 'An eye for an eye and a tooth for a tooth.' But I say to you, Do not resist an evildoer. But if anyone strikes you on the right cheek, turn the other also; and if anyone wants to sue you and take your coat, give your cloak as well; and if anyone forces you to go one mile, go also the second mile. Give to everyone who begs from you, and do not refuse anyone who wants to borrow from you. You have heard that it was said, 'You shall love your neighbor and hate your enemy.' But I say to you, Love your enemies and pray for those who persecute you, so that you may be children of your Father in heaven; for he makes his sun rise on the evil and on the good, and sends rain on the righteous and on the unrighteous. For if you love those who love you, what reward do you have? Do not even the tax collectors do the same? And if you greet only your brothers and sisters, what more are you doing than others? Do not even the Gentiles do the same? Be perfect, therefore, as your heavenly Father is perfect."

- I am to be as perfect as God the Father! Is Jesus being unreasonable, asking too much of me? Jesus portrays God as a loving and proud Father who sees himself in me and in each of his sons and daughters. So he expects that I, a dearly loved child of his, created in his image, will be good to all my brothers and sisters, even my "enemies" and persecutors.

- I am not to retaliate, but should give, share, lend, and go the extra mile. How do I see myself doing one of these in the days to come?

Monday 24th February
Mark 9:14–29

When they came to the disciples, they saw a great crowd around them, and some scribes arguing with them. When the whole crowd saw him, they were immediately overcome with awe, and they ran forward to greet him. He asked them, "What are you arguing about with them?" Someone from the crowd answered him, "Teacher, I brought you my son; he has a spirit that makes him unable to speak; and whenever it seizes him, it dashes him down; and he foams and grinds his teeth and becomes rigid;

and I asked your disciples to cast it out, but they could not do so." He answered them, "You faithless generation, how much longer must I be among you? How much longer must I put up with you? Bring him to me." And they brought the boy to him. When the spirit saw him, immediately it convulsed the boy, and he fell on the ground and rolled about, foaming at the mouth. Jesus asked the father, "How long has this been happening to him?" And he said, "From childhood. It has often cast him into the fire and into the water, to destroy him; but if you are able to do anything, have pity on us and help us." Jesus said to him, "If you are able!—All things can be done for the one who believes." Immediately the father of the child cried out, "I believe; help my unbelief!" When Jesus saw that a crowd came running together, he rebuked the unclean spirit, saying to it, "You spirit that keeps this boy from speaking and hearing, I command you, come out of him, and never enter him again!" After crying out and convulsing him terribly, it came out, and the boy was like a corpse, so that most of them said, "He is dead." But Jesus took him by the hand and lifted him up, and he was able to stand. When he had entered the house, his disciples asked him privately, "Why could we not cast it out?" He said to them, "This kind can come out only through prayer."

- Notice Jesus' impatience in this situation. In it we can find resonance with our own human impatience and also find the strength to persevere. Doubt can be an important part of belief and can add to our growth.

- Jesus' disciples prove to be a disappointment. Lord, I sometimes feel let down and disappointed by the church or its ministers. When I am discouraged, help me to look beyond the institution and its ministers. Let me turn in faith to you, O healer and giver of life.

Tuesday 25th February
Mark 9:30–37

They went on from there and passed through Galilee. He did not want anyone to know it; for he was teaching his disciples, saying to them, "The Son of Man is to be betrayed into human hands, and they will kill him, and three days after being killed, he will rise again." But they did not understand what he was saying and were afraid to ask him. Then they came to Capernaum; and when he was in the house he asked them, "What were you arguing about on the way?" But they were silent, for on the way they had argued with one another who was the greatest. He sat down, called the twelve, and said to them, "Whoever wants to be first must be last of all and servant of all." Then he took a little child and put it among them; and taking it in his arms, he said to them, "Whoever welcomes one such child in my name welcomes me, and whoever welcomes me welcomes not me but the one who sent me."

- The disciples are on the way to Jerusalem with Jesus. They cannot accept that such a dreadful fate awaits him there: betrayal and death. They are in shock, distraught, squabbling among themselves. How would I react if I were one of the disciples and learned that Jesus would be killed soon?

- Do I seek to be important, wealthy, a celebrity? In welcoming a little child, Jesus reminds us that greatness is to be found in loving service of the weaker members of the community.

Wednesday 26th February
Ash Wednesday
Matthew 6:1–6, 16–18

"Beware of practicing your piety before others in order to be seen by them; for then you have no reward from your Father in heaven. So whenever you give alms, do not sound a trumpet before you, as the hypocrites do in the synagogues and in the streets, so that they may be praised by others. Truly I tell you, they have received their reward. But when you give alms, do not let your left hand know what your right hand is doing, so that your alms may be done in secret; and your Father who sees in secret will reward you. And whenever you pray, do not be like the hypocrites; for they love to stand and pray in the synagogues and at the street corners, so that they may be seen by others. Truly I tell you, they have received their reward. But whenever you pray, go into your room and shut the door and pray to your Father who is in secret; and your Father who sees in secret will reward you. And whenever you fast, do not look dismal, like the hypocrites, for they disfigure their faces so as to show others that they are fasting. Truly I tell you, they have received their reward. But when you fast, put oil on your head and wash your face, so that your fasting may be seen not by others but by your Father who is in secret; and your Father who sees in secret will reward you."

- Today is Ash Wednesday, the beginning of Lent, when we prepare for the celebration of Holy Week and Easter. Let's increase our times of prayer during these six weeks of Lent.

- Why do you think Jesus encourages us to be private in our prayers? What do you see as the dangers of making our inner life more public?

Thursday 27th February
Luke 9:22–25

[Jesus said to his disciples:] "The Son of Man must undergo great suffering, and be rejected by the elders, chief priests, and scribes, and be killed, and on the third day be raised." Then he said to them all, "If any want to become my followers, let them deny themselves and take up their cross daily and follow me. For those who want to save their life will lose it, and those who lose their life for my sake will save it. What does it profit them if they gain the whole world, but lose or forfeit themselves?"

- Life holds so many challenges: the losses and daily disappointments that come my way. Do I despair, fall apart, and give up? Or do I rise to challenges and shoulder my crosses with courage, knowing that Jesus shares the load, thereby filling me with contentment, even joy?

- What do I think Jesus means by the statement, "those who lose their life for my sake will save it"? I ponder this statement in my prayer today.

Friday 28th February
Matthew 9:14–15

Then the disciples of John came to Jesus, saying, "Why do we and the Pharisees fast often, but your disciples do not fast?" And Jesus said to them, "The wedding guests cannot mourn as long as the bridegroom is with them, can they? The days will come when the bridegroom is taken away from them, and then they will fast."

- Spend some time each day allowing the joy of God to fill your heart. Spend some time mourning with him, as joy is lost for so many. Any fasting is to remind us that the Lord of all joy suffers in his people, perhaps in people who are near to us. Prayer brings us near to others and near to God.

- Here Jesus uses the notion of fasting to reveal that the God whom the Jews hunger for has arrived. Rejoicing, not mourning, is the appropriate response to the presence of divine mercy revealed in Jesus. Lord, this Lent may my prayer and my fasting reveal my inner hunger for you.

Saturday 29th February
Luke 5:27–32

After this he went out and saw a tax collector named Levi, sitting at the tax booth; and he said to him, "Follow me." And he got up, left everything, and followed him. Then Levi gave a great banquet for him in his house; and there was a large crowd of tax collectors and others sitting at the table with them. The Pharisees and their scribes were complaining to his disciples, saying, "Why do you eat and drink with tax collectors and sinners?" Jesus answered, "Those who are well have no need of a physician, but those who are sick; I have come to call not the righteous but sinners to repentance."

- "Who? . . . me?" Levi, a despised tax collector for the hated Romans, must have been astonished that Jesus should want him as a disciple. Are you seated at your table just now? Hear Jesus knock, asking, "May I come in?"

- Or, sit at table in Levi's house and join in the great banquet with Jesus and all the other guests. How much Jesus loves to socialize at meals, to meet people where they are most at home or in places of joyful nourishment!

March 1—March 7

Something to think and pray about each day this week:

A public faith life may bruise your head. It can embarrass you, challenge you, and create large amounts of anxiety and fear—on buses, in restaurants, along roads, or in Wiccan barns filled with wands. This is even more difficult if you are twenty-seven and some of your friends look at you the way you looked at the Wiccan warlock selling toads. Yet, along with its bumps and bruises, toads and dirty looks, the key ingredients to having a public faith life still include generous heapings of joy and grace, love, wonder, and strength—the strength to sometimes do things you never thought you could do.

—Matt Weber, *Fearing the Stigmata*

The Presence of God

I pause for a moment and think of the love and the grace that God showers on me. I am created in the image and likeness of God; I am God's dwelling place.

Freedom

Lord, you granted me the great gift of freedom. In these times, O Lord, grant that I may be free from any form of racism or intolerance. Remind me that we are all equal in your loving eyes.

Consciousness

Knowing that God loves me unconditionally, I can afford to be honest about how I am.
How has the day been, and how do I feel now? I share my feelings openly with the Lord.

The Word

I take my time to read the word of God slowly, a few times, allowing myself to dwell on anything that strikes me. (Please turn to the Scripture on the following pages. Inspiration points are there, should you need them. When you are ready, return here to continue.)

Conversation

Sometimes I wonder what I might say if I were to meet you in person, Lord.
I think I might say, "Thank you" because you are always there for me.

Conclusion

I thank God for these moments we have spent together and for any insights I have been given concerning the text.

Sunday 1st March
First Sunday of Lent
Matthew 4:1–11

Then Jesus was led up by the Spirit into the wilderness to be tempted by the devil. He fasted forty days and forty nights, and afterwards he was famished. The tempter came and said to him, "If you are the Son of God, command these stones to become loaves of bread." But he answered, "It is written, 'One does not live by bread alone, but by every word that comes from the mouth of God.'" Then the devil took him to the holy city and placed him on the pinnacle of the temple, saying to him, "If you are the Son of God, throw yourself down; for it is written, 'He will command his angels concerning you,' and 'On their hands they will bear you up, so that you will not dash your foot against a stone.'" Jesus said to him, "Again it is written, 'Do not put the Lord your God to the test.'" Again, the devil took him to a very high mountain and showed him all the kingdoms of the world and their splendor; and he said to him, "All these I will give you, if you will fall down and worship me." Jesus said to him, "Away with you, Satan! for it is written, 'Worship the Lord your God, and serve only him.'" Then the devil left him, and suddenly angels came and waited on him.

- At his baptism by John, Jesus had heard the voice of God the Father identifying him, a young village workman, as his beloved Son. During his temptation, he must have reflected on the challenges of this radically new mission. Am I tempted, like Jesus here, to put my needs first or to seek power that will make it possible for me to accomplish my goals?

- Do I want to attract notice, to be popular? A sense of power is intoxicating. Do I want to be influential, dominating others rather than serving them?

Monday 2nd March
Matthew 25:31–46

"When the Son of Man comes in his glory, and all the angels with him, then he will sit on the throne of his glory. All the nations will be gathered before him, and he will separate people one from another as a shepherd separates the sheep from the goats, and he will put the sheep at his right hand and the goats at the left. Then the king will say to those at his right hand, 'Come, you that are blessed by my Father, inherit the kingdom prepared for you from the foundation of the world; for I was hungry and you gave me food, I was thirsty and you gave me something to drink, I was a stranger and you welcomed me, I was naked and you gave me clothing, I was sick and you took care of me, I was in prison and you visited me.' Then the righteous will answer him, 'Lord, when was it that we saw you hungry and gave you food, or thirsty and gave you something to drink? And when was it that we saw you a stranger and welcomed you, or naked and gave you clothing? And when was it that we saw you sick or in prison and visited you?' And the king will answer them, 'Truly I tell you, just as you did it to one of the least of these who are members of my family, you did it to me.' Then he will say to those at his left hand, 'You that are accursed, depart from me into the eternal fire prepared for the devil and his angels; for I was hungry and you gave me no food, I was thirsty and you gave me nothing to drink, I was a stranger and you did not welcome me, naked and you did not give me clothing, sick and in prison and you did not visit me.' Then they also will answer, 'Lord, when was it that we saw you hungry or thirsty or a stranger or naked or sick or in prison, and did not take care of you?' Then he will answer them, 'Truly I tell you, just as you did not do it to one of the least of these, you did not do it to me.' And these will go away into eternal punishment, but the righteous into eternal life."

- The Father delights in people who show kindly, compassionate, practical love to those in need.

- Saint Matthew's hearers struggled with what would happen to non-Jews, because they themselves were the Chosen People. Jesus says that with his coming into the world, everyone is a "chosen" person. Everyone is to be treated with limitless respect. Jesus is already present, but in disguise, in every person. What do I see when I see the needy? Do I focus on the hidden glory of others? How would I fare if human history were to be terminated today?

Tuesday 3rd March
Matthew 6:7–15

Jesus said, "When you are praying, do not heap up empty phrases as the Gentiles do; for they think that they will be heard because of their many words. Do not be like them, for your Father knows what you need before you ask him. Pray then in this way: 'Our Father in heaven, hallowed be your name. Your kingdom come. Your will be done, on earth as it is in heaven. Give us this day our daily bread. And forgive us our debts, as we also have forgiven our debtors. And do not bring us to the time of trial, but rescue us from the evil one.' For if you forgive others their trespasses, your heavenly Father will also forgive you; but if you do not forgive others, neither will your Father forgive your trespasses."

• Jesus addressed the Father in his native Aramaic language as "Abba," a child's term of endearment, like Papa, Mama, Dada. The Lord's Prayer flows from the Jewish synagogue prayers that Jesus would have recited. It's not just a prayer for Jews or Christians but is appropriate for all believers in God.

• True prayer is simple and trusting, sometimes without words: "Be still and know that I am God" (Psalm 46:10). It can be good to dwell on a phrase or to savor a single word.

Wednesday 4th March
Luke 11:29–32

When the crowds were increasing, he began to say, "This generation is an evil generation; it asks for a sign, but no sign will be given to it except the sign of Jonah. For just as Jonah became a sign to the people of Nineveh, so the Son of Man will be to this generation. The queen of the South will rise at the judgment with the people of this generation and condemn them, because she came from the ends of the earth to listen to the wisdom of Solomon, and see, something greater than Solomon is here! The people of Nineveh will rise up at the judgment with this generation and condemn it, because they repented at the proclamation of Jonah, and see, something greater than Jonah is here!"

• People are coming to Jesus looking for signs. He compares himself to Solomon and Jonah, who were signs from God in their lifetimes. He, however, speaks with greater authority than these. What signs in your life are leading you to Jesus? Who are your advisors, and whose voice do you listen to when you think about the deep meaning of your life?

- Jesus tells it as it is. When "the crowds were increasing," he challenged them to ask themselves why they were coming to see and listen to him. Why do I come to prayer each day? Something greater is here.

Thursday 5th March
Matthew 7:7–12

"Ask, and it will be given to you; search, and you will find; knock, and the door will be opened for you. For everyone who asks receives, and everyone who searches finds, and for everyone who knocks, the door will be opened. Is there anyone among you who, if your child asks for bread, will give a stone? Or if the child asks for a fish, will give a snake? If you then, who are evil, know how to give good gifts to your children, how much more will your Father in heaven give good things to those who ask him! In everything do to others as you would have them do to you; for this is the law and the prophets."

- In these short instructions for prayer, Jesus invites us to come before God with expectant hearts, asking for what we need. God is always listening to our prayers. "All things can be done for the one who believes" (Mark 9:23).
- Parent/child is only a metaphor for what happens in prayer. I know, Lord, that you always hear my cry, but I do not always understand your answer. I will still go on praying to you, happy to fall back on the "Our Father."

Friday 6th March
Matthew 5:20–26

"For I tell you, unless your righteousness exceeds that of the scribes and Pharisees, you will never enter the kingdom of heaven. You have heard that it was said to those of ancient times, 'You shall not murder'; and 'whoever murders shall be liable to judgment.' But I say to you that if you are angry with a brother or sister, you will be liable to judgment; and if you insult a brother or sister, you will be liable to the council; and if you say, 'You fool,' you will be liable to the hell of fire. So when you are offering your gift at the altar, if you remember that your brother or sister has something against you, leave your gift there before the altar and go;

first be reconciled to your brother or sister, and then come and offer your gift. Come to terms quickly with your accuser while you are on the way to court with him, or your accuser may hand you over to the judge, and the judge to the guard, and you will be thrown into prison. Truly I tell you, you will never get out until you have paid the last penny."

- Jesus' message goes deeper than adherence to the letter of the law, which the Pharisees were preoccupied with. It is about embracing the gospel values of forgiveness and reconciliation.

- The standards operating in the kingdom of heaven are high! Jesus does not dismiss Old Testament teaching but goes to the root of things. We can be smug and content with our conventional good behavior. However, Jesus says to us, "But what about your anger? What about insulting someone? Do you despise anyone, ever?"

Saturday 7th March
Matthew 5:43–48

"You have heard that it was said, 'You shall love your neighbor and hate your enemy.' But I say to you, Love your enemies and pray for those who persecute you, so that you may be children of your Father in heaven; for he makes his sun rise on the evil and on the good, and sends rain on the righteous and on the unrighteous. For if you love those who love you, what reward do you have? Do not even the tax collectors do the same? And if you greet only your brothers and sisters, what more are you doing than others? Do not even the Gentiles do the same? Be perfect, therefore, as your heavenly Father is perfect."

- Jesus teaches his followers about a new criterion of love that is to be the standard for the early Christian community and for us. It is not enough to love those who love you. To truly live as a disciple of Jesus demands that we reach out with an all-embracing love to others, including those who make life difficult for us.

- "If we love one another, God lives in us, and his love is perfected in us" (1 John 4:12). Contemplate the wonder of God's unconditional love for you and ask for the grace to radiate that love in the different situations and activities of your day.

March 8—March 14

Something to think and pray about each day this week:

Be who only you are. Rise to what you dream. Do not cease to dream. Do not despair even though pain comes hand in hand with joy. That is the nature of the gift we were given. It is the most amazing and extraordinary and confusing and complicated gift that ever was. Never take it for granted, not for an instant, not for the seventh of a second. The price for it is your attentiveness and generosity and kindness and mercy. Also humor. Humor will destroy the brooding castles of the murderers and chase their armies wailing into the darkness. What you do now, today, in these next few minutes, matters more than I can tell you. It advances the universe two inches. If we are our best selves, there will come a world where children do not weep and war is a memory and violence is a joke no one tells, having forgotten the words. You and I know this is possible. It is what He said could happen if we loved well. He did not mean loving only the people you know. He meant every idiot and liar and thief and blowhard and even your cousin. I do not know how that could be so, but I know it is so. So do you. Let us begin again, you and me, this afternoon. Ready?

—Brian Doyle, *The Thorny Grace of It*

The Presence of God
Dear Jesus, today I call on you, but not to ask for anything. I'd like only to dwell in your presence. May my heart respond to your love.

Freedom
God my creator, you gave me life and the gift of freedom. Through your love I exist in this world. May I never take the gift of life for granted. May I always respect others' right to life.

Consciousness
I ask how I am today. Am I particularly tired, stressed, or anxious? If any of these characteristics apply, can I try to let go of the concerns that disturb me?

The Word
The word of God comes down to us through the Scriptures. May the Holy Spirit enlighten my mind and my heart to respond to the Gospel teachings. (Please turn to the Scripture on the following pages. Inspiration points are there, should you need them. When you are ready, return here to continue.)

Conversation
I begin to talk with Jesus about the Scripture I have just read. What part of it strikes a chord in me? Perhaps the words of a friend—or some story I have heard recently—will rise to the surface in my consciousness. If so, does the story throw light on what the Scripture passage may be saying to me?

Conclusion
Glory be to the Father, and to the Son, and to the Holy Spirit,
As it was in the beginning, is now and ever shall be,
World without end. Amen.

Sunday 8th March
Second Sunday of Lent
Matthew 17:1–9

Six days later, Jesus took with him Peter and James and his brother John and led them up a high mountain, by themselves. And he was transfigured before them, and his face shone like the sun, and his clothes became dazzling white. Suddenly there appeared to them Moses and Elijah, talking with him. Then Peter said to Jesus, "Lord, it is good for us to be here; if you wish, I will make three dwellings here, one for you, one for Moses, and one for Elijah." While he was still speaking, suddenly a bright cloud overshadowed them, and from the cloud a voice said, "This is my Son, the Beloved; with him I am well pleased; listen to him!" When the disciples heard this, they fell to the ground and were overcome by fear. But Jesus came and touched them, saying, "Get up and do not be afraid." And when they looked up, they saw no one except Jesus himself alone. As they were coming down the mountain, Jesus ordered them, "Tell no one about the vision until after the Son of Man has been raised from the dead."

- The disciples see Jesus revealed in all his divine glory. It is a special moment for them, as Peter confirms: "it is good for us to be here." The voice of God the Father resounding from the cloud has an important message to convey to the disciples, and us: "Listen to him." A listening heart is a heart warmed by the love of God and taught by his words. The one we listen to is the Son of God: Jesus, transfigured in his humanity.

- Prayer is better described as listening than speaking. Spend some time in prayer just listening to the mood of love and peace in God's presence.

Monday 9th March
Luke 6:36–38

[Jesus said to the disciples,] "Be merciful, just as your Father is merciful. Do not judge, and you will not be judged; do not condemn, and you will not be condemned. Forgive, and you will be forgiven; give, and it will be given to you. A good measure, pressed down, shaken together, running over, will be put into your lap; for the measure you give will be the measure you get back."

- What a beautiful, challenging Lenten program! Let us strive each day for the remainder of Lent not to judge or condemn; to forgive and tell others that they are forgiven; and to do one daily act of generosity. What transformed people we will be by Easter!

- Jesus stresses once again the primary importance of good relationships with others. The world would be a different place if we were merciful and noncondemning. Lord, my poor heart is very small, and it can also be very hard. Your heart is large and also very tender and compassionate. When I try to forgive others, my heart becomes a bit more like yours, and you swamp me with your overflowing generosity.

Tuesday 10th March
Matthew 23:1–12

Then Jesus said to the crowds and to his disciples, "The scribes and the Pharisees sit on Moses' seat; therefore, do whatever they teach you and follow it; but do not do as they do, for they do not practice what they teach. They tie up heavy burdens, hard to bear, and lay them on the shoulders of others; but they themselves are unwilling to lift a finger to move them. They do all their deeds to be seen by others; for they make their phylacteries broad and their fringes long. They love to have the place of honor at banquets and the best seats in the synagogues, and to be greeted with respect in the marketplaces, and to have people call them rabbi. But you are not to be called rabbi, for you have one teacher, and you are all students. And call no one your father on earth, for you have one Father—the one in heaven. Nor are you to be called instructors, for you have one instructor, the Messiah. The greatest among you will be your servant. All who exalt themselves will be humbled, and all who humble themselves will be exalted."

- The Pharisees had great clarity about their beliefs: they allowed their belief in God to speak to them about their own worthiness and to judge the unworthiness of others. Our religious acts and attitudes are our attempts to recognize God's presence and power. In hearing God's response, we are rescued from proclaiming ourselves.

- I pray not for certainty, but for humility. I ask God to let me know that, in being least, I can allow God to raise me up. This is the only promotion that matters!

Wednesday 11th March
Matthew 20:17–28

While Jesus was going up to Jerusalem, he took the twelve disciples aside by themselves, and said to them on the way, "See, we are going up to Jerusalem, and the Son of Man will be handed over to the chief priests and scribes, and they will condemn him to death; then they will hand him over to the Gentiles to be mocked and flogged and crucified; and on the third day he will be raised." Then the mother of the sons of Zebedee came to him with her sons, and kneeling before him, she asked a favor of him. And he said to her, "What do you want?" She said to him, "Declare that these two sons of mine will sit, one at your right hand and one at your left, in your kingdom." But Jesus answered, "You do not know what you are asking. Are you able to drink the cup that I am about to drink?" They said to him, "We are able." He said to them, "You will indeed drink my cup, but to sit at my right hand and at my left, this is not mine to grant, but it is for those for whom it has been prepared by my Father." When the ten heard it, they were angry with the two brothers. But Jesus called them to him and said, "You know that the rulers of the Gentiles lord it over them, and their great ones are tyrants over them. It will not be so among you; but whoever wishes to be great among you must be your servant, and whoever wishes to be first among you must be your slave; just as the Son of Man came not to be served but to serve, and to give his life a ransom for many."

- Jesus describes vividly the degrading ways in which he will be treated in his Passion. He does this to strengthen his disciples. When we decide to act lovingly in all we do, we become vulnerable. People will take advantage of us. But love will have the final word. We will be raised up as Jesus was. I thank God for this.

- Jesus, you abhor all forms of domination. The kingdom of God is to be a domination-free community. I can see how Christian churches fall into the trap of domination. But do I dominate anyone? Even in an argument? Do I even think I am better than anyone else?

Thursday 12th March
Luke 16:19–31

Jesus said to the Pharisees, "There was a rich man who was dressed in purple and fine linen and who feasted sumptuously every day. And at his gate lay a poor man named Lazarus, covered with sores, who longed to satisfy his hunger with what fell from the rich man's table; even the dogs would come and lick his sores. The poor man died and was carried away by the angels to be with Abraham. The rich man also died and was buried. In Hades, where he was being tormented, he looked up and saw Abraham far away with Lazarus by his side. He called out, 'Father Abraham, have mercy on me, and send Lazarus to dip the tip of his finger in water and cool my tongue; for I am in agony in these flames.' But Abraham said, 'Child, remember that during your lifetime you received your good things, and Lazarus in like manner evil things; but now he is comforted here, and you are in agony. Besides all this, between you and us a great chasm has been fixed, so that those who might want to pass from here to you cannot do so, and no one can cross from there to us.' He said, 'Then, father, I beg you to send him to my father's house—for I have five brothers—that he may warn them, so that they will not also come into this place of torment.' Abraham replied, 'They have Moses and the prophets; they should listen to them.' He said, 'No, father Abraham; but if someone goes to them from the dead, they will repent.' He said to him, 'If they do not listen to Moses and the prophets, neither will they be convinced even if someone rises from the dead.'"

- The poor are brought straight into the kingdom of God, while the rich have to endure the pain of conversion. I ponder the mysterious workings of God's providence. I pray for the rich that they be converted, and I ask to be shown how to share my own possessions with the needy.

- During Lent I try to hear the call to come back home to God. I join the great pilgrimage of people who, through the ages, have been called by Moses and the prophets to listen to the word of the Lord.

Friday 13th March
Matthew 21:33–43, 45–46

"Listen to another parable. There was a landowner who planted a vineyard, put a fence around it, dug a wine press in it, and built a watchtower. Then he leased it to tenants and went to another country. When the harvest time had come, he sent his slaves to the tenants to collect his produce. But the tenants seized his slaves and beat one, killed another, and stoned another. Again he sent other slaves, more than the first; and they treated them in the same way. Finally he sent his son to them, saying, 'They will respect my son.' But when the tenants saw the son, they said to themselves, 'This is the heir; come, let us kill him and get his inheritance.' So they seized him, threw him out of the vineyard, and killed him. Now when the owner of the vineyard comes, what will he do to those tenants?" They said to him, "He will put those wretches to a miserable death, and lease the vineyard to other tenants who will give him the produce at the harvest time." Jesus said to them, "Have you never read in the scriptures: 'The stone that the builders rejected / has become the cornerstone; this was the Lord's doing, / and it is amazing in our eyes'? Therefore I tell you, the kingdom of God will be taken away from you and given to a people that produces the fruits of the kingdom." When the chief priests and the Pharisees heard his parables, they realized that he was speaking about them. They wanted to arrest him, but they feared the crowds, because they regarded him as a prophet.

- We are the tenants in the parable. God provides everything we need to make our vineyard prosper. God gives us the freedom to run the vineyard as we choose—but it is God's. This is what prayer is about— coming to know the mind of God about our lives. What fruits will I produce for the Lord?

- One of the saddest statements in the Gospels is this innocent comment by the father: "They will respect my son." I am frightened to think what would happen if Jesus came into our world today. His message about the kingdom of God would put him in direct opposition to so many other kingdoms. He would become an enemy to be got rid of. Jesus, you were thrown out and killed. But you took no revenge. Instead, by your love you reconciled everyone with God. May I always wish others well and pray for them, even if they hurt me.

Saturday 14th March
Luke 15:1–3, 11–32

Now all the tax collectors and sinners were coming near to listen to him. And the Pharisees and the scribes were grumbling and saying, "This fellow welcomes sinners and eats with them." So he told them this parable: "There was a man who had two sons. The younger of them said to his father, 'Father, give me the share of the property that will belong to me.' So he divided his property between them. A few days later the younger son gathered all he had and traveled to a distant country, and there he squandered his property in dissolute living. When he had spent everything, a severe famine took place throughout that country, and he began to be in need. So he went and hired himself out to one of the citizens of that country, who sent him to his fields to feed the pigs. He would gladly have filled himself with the pods that the pigs were eating; and no one gave him anything. But when he came to himself he said, 'How many of my father's hired hands have bread enough and to spare, but here I am dying of hunger! I will get up and go to my father, and I will say to him, "Father, I have sinned against heaven and before you; I am no longer worthy to be called your son; treat me like one of your hired hands."' So he set off and went to his father. But while he was still far off, his father saw him and was filled with compassion; he ran and put his arms around him and kissed him. Then the son said to him, 'Father, I have sinned against heaven and before you; I am no longer worthy to be called your son.' But the father said to his slaves, 'Quickly, bring out a robe—the best one—and put it on him; put a ring on his finger and sandals on his feet. And get the fatted calf and kill it, and let us eat and celebrate; for this son of mine was dead and is alive again; he was lost and is found!' And they began to celebrate. Now his elder son was in the field; and when he came and approached the house, he heard music and dancing. He called one of the slaves and asked what was going on. He replied, 'Your brother has come, and your father has killed the fatted calf, because he has got him back safe and sound.' Then he became angry and refused to go in. His father came out and began to plead with him. But he answered his father, 'Listen! For all these years I have been working like a slave for you, and I have never disobeyed your command; yet you have never given me even a young goat so that I might celebrate with my friends. But when this son of yours came back, who has devoured your property with prostitutes, you killed the fatted calf for him!' Then the father said to him, 'Son, you are always with me, and all that is mine is yours. But we had to celebrate and rejoice, because this brother of yours was dead and has come to life; he was lost and has been found.'"

- Jesus told a rather elaborate story. If you could not use a story but had to create a rational argument, how would you explain what Jesus was trying to say?

- Jesus, remind me that I am part of the eternal sacred story. And teach me how to communicate to others that their individual stories are also sacred.

March 15—March 21

Something to think and pray about each day this week:

Jesus clearly called us to compassionate service, especially for the people most in need. Melding our "being" with our "doing" proves a constant challenge. Ignatius reached a balance of prayer and action, realizing that one without the other puts our spirituality out of harmony.

Pedro Arrupe, former superior general of the Jesuits, remarked:

> "Service is the key idea of the charism of Ignatius. It is an idea whose moving power achieved in the life and spirituality of Ignatius—even in his mystical phase—a total realization: unconditioned and limitless service, service that is large-hearted and humble. It could be said that even the Trinitarian "lights," which enriched his mystical life, rather than leading to a passive and contemplative quieting, spurred him to a greater service of this God he contemplated with such great love and reverence."
> (*Challenge*, 254)

—Jacqueline Bergan and Marie Schwan, CSJ,
Praying with Ignatius of Loyola

The Presence of God
I remind myself that, as I sit here now,
God is gazing on me with love and holding me in being.
I pause for a moment and think of this.

Freedom
"There are very few people who realize what God would make of them if they abandoned themselves into his hands, and let themselves be formed by his grace" (Saint Ignatius). I ask for the grace to trust myself totally to God's love.

Consciousness
Where do I sense hope, encouragement, and growth in my life? By looking back over the past few months, I may be able to see which activities and occasions have produced rich fruit. If I do notice such areas, I will determine to give those areas both time and space in the future.

The Word
Lord Jesus, you became human to communicate with me.
You walked and worked on this earth.
You endured the heat and struggled with the cold.
All your time on this earth was spent in caring for humanity.
You healed the sick, you raised the dead.
Most important of all, you saved me from death.
(Please turn to the Scripture on the following pages. Inspiration points are there, should you need them. When you are ready, return here to continue.)

Conversation
What is stirring in me as I pray? Am I consoled, troubled, left cold? I imagine Jesus standing or sitting at my side, and I share my feelings with him.

Conclusion
Glory be to the Father, and to the Son, and to the Holy Spirit,
As it was in the beginning, is now and ever shall be,
World without end. Amen.

Sunday 15th March
Third Sunday of Lent
John 4:5–15, 19b–26, 39a, 40–42

So he came to a Samaritan city called Sychar, near the plot of ground that
Jacob had given to his son Joseph. Jacob's well was there, and Jesus, tired
out by his journey, was sitting by the well. It was about noon. A Samaritan
woman came to draw water, and Jesus said to her, "Give me a drink." (His
disciples had gone to the city to buy food.) The Samaritan woman said to
him, "How is it that you, a Jew, ask a drink of me, a woman of Samaria?"
(Jews do not share things in common with Samaritans.) Jesus answered
her, "If you knew the gift of God, and who it is that is saying to you,
'Give me a drink,' you would have asked him, and he would have given
you living water." The woman said to him, "Sir, you have no bucket, and
the well is deep. Where do you get that living water? Are you greater than
our ancestor Jacob, who gave us the well, and with his sons and his flocks
drank from it?" Jesus said to her, "Everyone who drinks of this water will
be thirsty again, but those who drink of the water that I will give them
will never be thirsty. The water that I will give will become in them a
spring of water gushing up to eternal life." The woman said to him, "Sir,
give me this water, so that I may never be thirsty or have to keep coming
here to draw water." . . . The woman said to him, "Sir, I see that you
are a prophet. Our ancestors worshiped on this mountain, but you say
that the place where people must worship is in Jerusalem." Jesus said to
her, "Woman, believe me, the hour is coming when you will worship the
Father neither on this mountain nor in Jerusalem. You worship what you
do not know; we worship what we know, for salvation is from the Jews.
But the hour is coming, and is now here, when the true worshipers will
worship the Father in spirit and truth, for the Father seeks such as these to
worship him. God is spirit, and those who worship him must worship in
spirit and truth." The woman said to him, "I know that Messiah is coming" (who is called Christ). "When he comes, he will proclaim all things
to us." Jesus said to her, "I am he, the one who is speaking to you." . . .
Many Samaritans from that city believed in him because of the woman's
testimony. . . . So when the Samaritans came to him, they asked him to
stay with them; and he stayed there two days. And many more believed
because of his word. They said to the woman, "It is no longer because of

what you said that we believe, for we have heard for ourselves, and we know that this is truly the Savior of the world."

- Jesus begins with his own physical thirst and ends up talking about the woman's soul thirst. What can I learn from this conversation about sharing the Good News?

- In speaking with a woman to whom he was not related, and to a Samaritan, who was considered apostate by the Jewish community, Jesus crossed two cultural boundaries. What boundaries do I face in a normal day?

Monday 16th March
Luke 4:24–30

And he said, "Truly I tell you, no prophet is accepted in the prophet's hometown. But the truth is, there were many widows in Israel in the time of Elijah, when the heaven was shut up three years and six months, and there was a severe famine over all the land; yet Elijah was sent to none of them except to a widow at Zarephath in Sidon. There were also many lepers in Israel in the time of the prophet Elisha, and none of them was cleansed except Naaman the Syrian." When they heard this, all in the synagogue were filled with rage. They got up, drove him out of the town, and led him to the brow of the hill on which their town was built, so that they might hurl him off the cliff. But he passed through the midst of them and went on his way.

- The people in question here were jealous for their community of faith. Jesus was including all nationalities in the care and the saving love of God. His audience was jealous of their own relationship with God and used it in many ordinary ways to keep others out of favor. They denied human rights to anyone outside their circle. Which people did my community teach me to exclude when I was growing up and learning who was "in" and who was "out"?

- Jesus is the one of universal welcome, his heart open in prayer and life to all, no matter their creed, nation, gender, age or any of the categories with which we are divided from one another. I ask him to open my heart to be as welcoming as his.

Tuesday 17th March

Matthew 18:21–35

Then Peter came and said to him, "Lord, if another member of the church sins against me, how often should I forgive? As many as seven times?" Jesus said to him, "Not seven times, but, I tell you, seventy-seven times. For this reason the kingdom of heaven may be compared to a king who wished to settle accounts with his slaves. When he began the reckoning, one who owed him ten thousand talents was brought to him; and, as he could not pay, his lord ordered him to be sold, together with his wife and children and all his possessions, and payment to be made. So the slave fell on his knees before him, saying, 'Have patience with me, and I will pay you everything.' And out of pity for him, the lord of that slave released him and forgave him the debt. But that same slave, as he went out, came upon one of his fellow slaves who owed him a hundred denarii; and seizing him by the throat, he said, 'Pay what you owe.' Then his fellow slave fell down and pleaded with him, 'Have patience with me, and I will pay you.' But he refused; then he went and threw him into prison until he should pay the debt. When his fellow slaves saw what had happened, they were greatly distressed, and they went and reported to their lord all that had taken place. Then his lord summoned him and said to him, 'You wicked slave! I forgave you all that debt because you pleaded with me. Should you not have had mercy on your fellow slave, as I had mercy on you?' And in anger his lord handed him over to be tortured until he should pay his entire debt. So my heavenly Father will also do to every one of you, if you do not forgive your brother or sister from your heart."

- Forgiveness is never easy. Surely to forgive one's brother or sister up to seven times is pretty generous! After all, there has to be a limit, at least so Peter thought!

- Not so, according to Jesus: seventy-seven times. No limit, endless and ongoing. This is how the Lord loves you. "I forgave you all that debt" (Matthew 18:32). Thank you, Lord, for forgiving me seventy-seven times and more. Give me the grace to forgive someone today.

Wednesday 18th March
Matthew 5:17–19

Jesus said to the crowds, "Do not think that I have come to abolish the law or the prophets; I have come not to abolish but to fulfill. For truly I tell you, until heaven and earth pass away, not one letter, not one stroke of a letter, will pass from the law until all is accomplished. Therefore, whoever breaks one of the least of these commandments, and teaches others to do the same, will be called least in the kingdom of heaven; but whoever does them and teaches them will be called great in the kingdom of heaven."

- It is not so easy to pray this gospel! "Do not think that I have come to abolish the law or the prophets." The heart of the Law was and is: "You must love the Lord your God with all your heart, and with all your soul, and with all your mind . . . [and] your neighbor as yourself" (Matthew 22:37, 39). Observing external laws is not enough. Jesus wants listening hearts, courageous, generous, and discerning. Hearts like his. Are you ever called to be prophetic by rising above peer pressure and speaking the truth in your heart?

- Lord, you were not turning your back on the past but deepening our sense of where we stand before God: not as scrupulous rule keepers but as loving children.

Thursday 19th March
Saint Joseph, Spouse of the Blessed Virgin Mary
Matthew 1:16, 18-21, 24a

[A]nd Jacob [was] the father of Joseph the husband of Mary, of whom Jesus was born, who is called the Messiah. . . . Now the birth of Jesus the Messiah took place in this way. When his mother Mary had been engaged to Joseph, but before they lived together, she was found to be with child from the Holy Spirit. Her husband Joseph, being a righteous man and unwilling to expose her to public disgrace, planned to dismiss her quietly. But just when he had resolved to do this, an angel of the Lord appeared to him in a dream and said, "Joseph, son of David, do not be afraid to take Mary as your wife, for the child conceived in her is from the Holy Spirit. She will bear a son, and you are to name him Jesus, for he will save his people from their sins." . . . When Joseph awoke from sleep, he did as the angel of the Lord commanded him.

- God called Joseph to let go of his own plans and put himself at the service of Jesus and Mary. We hear no words from Joseph in the Gospels, only mention of his being a just and generous man: his taking Mary into his home and his protection of Mary and Jesus. Joseph passed years in Nazareth, his faithfulness expressed in routine services that never drew attention to himself.

- Yet he had one important commission: "you are to name him Jesus, for he will save his people from their sins." Spend time resting in Joseph's company. He understands your daily tasks. Let him look lovingly at you and all you must do today. Be at ease in the presence of the one who lived in the presence of Jesus and Mary.

Friday 20th March
Mark 12:28–34

One of the scribes came near and heard them disputing with one another, and seeing that Jesus answered them well, he asked him, "Which commandment is the first of all?" Jesus answered, "The first is, 'Hear, O Israel: the Lord our God, the Lord is one; you shall love the Lord your God with all your heart, and with all your soul, and with all your mind, and with all your strength.' The second is this, 'You shall love your neighbor as yourself.' There is no other commandment greater than these." Then the scribe said to him, "You are right, Teacher; you have truly said that 'he is one, and besides him there is no other'; and 'to love him with all the heart, and with all the understanding, and with all the strength,' and 'to love one's neighbor as oneself,'—this is much more important than all whole burnt offerings and sacrifices." When Jesus saw that he answered wisely, he said to him, "You are not far from the kingdom of God." After that no one dared to ask him any question.

- The first commandment is to love God with all we have—not only with our hearts, but with our limbs. We need to embrace the Almighty in all we do. We are called to give him total love in a spirit of adoration.

- There are two commandments, even if they merge together. We have to love our neighbor (all people) as being part of ourselves. Especially their sufferings need to impinge on us. Our love should not be only for those who please us but also for those we don't like or who may be hostile to us. The most important thing in life is to have a loving heart, which is very demanding.

Saturday 21st March

Luke 18:9–14

He also told this parable to some who trusted in themselves that they were righteous and regarded others with contempt: "Two men went up to the temple to pray, one a Pharisee and the other a tax collector. The Pharisee, standing by himself, was praying thus, 'God, I thank you that I am not like other people: thieves, rogues, adulterers, or even like this tax collector. I fast twice a week; I give a tenth of all my income.' But the tax collector, standing far off, would not even look up to heaven, but was beating his breast and saying, 'God, be merciful to me, a sinner!' I tell you, this man went down to his home justified rather than the other; for all who exalt themselves will be humbled, but all who humble themselves will be exalted."

• The contrast between Pharisee and publican has entered so deeply into our culture that it is sometimes reversed, and people are more anxious to hide at the back of the church than to be in the front pews.

• How does the story strike me? I would hate to be the object of people's contempt. But Lord, if they knew me as you do, they might be right to feel contempt. And I have no right to look down on those whose sins are paraded in the media. Be merciful to me.

March 22—March 28

Something to think and pray about each day this week:

You can't lead others if you can't lead yourself. But you can't lead others if you use power primarily to serve yourself and your ego. Leadership is not about you, it's about the rest of us—your family, community, colleagues, or customers.

"Get over yourself" is how we blunt New Yorkers put it. Pope Francis employs a richer concept: "Authentic power is service." The two phrases encapsulate a paradox of leadership. Leaders must dig deep within themselves, but that inward journey ultimately inspires them to leap beyond the shortsighted horizons that diminish so many leaders, who never see beyond my department, my company, my money, me, me, me.

Good leaders see farther. They feel called to transcend themselves and serve a greater mission than self-interest alone.

—Chris Lowney, *Pope Francis: Why He Leads the Way He Leads*

The Presence of God
I pause for a moment
and reflect on God's life-giving presence
in every part of my body,
in everything around me,
in the whole of my life.

Freedom
Many countries are at this moment suffering the agonies of war. I bow my head in thanksgiving for my freedom. I pray for all prisoners and captives.

Consciousness
Knowing that God loves me unconditionally, I look honestly over the past day, its events, and my feelings. Do I have something to be grateful for? Then I give thanks. Is there something I am sorry for? Then I ask forgiveness.

The Word
Now I turn to the Scripture set out for me this day. I read slowly over the words and see if any sentence or sentiment appeals to me. (Please turn to the Scripture on the following pages. Inspiration points are there, should you need them. When you are ready, return here to continue.)

Conversation
I know with certainty that there were times when you carried me, Lord. There were times when it was through your strength that I got through the dark times in my life.

Conclusion
Glory be to the Father, and to the Son, and to the Holy Spirit,
As it was in the beginning, is now and ever shall be,
World without end. Amen.

Sunday 22nd March
Fourth Sunday of Lent

John 9:1–41

As he walked along, he saw a man blind from birth. His disciples asked him, "Rabbi, who sinned, this man or his parents, that he was born blind?" Jesus answered, "Neither this man nor his parents sinned; he was born blind so that God's works might be revealed in him. We must work the works of him who sent me while it is day; night is coming when no one can work. As long as I am in the world, I am the light of the world." When he had said this, he spat on the ground and made mud with the saliva and spread the mud on the man's eyes, saying to him, "Go, wash in the pool of Siloam" (which means Sent). Then he went and washed and came back able to see. The neighbors and those who had seen him before as a beggar began to ask, "Is this not the man who used to sit and beg?" Some were saying, "It is he." Others were saying, "No, but it is someone like him." He kept saying, "I am the man." But they kept asking him, "Then how were your eyes opened?" He answered, "The man called Jesus made mud, spread it on my eyes, and said to me, 'Go to Siloam and wash.' Then I went and washed and received my sight." They said to him, "Where is he?" He said, "I do not know." They brought to the Pharisees the man who had formerly been blind. Now it was a sabbath day when Jesus made the mud and opened his eyes. Then the Pharisees also began to ask him how he had received his sight. He said to them, "He put mud on my eyes. Then I washed, and now I see." Some of the Pharisees said, "This man is not from God, for he does not observe the sabbath." But others said, "How can a man who is a sinner perform such signs?" And they were divided. So they said again to the blind man, "What do you say about him? It was your eyes he opened." He said, "He is a prophet." The Jews did not believe that he had been blind and had received his sight until they called the parents of the man who had received his sight and asked them, "Is this your son, who you say was born blind? How then does he now see?" His parents answered, "We know that this is our son, and that he was born blind; but we do not know how it is that now he sees, nor do we know who opened his eyes. Ask him; he is of age. He will speak for himself." His parents said this because they were afraid of the

Jews; for the Jews had already agreed that anyone who confessed Jesus to be the Messiah would be put out of the synagogue. Therefore his parents said, "He is of age; ask him." So for the second time they called the man who had been blind, and they said to him, "Give glory to God! We know that this man is a sinner." He answered, "I do not know whether he is a sinner. One thing I do know, that though I was blind, now I see." They said to him, "What did he do to you? How did he open your eyes?" He answered them, "I have told you already, and you would not listen. Why do you want to hear it again? Do you also want to become his disciples?" Then they reviled him, saying, "You are his disciple, but we are disciples of Moses. We know that God has spoken to Moses, but as for this man, we do not know where he comes from." The man answered, "Here is an astonishing thing! You do not know where he comes from, and yet he opened my eyes. We know that God does not listen to sinners, but he does listen to one who worships him and obeys his will. Never since the world began has it been heard that anyone opened the eyes of a person born blind. If this man were not from God, he could do nothing." They answered him, "You were born entirely in sins, and are you trying to teach us?" And they drove him out. Jesus heard that they had driven him out, and when he found him, he said, "Do you believe in the Son of Man?" He answered, "And who is he, sir? Tell me, so that I may believe in him." Jesus said to him, "You have seen him, and the one speaking with you is he." He said, "Lord, I believe." And he worshiped him.

- The opening question of the disciples was, "Who is to blame?" This is a common question in the media today; perhaps it is part of my own vocabulary. Jesus reminds us that sometimes no one is to blame but that difficult situations present an opportunity for us to be drawn into God's presence.

- Lord there were times I was lost and found, was blind and then could see. Thank you. The man's blindness is cured, but the blindness of those who won't believe in Jesus remains. I think of how I grope, stumble, and am unsure of my direction unless I can rely on Jesus, the light of the world.

Monday 23rd March

John 4:43–54

When the two days were over, he went from that place to Galilee (for Jesus himself had testified that a prophet has no honor in the prophet's own country). When he came to Galilee, the Galileans welcomed him, since they had seen all that he had done in Jerusalem at the festival; for they too had gone to the festival. Then he came again to Cana in Galilee where he had changed the water into wine. Now there was a royal official whose son lay ill in Capernaum. When he heard that Jesus had come from Judea to Galilee, he went and begged him to come down and heal his son, for he was at the point of death. Then Jesus said to him, "Unless you see signs and wonders you will not believe." The official said to him, "Sir, come down before my little boy dies." Jesus said to him, "Go; your son will live." The man believed the word that Jesus spoke to him and started on his way. As he was going down, his slaves met him and told him that his child was alive. So he asked them the hour when he began to recover, and they said to him, "Yesterday at one in the afternoon the fever left him." The father realized that this was the hour when Jesus had said to him, "Your son will live." So he himself believed, along with his whole household. Now this was the second sign that Jesus did after coming from Judea to Galilee.

- This man believed Jesus' word *without* signs and wonders. His believing was followed by the wonder of his son's recovery, which led to his whole household believing.

- This is the first recorded healing miracle of Jesus. Do I believe in miracles? More important, do I believe that Jesus is "the greatest miracle of the universe? He is all the love of God contained in a human heart and a human face" (Pope Benedict XVI).

Tuesday 24th March

John 5:1–16

After this there was a festival of the Jews, and Jesus went up to Jerusalem. Now in Jerusalem by the Sheep Gate there is a pool, called in Hebrew Beth-zatha, which has five porticoes. In these lay many invalids—blind, lame, and paralyzed. One man was there who had been ill for thirty-eight years. When Jesus saw him lying there and knew that he had been there a long time, he said to him, "Do you want to be made well?" The sick man answered him, "Sir, I have no one to put me into the pool when the water is stirred up; and while I am making my way, someone else steps down ahead of me." Jesus said to him, "Stand up, take your mat and walk." At once the man was made well, and he took up his mat and began to walk. Now that day was a sabbath. So the Jews said to the man who had been cured, "It is the sabbath; it is not lawful for you to carry your mat." But he answered them, "The man who made me well said to me, 'Take up your mat and walk.'" They asked him, "Who is the man who said to you, 'Take it up and walk'?" Now the man who had been healed did not know who it was, for Jesus had disappeared in the crowd that was there. Later Jesus found him in the temple and said to him, "See, you have been made well! Do not sin any more, so that nothing worse happens to you." The man went away and told the Jews that it was Jesus who had made him well. Therefore the Jews started persecuting Jesus, because he was doing such things on the sabbath.

- The man on the mat is obviously ill, and yet Jesus asks if he wants to be made well. In truth, sometimes we prefer to remain as we are rather than change for the better. We fear what the change will bring, or we have grown comfortable with our "illness." I imagine Jesus asking me, right now, "Do you want to be made well?" What is my response?

- By healing people on the Sabbath, Jesus was breaking not the law of Moses but subsequent laws created to help people know how to fulfill the law of Moses. It can seem simpler to stick with rigid and complicated systems than to rely on our own discernment of what God asks of us. What discernment is required of me today?

Wednesday 25th March
The Annunciation of the Lord
Luke 1:26–38

In the sixth month the angel Gabriel was sent by God to a town in Galilee called Nazareth, to a virgin engaged to a man whose name was Joseph, of the house of David. The virgin's name was Mary. And he came to her and said, "Greetings, favored one! The Lord is with you." But she was much perplexed by his words and pondered what sort of greeting this might be. The angel said to her, "Do not be afraid, Mary, for you have found favor with God. And now, you will conceive in your womb and bear a son, and you will name him Jesus. He will be great, and will be called the Son of the Most High, and the Lord God will give to him the throne of his ancestor David. He will reign over the house of Jacob forever, and of his kingdom there will be no end." Mary said to the angel, "How can this be, since I am a virgin?" The angel said to her, "The Holy Spirit will come upon you, and the power of the Most High will overshadow you; therefore the child to be born will be holy; he will be called Son of God. And now, your relative Elizabeth in her old age has also conceived a son; and this is the sixth month for her who was said to be barren. For nothing will be impossible with God." Then Mary said, "Here am I, the servant of the Lord; let it be with me according to your word." Then the angel departed from her.

- Like Mary, I came into the world for a purpose. That purpose probably will not be revealed to me as dramatically as it was to her. Perhaps she heard God's message so clearly because she was comfortable with silence. Too often I fear the emptiness, the darkness, the silence within me. Yet it is there that the Spirit lives and works, even when my prayer seems most arid. God, help me go daily into the quiet of my heart, to meet you there, in love and adoration.

- Mary did not receive the angel's message as a total surprise; she was ready to engage in conversation with God's messenger. I turn to God in my prayer and try to see God's finger at work in my life. I draw inspiration from Mary's disposition.

Thursday 26th March
John 5:31–47

"If I testify about myself, my testimony is not true. There is another who testifies on my behalf, and I know that his testimony to me is true. You sent messengers to John, and he testified to the truth. Not that I accept such human testimony, but I say these things so that you may be saved. He was a burning and shining lamp, and you were willing to rejoice for a while in his light. But I have a testimony greater than John's. The works that the Father has given me to complete, the very works that I am doing, testify on my behalf that the Father has sent me. And the Father who sent me has himself testified on my behalf. You have never heard his voice or seen his form, and you do not have his word abiding in you, because you do not believe him whom he has sent. You search the scriptures because you think that in them you have eternal life; and it is they that testify on my behalf. Yet you refuse to come to me to have life. I do not accept glory from human beings. But I know that you do not have the love of God in you. I have come in my Father's name, and you do not accept me; if another comes in his own name, you will accept him. How can you believe when you accept glory from one another and do not seek the glory that comes from the one who alone is God? Do not think that I will accuse you before the Father; your accuser is Moses, on whom you have set your hope. If you believed Moses, you would believe me, for he wrote about me. But if you do not believe what he wrote, how will you believe what I say?"

- Jesus appeals to the minds of those who seek to disregard him. He reminds them of what they have seen, of the witnesses they have heard, and of the words of the prophets. I pray that I be blessed with deeper faith as I review the evidence to which Jesus draws my attention. As I believe in Jesus who was sent by God, the word of God is alive in me.

- John the Baptist prepared the way for people to hear Jesus. He brought people near to God, and some of them recognized Jesus when he arrived. Some people we meet make it easier to recognize Jesus. It is good to have met people who are like Jesus—just as John the Baptist prepared the way of Jesus by the way he lived. Give thanks for such people in prayer!

Friday 27th March
John 7:1–2, 10, 25–30

After this Jesus went about in Galilee. He did not wish to go about in Judea because the Jews were looking for an opportunity to kill him. Now the Jewish festival of Booths was near. . . . But after his brothers had gone to the festival, then he also went, not publicly but as it were in secret. . . . Now some of the people of Jerusalem were saying, "Is not this the man whom they are trying to kill? And here he is, speaking openly, but they say nothing to him! Can it be that the authorities really know that this is the Messiah? Yet we know where this man is from; but when the Messiah comes, no one will know where he is from." Then Jesus cried out as he was teaching in the temple, "You know me, and you know where I am from. I have not come on my own. But the one who sent me is true, and you do not know him. I know him, because I am from him, and he sent me." Then they tried to arrest him, but no one laid hands on him, because his hour had not yet come.

- "Not publicly but as it were in secret"; Jesus never made himself the center. He was ever pointing to his Father and, toward the end of his life, speaking of the Spirit that was to come.

- "Yet we know where this man is from." In what ways do my biases—about a person's race, language, religion, or country of origin—prevent my listening to what the person actually says? I pray for openness to receive God's words when they reach me—and however they reach me.

Saturday 28th March
John 7:40–53

When they heard these words, some in the crowd said, "This is really the prophet." Others said, "This is the Messiah." But some asked, "Surely the Messiah does not come from Galilee, does he? Has not the scripture said that the Messiah is descended from David and comes from Bethlehem, the village where David lived?" So there was a division in the crowd because of him. Some of them wanted to arrest him, but no one laid hands on him. Then the temple police went back to the chief priests and Pharisees, who asked them, "Why did you not arrest him?" The police answered, "Never has anyone spoken like this!" Then the Pharisees replied, "Surely you have not been deceived too, have you? Has any one of the authorities or of the Pharisees believed in him? But this crowd, which does not know the law—they are accursed." Nicodemus, who had gone to Jesus before, and who was one of them, asked, "Our law does not judge people without first giving them a hearing to find out what they are doing, does it?" They replied, "Surely you are not also from Galilee, are you? Search and you will see that no prophet is to arise from Galilee." Then each of them went home.

- According to Meister Eckhart, the great medieval theologian and mystic, the Son of God is being born unceasingly: "If God stopped saying his Word, but for an instant even, heaven and earth would disappear."

That Word of God is spoken in my soul. When I stop to listen to it, I am in touch with the source of all creation.

- Prayer can allow us to be surprised by Jesus Christ—or to be questioned by him. We can end our prayer with the question, "Who is this man, and what have I learned about him today?" He gives no easy answers but walks with us while we ask the questions.

March 29—April 4

Something to think and pray about each day this week:

Real peace is not just a matter of structures and mechanisms. It rests, above all, on the adoption of a style of human coexistence marked by mutual acceptance and a capacity to forgive from the heart. We all need to be forgiven by others, so we must all be ready to forgive. Asking and granting forgiveness is something profoundly worthy of every one of us; sometimes it is the only way out of situations marked by age-old and violent hatred.

Forgiveness, in its truest and highest form, is a free act of love; but precisely because it is an act of love, it has its own intrinsic demands: the first of which is respect for the truth.

God alone is absolute truth, but He made the human heart open to the desire for truth, which He then fully revealed in His Incarnate Son. Hence, we are all called to live the truth. Forgiveness, far from precluding the search for truth, actually requires it. Evil that has been done must be acknowledged and, as far as possible, corrected.

—Saint John Paul II, *Go in Peace*

The Presence of God
God is with me, but even more astounding, God is within me.
Let me dwell for a moment on God's life-giving presence
in my body, in my mind, in my heart,
as I sit here, right now.

Freedom
Lord, may I never take the gift of freedom for granted. You gave me the great blessing of freedom of spirit. Fill my spirit with your peace and joy.

Consciousness
I remind myself that I am in the presence of God, who is my strength in times of weakness and my comforter in times of sorrow.

The Word
I take my time to read the word of God slowly, a few times, allowing myself to dwell on anything that strikes me. (Please turn to the Scripture on the following pages. Inspiration points are there, should you need them. When you are ready, return here to continue.)

Conversation
Jesus, you always welcomed little children when you walked on this earth. Teach me to have a childlike trust in you. Teach me to live in the knowledge that you will never abandon me.

Conclusion
Glory be to the Father, and to the Son, and to the Holy Spirit,
As it was in the beginning, is now and ever shall be,
World without end. Amen.

Sunday 29th March
Fifth Sunday of Lent
John 11:3–7, 17, 20–27, 33b–45

So the sisters sent a message to Jesus, "Lord, he whom you love is ill." But when Jesus heard it, he said, "This illness does not lead to death; rather it is for God's glory, so that the Son of God may be glorified through it." Accordingly, though Jesus loved Martha and her sister and Lazarus, after having heard that Lazarus was ill, he stayed two days longer in the place where he was. Then after this he said to the disciples, "Let us go to Judea again." . . . When Jesus arrived, he found that Lazarus had already been in the tomb four days. . . . When Martha heard that Jesus was coming, she went and met him, while Mary stayed at home. Martha said to Jesus, "Lord, if you had been here, my brother would not have died. But even now I know that God will give you whatever you ask of him." Jesus said to her, "Your brother will rise again." Martha said to him, "I know that he will rise again in the resurrection on the last day." Jesus said to her, "I am the resurrection and the life. Those who believe in me, even though they die, will live, and everyone who lives and believes in me will never die. Do you believe this?" She said to him, "Yes, Lord, I believe that you are the Messiah, the Son of God, the one coming into the world." . . . When Jesus saw [Mary] weeping, and the Jews who came with her also weeping, he was greatly disturbed in spirit and deeply moved. He said, "Where have you laid him?" They said to him, "Lord, come and see." Jesus began to weep. So the Jews said, "See how he loved him!" But some of them said, "Could not he who opened the eyes of the blind man have kept this man from dying?" Then Jesus, again greatly disturbed, came to the tomb. It was a cave, and a stone was lying against it. Jesus said, "Take away the stone." Martha, the sister of the dead man, said to him, "Lord, already there is a stench because he has been dead for four days." Jesus said to her, "Did I not tell you that if you believed, you would see the glory of God?" So they took away the stone. And Jesus looked upward and said, "Father, I thank you for having heard me. I knew that you always hear me, but I have said this for the sake of the crowd standing here, so that they may believe that you sent me." When he had said this, he cried with a loud voice, "Lazarus, come out!" The dead man came out, his hands and feet bound with strips of cloth, and his face wrapped in a cloth. Jesus said to them, "Unbind him, and let him go." Many of the Jews therefore, who had come with Mary and had seen what Jesus did, believed in him.

- I hear you asking me the same question, Lord: "Do you believe that I am the resurrection and the life?" In the long run, nothing is more important than my answer to this. I cannot grasp your words in my imagination, Lord, but I believe. Help my unbelief.

- "Unbind him, and let him go." Even a man resurrected from the dead needed the help of community. Show me, Lord, how I can participate in others' unbinding and freedom.

Monday 30th March
John 8:1–11

Jesus went to the Mount of Olives. Early in the morning Jesus came again to the temple. All the people came to him and he sat down and began to teach them. The scribes and the Pharisees brought a woman who had been caught in adultery; and making her stand before all of them, they said to him, "Teacher, this woman was caught in the very act of committing adultery. Now in the law Moses commanded us to stone such women. Now what do you say?" They said this to test him, so that they might have some charge to bring against him. Jesus bent down and wrote with his finger on the ground. When they kept on questioning him, he straightened up and said to them, "Let anyone among you who is without sin be the first to throw a stone at her." And once again he bent down and wrote on the ground. When they heard it, they went away, one by one, beginning with the elders; and Jesus was left alone with the woman standing before him. Jesus straightened up and said to her, "Woman, where are they? Has no one condemned you?" She said, "No one, sir." And Jesus said, "Neither do I condemn you. Go your way, and from now on do not sin again."

- We have all sinned. We have all experienced overwhelming shame. Even if the sin is not discovered, our self-accusatory voice can become so loud in our head that it drowns out the gentle voice of Jesus, telling us to begin again.

- If we cannot believe ourselves forgiven, how will we ever be able to move out of what the philosopher Ivan Illich describes as "our self-imposed cages"? Lord, you who opened the ears of the deaf and the eyes of the blind, let me hear your words of forgiveness; let me see and believe in the possibility of a better life.

Tuesday 31st March
John 8:21–30

Again he said to them, "I am going away, and you will search for me, but you will die in your sin. Where I am going, you cannot come." Then the Jews said, "Is he going to kill himself? Is that what he means by saying, 'Where I am going, you cannot come'?" He said to them, "You are from below, I am from above; you are of this world, I am not of this world. I told you that you would die in your sins, for you will die in your sins unless you believe that I am he." They said to him, "Who are you?" Jesus said to them, "Why do I speak to you at all? I have much to say about you and much to condemn; but the one who sent me is true, and I declare to the world what I have heard from him." They did not understand that he was speaking to them about the Father. So Jesus said, "When you have lifted up the Son of Man, then you will realize that I am he, and that I do nothing on my own, but I speak these things as the Father instructed me. And the one who sent me is with me; he has not left me alone, for I always do what is pleasing to him." As he was saying these things, many believed in him.

- "I am going away, and you will search for me, but you will die in your sin." The time to search for Jesus is now. If I want to see how closely my daily life is aligned with my life priorities, I need only ask myself one question: "How do I spend my time?" What do I do most, and what are the things I postpone? What do I think about most? Aspire to most?

- If our hearts and our lives are tied to this world, can we really be seeking Christ?

Wednesday 1st April
John 8:31–42

Then Jesus said to the Jews who had believed in him, "If you continue in my word, you are truly my disciples; and you will know the truth, and the truth will make you free." They answered him, "We are descendants of Abraham and have never been slaves to anyone. What do you mean by saying, 'You will be made free'?" Jesus answered them, "Very truly, I tell you, everyone who commits sin is a slave to sin. The slave does not have a permanent place in the household; the son has a place there forever. So if the Son makes you free, you will be free indeed. I know that you are descendants of Abraham; yet you look for an opportunity to kill me, because there is no place in you for my word. I declare what I have seen in the Father's presence; as for you, you should do what you have heard from the Father." They answered him, "Abraham is our father." Jesus said to them, "If you were Abraham's children, you would be doing what Abraham did, but now you are trying to kill me, a man who has told you the truth that I heard from God. This is not what Abraham did. You are indeed doing what your father does." They said to him, "We are not illegitimate children; we have one father, God himself." Jesus said to them, "If God were your Father, you would love me, for I came from God and now I am here. I did not come on my own, but he sent me."

- "Abiding" ("continue in") means that we draw life from the word of God. This life is Christ himself; he is the love of the Father. Being a disciple, a listener, is living and abiding in truth, knowing that the Jesus of our prayer comes from God and is with God.

- Our love indicates our spiritual pedigree. Jesus, help me follow you and thus accept truth and demonstrate it through love.

Thursday 2nd April
John 8:51–59

Jesus said, "Very truly, I tell you, whoever keeps my word will never see death." The Jews said to him, "Now we know that you have a demon. Abraham died, and so did the prophets; yet you say, 'Whoever keeps my word will never taste death.' Are you greater than our father Abraham, who died? The prophets also died. Who do you claim to be?" Jesus answered, "If I glorify myself, my glory is nothing. It is my Father who glorifies me, he of whom you say, 'He is our God,' though you do not know him. But I know him; if I were to say that I do not know him, I would be a liar like you. But I do know him and I keep his word. Your ancestor Abraham rejoiced that he would see my day; he saw it and was glad." Then the Jews said to him, "You are not yet fifty years old, and have you seen Abraham?" Jesus said to them, "Very truly, I tell you, before

Abraham was, I am." So they picked up stones to throw at him, but Jesus hid himself and went out of the temple.

- The wilderness inside us is a place of testing, where the power of false gods is broken. It is a place of encounter with ourselves, with our inner demons, and with God. To enter it, we must be silent and alone, leaving behind our elaborately constructed avoidance techniques, safety nets, and empty spiritual practices. Only through making ourselves vulnerable to our own pain and fear can we make ourselves open to the experience of loving and of being loved.

- Note yet another "I am" statement: *Before Abraham was, I am.* Jesus claims both preexistence and oneness with God. How does such information influence the way I think about life and death and what it means to be a spiritual being?

Friday 3rd April
John 10:31–42

The Jews took up stones again to stone him. Jesus replied, "I have shown you many good works from the Father. For which of these are you going to stone me?" The Jews answered, "It is not for a good work that we are going to stone you, but for blasphemy, because you, though only a human being, are making yourself God." Jesus answered, "Is it not written in your law, 'I said, you are gods'? If those to whom the word of God came were called 'gods'—and the scripture cannot be annulled—can you say that the one whom the Father has sanctified and sent into the world is blaspheming because I said, 'I am God's Son'? If I am not doing the works of my Father, then do not believe me. But if I do them, even though you do not believe me, believe the works, so that you may know and understand that the Father is in me and I am in the Father." Then they tried to arrest him again, but he escaped from their hands. He went away again across the Jordan to the place where John had been baptizing earlier, and he remained there. Many came to him, and they were saying, "John performed no sign, but everything that John said about this man was true." And many believed in him there.

- Jesus often impresses upon us the need to act upon his word. One can argue with words, but deeds cannot be contradicted. They speak for themselves. The Word is planted deep in me, and I pray in the words of the apostle James, "Let me be a doer of the word, and not a forgetful hearer." The world watches the deeds of Christians—and often is not impressed.

- The people in today's reading condemn Jesus because of their particular image of God. What is my image of God? Have I ever condemned someone because I nursed a warped image of God?

Saturday 4th April
John 11:45–56

Many of the Jews therefore, who had come with Mary and had seen what Jesus did, believed in him. But some of them went to the Pharisees and told them what he had done. So the chief priests and the Pharisees called a meeting of the council, and said, "What are we to do? This man is performing many signs. If we let him go on like this, everyone will believe in him, and the Romans will come and destroy both our holy place and our nation." But one of them, Caiaphas, who was high priest that year, said to them, "You know nothing at all! You do not understand that it is better for you to have one man die for the people than to have the whole nation destroyed." He did not say this on his own, but being high priest that year he prophesied that Jesus was about to die for the nation, and not for the nation only, but to gather into one the dispersed children of God. So from that day on they planned to put him to death. Jesus therefore no longer walked about openly among the Jews, but went from there to a town called Ephraim in the region near the wilderness; and he remained there with the disciples. Now the Passover of the Jews was near, and many went up from the country to Jerusalem before the Passover to purify themselves. They were looking for Jesus and were asking one another as they stood in the temple, "What do you think? Surely he will not come to the festival, will he?"

- Caiaphas was a Sadducee. He was also ruthless, political, and determined to buttress the status quo and the privileges of his wealthy class. He used the argument of the powerful in every age: we must eliminate the awkward troublemaker in the name of the common good—in this case, "the common good" meaning the comfort of the Sadducees. But he spoke wiser than he knew. One man, Jesus, was to die for the people, and for me.

- Caiaphas is afraid that the popularity of Jesus will draw down the wrath of Rome and destroy both the temple—the holy place—and the nation. In his blindness he cannot see that the Jewish people are themselves the temple. Do I appreciate that I, too, am a temple of the living God? Lord, take away my blindness so that I can see myself as you see me.

Holy Week
April 5—April 11

Something to think and pray about each day this week:

Ingenuity blossoms when the personal freedom to pursue opportunities is linked to a profound trust and optimism that the world presents plenty of them. Imagination, creativity, adaptability, and rapid response become the keys for finding and unlocking those opportunities.

—Chris Lowney, *Heroic Leadership*

The Presence of God

Dear Lord, as I come to you today, fill my heart, my whole being, with the wonder of your presence. Help me remain receptive to you as I put aside the cares of this world. Fill my mind with your peace.

Freedom

Lord, grant me the grace to be free from the excesses of this life. Let me not get caught up with the desire for wealth. Keep my heart and mind free to love and serve you.

Consciousness

I exist in a web of relationships: links to nature, people, God.
I trace out these links, giving thanks for the life that flows through them.
Some links are twisted or broken; I may feel regret, anger, disappointment.
I pray for the gift of acceptance and forgiveness.

The Word

God speaks to each of us individually. I listen attentively to hear what he is saying to me. Read the text a few times, then listen. (Please turn to the Scripture on the following pages. Inspiration points are there, should you need them. When you are ready, return here to continue.)

Conversation

Jesus, you speak to me through the words of the Gospels. May I respond to your call today. Teach me to recognize your hand at work in my daily living.

Conclusion

I thank God for these moments we have spent together and for any insights I have been given concerning the text.

Sunday 5th April
Palm Sunday of the Passion of the Lord
Matthew 27:45–54

From noon on, darkness came over the whole land until three in the afternoon. And about three o'clock Jesus cried with a loud voice, "Eli, Eli, lema sabachthani?" that is, "My God, my God, why have you forsaken me?" When some of the bystanders heard it, they said, "This man is calling for Elijah." At once one of them ran and got a sponge, filled it with sour wine, put it on a stick, and gave it to him to drink. But the others said, "Wait, let us see whether Elijah will come to save him." Then Jesus cried again with a loud voice and breathed his last. At that moment the curtain of the temple was torn in two, from top to bottom. The earth shook, and the rocks were split. The tombs also were opened, and many bodies of the saints who had fallen asleep were raised. After his resurrection they came out of the tombs and entered the holy city and appeared to many. Now when the centurion and those with him, who were keeping watch over Jesus, saw the earthquake and what took place, they were terrified and said, "Truly this man was God's Son!"

- People expected the Messiah to be a hero figure—one whom Elijah would miraculously deliver at the last minute. Indeed, if Jesus had been delivered from the cross, no doubt the religious leaders who put him there would have proclaimed him the Messiah. But Jesus is not a savior who delivers himself from the reality humanity must face. His life demonstrated the holy nature—made in God's image—of the human race. And Jesus of Nazareth would make redemptive even the act of dying.

- Watch the scene here: the death of the good man. Allow yourself to be touched by it; let Jesus die for you and for all. Then look at the one guarding the cross—the one who says that this Man was God's Son. In prayer express your belief and faith in this truth.

Monday 6th April
John 12:1–11

Six days before the Passover Jesus came to Bethany, the home of Lazarus, whom he had raised from the dead. There they gave a dinner for him. Martha served, and Lazarus was one of those at the table with him. Mary took a pound of costly perfume made of pure nard, anointed Jesus' feet, and wiped them with her hair. The house was filled with the fragrance of the perfume. But Judas Iscariot, one of his disciples (the one who was about to betray him), said, "Why was this perfume not sold for three hundred denarii and the money given to the poor?" (He said this not because he cared about the poor, but because he was a thief; he kept the common purse and used to steal what was put into it.) Jesus said, "Leave her alone. She bought it so that she might keep it for the day of my burial. You always have the poor with you, but you do not always have me." When the great crowd of the Jews learned that he was there, they came not only because of Jesus but also to see Lazarus, whom he had raised from the dead. So the chief priests planned to put Lazarus to death as well, since it was on account of him that many of the Jews were deserting and were believing in Jesus.

- We join the dinner party and are struck by the surpassing generosity of Mary's gesture, and then by the bitter begrudging with which Judas interprets the gift. We might allow moments of prayer this week to reach the zones within us that need tolerance, healing, and forgiveness.

- The generosity of Mary appeared wasteful and misplaced. Mary knew that Jesus was worthy of her honor and service, even when it cost. She was not held back by the judgments of others. Jesus, may I give to you freely and not care about others' opinions and reactions.

Tuesday 7th April
John 13:21–33, 36–38

After saying this Jesus was troubled in spirit, and declared, "Very truly, I tell you, one of you will betray me." The disciples looked at one another, uncertain of whom he was speaking. One of his disciples—the one whom Jesus loved—was reclining next to him; Simon Peter therefore motioned to him to ask Jesus of whom he was speaking. So while reclining next to Jesus, he asked him, "Lord, who is it?" Jesus answered, "It is the one to whom I give this piece of bread when I have dipped it in the dish." So when he had dipped the piece of bread, he gave it to Judas son of Simon Iscariot. After he received the piece of bread, Satan entered into him. Jesus said to him, "Do quickly what you are going to do." Now no one at the table knew why he said this to him. Some thought that, because Judas had the common purse, Jesus was telling him, "Buy what we need for the festival"; or, that he should give something to the poor. So, after receiving the piece of bread, he immediately went out. And it was night. When he had gone out, Jesus said, "Now the Son of Man has been glorified, and God has been glorified in him. If God has been glorified in him, God will also glorify him in himself and will glorify him at once. Little children, I am with you only a little longer. You will look for me; and as I said to the Jews so now I say to you, 'Where I am going, you cannot come.'" . . . Simon Peter said to him, "Lord, where are you going?" Jesus answered, "Where I am going, you cannot follow me now; but you will follow afterward." Peter said to him, "Lord, why can I not follow you now? I will lay down my life for you." Jesus answered, "Will you lay down your life for me? Very truly, I tell you, before the cock crows, you will have denied me three times."

- We rightly hesitate to answer affirmatively the question: "Will you lay down your life for me?" But there is no ambivalence in Jesus. He has already decided to lay down his life for us, in purest love.

- Imagine yourself at the table during the Last Supper. Are you picking up the tensions among the other participants? Do you notice how Jesus is troubled in spirit? Let the drama of the scene draw you into it. What are your predominant feelings? Speak freely to Jesus about the whole situation and your reactions to it.

Wednesday 8th April
Matthew 26:14–25

Then one of the twelve, who was called Judas Iscariot, went to the chief priests and said, "What will you give me if I betray him to you?" They paid him thirty pieces of silver. And from that moment he began to look for an opportunity to betray him. On the first day of Unleavened Bread the disciples came to Jesus, saying, "Where do you want us to make the preparations for you to eat the Passover?" He said, "Go into the city to a certain man, and say to him, 'The Teacher says, My time is near; I will keep the Passover at your house with my disciples.'" So the disciples did as Jesus had directed them, and they prepared the Passover meal. When it was evening, he took his place with the twelve; and while they were eating, he said, "Truly I tell you, one of you will betray me." And they became greatly distressed and began to say to him one after another, "Surely not I, Lord?" He answered, "The one who has dipped his hand into the bowl with me will betray me. The Son of Man goes as it is written of him, but woe to that one by whom the Son of Man is betrayed! It would have been better for that one not to have been born." Judas, who betrayed him, said, "Surely not I, Rabbi?" He replied, "You have said so."

- In some places this day is known as Spy Wednesday. Judas is the spy or sly, sneaky person who secretly approaches the chief priests with the intention of betraying Jesus to them. Jesus uses only words to persuade Judas not to carry out his pact with the chief priests. He takes no other measures to prevent his arrest. What is your reaction to this?

- Like us, Judas didn't see that it is we, not God, who must change. The real sin of Judas was not his betrayal but his rejection of the light. Judas refused to believe in the possibility of forgiveness. Let us not imitate him. No matter what wrong we have done, we can turn to Jesus for forgiveness and healing.

Thursday 9th April
Holy Thursday
John 13:1–15

Now before the festival of the Passover, Jesus knew that his hour had come to depart from this world and go to the Father. Having loved his own who were in the world, he loved them to the end. The devil had already put it into the heart of Judas son of Simon Iscariot to betray him. And during supper Jesus, knowing that the Father had given all things into his hands, and that he had come from God and was going to God, got up from the table, took off his outer robe, and tied a towel around himself. Then he poured water into a basin and began to wash the disciples' feet and to wipe them with the towel that was tied around him. He came to Simon Peter, who said to him, "Lord, are you going to wash my feet?" Jesus answered, "You do not know now what I am doing, but later you will understand." Peter said to him, "You will never wash my feet." Jesus answered, "Unless I wash you, you have no share with me." Simon Peter said to him, "Lord, not my feet only but also my hands and my head!" Jesus said to him, "One who has bathed does not need to wash, except for the feet, but is entirely clean. And you are clean, though not all of you." For he knew who was to betray him; for this reason he said, "Not all of you are clean." After he had washed their feet, had put on his robe, and had returned to the table, he said to them, "Do you know what I have done to you? You call me Teacher and Lord—and you are right, for that is what I am. So if I, your Lord and Teacher, have washed your feet, you also ought to wash one another's feet. For I have set you an example, that you also should do as I have done to you."

• Jesus kneels at my feet, as he did at Peter's, and he addresses the same words to me: "Unless I wash you, you have no share with me." But have I the courage and the generosity to accept his forgiveness and unconditional love?

• Lord, let my response to your love always be an unfaltering "Yes!"

Friday 10th April
Good Friday
John 18:1—19:42

After Jesus had spoken these words, he went out with his disciples across the Kidron valley to a place where there was a garden, which he and his disciples entered. Now Judas, who betrayed him, also knew the place, because Jesus often met there with his disciples. So Judas brought a detachment of soldiers together with police from the chief priests and the Pharisees, and they came there with lanterns and torches and weapons. Then Jesus, knowing all that was to happen to him, came forward and asked them, "Whom are you looking for?" They answered, "Jesus of Nazareth." Jesus replied, "I am he." Judas, who betrayed him, was standing with them. When Jesus said to them, "I am he," they stepped back and fell to the ground. Again he asked them, "Whom are you looking for?" And they said, "Jesus of Nazareth." Jesus answered, "I told you that I am he. So if you are looking for me, let these men go." This was to fulfill the word that he had spoken, "I did not lose a single one of those whom you gave me." Then Simon Peter, who had a sword, drew it, struck the high priest's slave, and cut off his right ear. The slave's name was Malchus. Jesus said to Peter, "Put your sword back into its sheath. Am I not to drink the cup that the Father has given me?"

So the soldiers, their officer, and the Jewish police arrested Jesus and bound him. First they took him to Annas, who was the father-in-law of Caiaphas, the high priest that year. Caiaphas was the one who had advised the Jews that it was better to have one person die for the people.

Simon Peter and another disciple followed Jesus. Since that disciple was known to the high priest, he went with Jesus into the courtyard of the high priest, but Peter was standing outside at the gate. So the other disciple, who was known to the high priest, went out, spoke to the woman who guarded the gate, and brought Peter in. The woman said to Peter, "You are not also one of this man's disciples, are you?" He said, "I am not." Now the slaves and the police had made a charcoal fire because it was cold, and they were standing around it and warming themselves. Peter also was standing with them and warming himself.

Then the high priest questioned Jesus about his disciples and about his teaching. Jesus answered, "I have spoken openly to the world; I have always taught in synagogues and in the temple, where all the Jews come together. I have said nothing in secret. Why do you ask me? Ask those who heard what I said to them; they know what I said." When he had said this, one of the police standing nearby struck Jesus on the face, saying, "Is that how you answer the high priest?" Jesus answered, "If I have spoken wrongly, testify to the wrong. But if I have spoken rightly, why do you strike me?" Then Annas sent him bound to Caiaphas the high priest.

Now Simon Peter was standing and warming himself. They asked him, "You are not also one of his disciples, are you?" He denied it and said, "I am not." One of the slaves of the high priest, a relative of the man whose ear Peter had cut off, asked, "Did I not see you in the garden with him?" Again Peter denied it, and at that moment the cock crowed.

Then they took Jesus from Caiaphas to Pilate's headquarters. It was early in the morning. They themselves did not enter the headquarters, so as to avoid ritual defilement and to be able to eat the Passover. So Pilate went out to them and said, "What accusation do you bring against this man?" They answered, "If this man were not a criminal, we would not have handed him over to you." Pilate said to them, "Take him yourselves and judge him according to your law." The Jews replied, "We are not permitted to put anyone to death." (This was to fulfill what Jesus had said when he indicated the kind of death he was to die.)

Then Pilate entered the headquarters again, summoned Jesus, and asked him, "Are you the King of the Jews?" Jesus answered, "Do you ask this on your own, or did others tell you about me?" Pilate replied, "I am not a Jew, am I? Your own nation and the chief priests have handed you over to me. What have you done?" Jesus answered, "My kingdom is not from this world. If my kingdom were from this world, my followers would be fighting to keep me from being handed over to the Jews. But as it is, my kingdom is not from here." Pilate asked him, "So you are a king?" Jesus answered, "You say that I am a king. For this I was born, and for this I came into the world, to testify to the truth. Everyone who belongs to the truth listens to my voice." Pilate asked him, "What is truth?"

After he had said this, he went out to the Jews again and told them, "I find no case against him." But you have a custom that I release someone for you at the Passover. Do you want me to release for you the King of the Jews?" They shouted in reply, "Not this man, but Barabbas!" Now Barabbas was a bandit.

Then Pilate took Jesus and had him flogged. And the soldiers wove a crown of thorns and put it on his head, and they dressed him in a purple robe. They kept coming up to him, saying, "Hail, King of the Jews!" and striking him on the face. Pilate went out again and said to them, "Look, I am bringing him out to you to let you know that I find no case against him." So Jesus came out, wearing the crown of thorns and the purple robe. Pilate said to them, "Here is the man!" When the chief priests and the police saw him, they shouted, "Crucify him! Crucify him!" Pilate said to them, "Take him yourselves and crucify him; I find no case against him." The Jews answered him, "We have a law, and according to that law he ought to die because he has claimed to be the Son of God."

Now when Pilate heard this, he was more afraid than ever. He entered his headquarters again and asked Jesus, "Where are you from?" But Jesus gave him no answer. Pilate therefore said to him, "Do you refuse to speak to me? Do you not know that I have power to release you, and power to crucify you?" Jesus answered him, "You would have no power over me unless it had been given you from above; therefore the one who handed me over to you is guilty of a greater sin." From then on Pilate tried to release him, but the Jews cried out, "If you release this man, you are no friend of the emperor. Everyone who claims to be a king sets himself against the emperor."

When Pilate heard these words, he brought Jesus outside and sat on the judge's bench at a place called The Stone Pavement, or in Hebrew Gabbatha. Now it was the day of Preparation for the Passover; and it was about noon. He said to the Jews, "Here is your King!" They cried out, "Away with him! Away with him! Crucify him!" Pilate asked them, "Shall I crucify your King?" The chief priests answered, "We have no king but the emperor." Then he handed him over to them to be crucified.

So they took Jesus; and carrying the cross by himself, he went out to what is called The Place of the Skull, which in Hebrew is called Golgotha. There they crucified him, and with him two others, one on either side, with Jesus between them. Pilate also had an inscription written and put on the cross. It read, "Jesus of Nazareth, the King of the Jews." Many of the Jews read this inscription, because the place where Jesus was crucified was near the city; and it was written in Hebrew, in Latin, and in Greek. Then the chief priests of the Jews said to Pilate, "Do not write, 'The King of the Jews,' but, 'This man said, I am King of the Jews.'" Pilate answered, "What I have written I have written." When the soldiers had crucified Jesus, they took his clothes and divided them into four parts, one for each soldier. They also took his tunic; now the tunic was seamless, woven in one piece from the top. So they said to one another, "Let us not tear it, but cast lots for it to see who will get it." This was to fulfill what the scripture says, "They divided my clothes among themselves, / and for my clothing they cast lots." And that is what the soldiers did.

Meanwhile, standing near the cross of Jesus were his mother, and his mother's sister, Mary the wife of Clopas, and Mary Magdalene. When Jesus saw his mother and the disciple whom he loved standing beside her, he said to his mother, "Woman, here is your son." Then he said to the disciple, "Here is your mother." And from that hour the disciple took her into his own home.

After this, when Jesus knew that all was now finished, he said (in order to fulfill the scripture), "I am thirsty." A jar full of sour wine was standing there. So they put a sponge full of the wine on a branch of hyssop and held it to his mouth. When Jesus had received the wine, he said, "It is finished." Then he bowed his head and gave up his spirit.

Since it was the day of Preparation, the Jews did not want the bodies left on the cross during the sabbath, especially because that sabbath was a day of great solemnity. So they asked Pilate to have the legs of the cru- cified men broken and the bodies removed. Then the soldiers came and broke the legs of the first and of the other who had been crucified with him. But when they came to Jesus and saw that he was already dead, they did not break his legs. Instead, one of the soldiers pierced his side with a spear, and at once blood and water came out. (He who saw this has testified so that you also may believe. His testimony is true, and he knows that he tells the truth.) These things occurred so that the scripture might be fulfilled, "None of his bones shall be broken." And again another passage of scripture says, "They will look on the one whom they have pierced."

After these things, Joseph of Arimathea, who was a disciple of Jesus, though a secret one because of his fear of the Jews, asked Pilate to let him take away the body of Jesus. Pilate gave him permission; so he came and removed his body. Nicodemus, who had at first come to Jesus by night, also came, bringing a mixture of myrrh and aloes, weighing about a hundred pounds. They took the body of Jesus and wrapped it with the spices in linen cloths, according to the burial custom of the Jews. Now there was a garden in the place where he was crucified, and in the garden there was a new tomb in which no one had ever been laid. And so, because it was the Jewish day of Preparation, and the tomb was nearby, they laid Jesus there.

- Good Friday puts the cross before me and challenges me not to look away. If I have followed Jesus' footsteps to Calvary, I do not have to fear because I, like him, am confident in God's enduring presence. Wherever there is suffering or pain, I seek the face of Jesus. I ask him for the strength I need to be a sign of hope wherever there is despair, to be a presence of love wherever it is most needed.

- All of us will one day give up our spirit. In prayer we can offer our death to God; we can do so with Mary: "Holy Mary, mother of God, pray for us, sinners; now and at the hour of our death."

Saturday 11th April
Holy Saturday
Matthew 28:1–10

After the sabbath, as the first day of the week was dawning, Mary Magdalene and the other Mary went to see the tomb. And suddenly there was a great earthquake; for an angel of the Lord, descending from heaven, came and rolled back the stone and sat on it. His appearance was like lightning, and his clothing white as snow. For fear of him the guards shook and became like dead men. But the angel said to the women, "Do not be afraid; I know that you are looking for Jesus who was crucified. He is not here; for he has been raised, as he said. Come, see the place where he lay. Then go quickly and tell his disciples, 'He has been raised from the dead, and indeed he is going ahead of you to Galilee; there you will see him.' This is my message for you." So they left the tomb quickly with fear and great joy, and ran to tell his disciples. Suddenly Jesus met them and said, "Greetings!" And they came to him, took hold of his feet, and worshiped him. Then Jesus said to them, "Do not be afraid; go and tell my brothers to go to Galilee; there they will see me."

- The angel and Jesus say to the women, "Do not be afraid." Change, revelation, and enlightenment tempt us to be anxious because we have encountered something so beyond our understanding. Jesus, help me remember "Do not be afraid" when I sense a transformation beginning in my life.

- Another point in common between the angel and Jesus is that they instructed the women to go tell the other disciples. Our life with Jesus is personal but not private; the Good News is meant to be shared. Am I willing to share this treasure in my life?

April 12—April 18

Something to think and pray about each day this week:

Decision making is a struggle, yet the Ignatian approach accepts the struggle wholeheartedly. In fact, the approach to decision making that Ignatius suggests depends on this struggle. It claims that the signs of God's direction for our lives are found precisely in the shifting movements of our divided hearts as spiritual forces struggle for mastery. Ignatian discernment teaches us to become aware of those movements, to reflect on them, and to interpret them. The battle is the problem, but it is also the solution.

—J. Michael Sparough, SJ, Jim Manney, and
Tim Hipskind, SJ, *What's Your Decision?*

The Presence of God

Dear Jesus, today I call on you, but not to ask for anything. I'd like only to dwell in your presence. May my heart respond to your love.

Freedom

God my creator, you gave me life and the gift of freedom. Through your love I exist in this world. May I never take the gift of life for granted. May I always respect others' right to life.

Consciousness

I ask how I am today. Am I particularly tired, stressed, or anxious? If any of these characteristics apply, can I try to let go of the concerns that disturb me?

The Word

The word of God comes down to us through the Scriptures. May the Holy Spirit enlighten my mind and my heart to respond to the Gospel teachings. (Please turn to the Scripture on the following pages. Inspiration points are there, should you need them. When you are ready, return here to continue.)

Conversation

I begin to talk with Jesus about the Scripture I have just read. What part of it strikes a chord in me? Perhaps the words of a friend—or some story I have heard recently—will rise to the surface in my consciousness. If so, does the story throw light on what the Scripture passage may be saying to me?

Conclusion

Glory be to the Father, and to the Son, and to the Holy Spirit,
As it was in the beginning, is now and ever shall be,
World without end. Amen.

Sunday 12th April
Easter Sunday of the Resurrection of the Lord
John 20:1–9

Early on the first day of the week, while it was still dark, Mary Magdalene came to the tomb and saw that the stone had been removed from the tomb. So she ran and went to Simon Peter and the other disciple, the one whom Jesus loved, and said to them, "They have taken the Lord out of the tomb, and we do not know where they have laid him." Then Peter and the other disciple set out and went toward the tomb. The two were running together, but the other disciple outran Peter and reached the tomb first. He bent down to look in and saw the linen wrappings lying there, but he did not go in. Then Simon Peter came, following him, and went into the tomb. He saw the linen wrappings lying there, and the cloth that had been on Jesus' head, not lying with the linen wrappings but rolled up in a place by itself. Then the other disciple, who reached the tomb first, also went in, and he saw and believed; for as yet they did not understand the scripture, that he must rise from the dead.

- "We proclaim the resurrection of Christ," says Pope Francis, "when his light illuminates the dark moments of our existence, and we are able to share it with others; when we know when to smile with those who smile, and weep with those who weep; when we accompany those who are sad and at risk of losing hope; when we recount our experience of Faith to those who are searching for meaning and happiness . . . and there—with our attitude, with our witness, with our life—we say 'Jesus is risen,' with our soul."

- Neither Peter nor John come to believe in the Resurrection without enduring confusion and uncertainty. But out of the confusion comes clarity. The empty tomb can only mean that Jesus is truly alive— raised and transformed by the Father. If Jesus is truly risen, then so are we. As we were one with him in his suffering, so are we now one with him in his risen joy. Alleluia!

Monday 13th April
Matthew 28:8–15

So they left the tomb quickly with fear and great joy, and ran to tell his disciples. Suddenly Jesus met them and said, "Greetings!" And they came to him, took hold of his feet, and worshiped him. Then Jesus said to them, "Do not be afraid; go and tell my brothers to go to Galilee; there they will see me." While they were going, some of the guard went into the city and told the chief priests everything that had happened. After the priests had assembled with the elders, they devised a plan to give a large sum of money to the soldiers, telling them, "You must say, 'His disciples came by night and stole him away while we were asleep.' If this comes to the governor's ears, we will satisfy him and keep you out of trouble." So they took the money and did as they were directed. And this story is still told among the Jews to this day.

- This reading tells of the cover-up orchestrated by the chief priests and elders. Bribery buys the silence of the soldiers, and further bribery is promised to make sure that the governor does not cause trouble. We are familiar with this pattern of corruption, are we not? But Jesus is still risen! Alleluia!

- Galilee was the backwater of Israel, a rural place where the poor and deprived lived. Yet it is the place where Jesus both began and ended his ministry. It is from here that he sends his disciples forth with the message of the Resurrection. Lord, you send me to the "Galilees" of my world, where you are often disguised in the poor, the deprived, the oppressed. Let me be a witness to you, an agent of hope and encouragement to all whom I meet.

Tuesday 14th April
John 20:11–18

But Mary stood weeping outside the tomb. As she wept, she bent over to look into the tomb; and she saw two angels in white, sitting where the body of Jesus had been lying, one at the head and the other at the feet. They said to her, "Woman, why are you weeping?" She said to them, "They have taken away my Lord, and I do not know where they have laid him." When she had said this, she turned around and saw Jesus standing there, but she did not know that it was Jesus. Jesus said to her, "Woman, why are you weeping? Whom are you looking for?" Supposing him to be the gardener, she said to him, "Sir, if you have carried him away, tell me where you have laid him, and I will take him away." Jesus said to her, "Mary!" She turned and said to him in Hebrew, "Rabbouni!" (which means Teacher). Jesus said to her, "Do not hold on to me, because I have not yet ascended to the Father. But go to my brothers and say to them, 'I am ascending to my Father and your Father, to my God and your God.'" Mary Magdalene went and announced to the disciples, "I have seen the Lord"; and she told them that he had said these things to her.

- Do we sometimes think the Lord has been taken away? Prayer and Christian life can be drab, dry, and tiresome. Institutional scandals drain our energy. Jesus' life in us is ever new. We are not to hold on to an "old" Jesus but rather to walk with him as he walks the new journey of life and prayer with us.

- What do I experience in this precious moment of encounter? Mary turned around and saw Jesus. I ask God to give me the strength I need always to be ready to turn around, to look again, that I may see and recognize Jesus' presence in my life.

Wednesday 15th April
Luke 24:13–35

Now on that same day two of them were going to a village called Emmaus, about seven miles from Jerusalem, and talking with each other about all these things that had happened. While they were talking and discussing, Jesus himself came near and went with them, but their eyes were kept from recognizing him. And he said to them, "What are you discussing with each other while you walk along?" They stood still, looking sad. Then one of them, whose name was Cleopas, answered him, "Are you the only stranger in Jerusalem who does not know the things that have taken place there in these days?" He asked them, "What things?" They replied, "The things about Jesus of Nazareth, who was a prophet mighty in deed and word before God and all the people, and how our chief priests and leaders handed him over to be condemned to death and crucified him. But we had hoped that he was the one to redeem Israel. Yes, and besides all this, it is now the third day since these things took place. Moreover, some women of our group astounded us. They were at the tomb early this morning, and when they did not find his body there, they came back and told us that they had indeed seen a vision of angels who said that he was alive. Some of those who were with us went to the tomb and found it just as the women had said; but they did not see him." Then he said to them, "Oh, how foolish you are, and how slow of heart to believe all that the prophets have declared! Was it not necessary that the Messiah should suffer these things and then enter into his glory?" Then beginning with Moses and all the prophets, he interpreted to them the things about himself in all the scriptures. As they came near the village to which they were going, he walked ahead as if he were going on. But they urged him strongly, saying, "Stay with us, because it is almost evening and the day is now nearly over." So he went in to stay with them. When he was at the table with them, he took bread, blessed and broke it, and gave it to them. Then their eyes were opened, and they recognized him; and he vanished from their sight. They said to each other, "Were not our hearts burning within us while he was talking to us on the road, while he was opening the scriptures to us?" That same hour they got up and returned to Jerusalem; and they found the eleven and their companions gathered together. They were saying, "The Lord has risen indeed, and he has appeared to Simon!" Then they told what had happened on the road, and how he had been made known to them in the breaking of the bread.

• Like Cleopas, I walk with you, Lord, but I do not always recognize you. Jesus, find me where I am. Draw near and walk with me. Open the Scriptures to me and help me recognize how my story comes to life as I listen to yours. Let me so hear your Good News that my heart may glow. Let me forget myself and receive your Spirit. You bring me the message of life, and you trust me to do for others what you want to do for me.

• Jesus, in times of disillusionment and faded dreams you stand at the door, waiting for me to invite you in. May the experience of your risen presence bring about a transformation in my daily engagement with others.

Thursday 16th April
Luke 24:35–48

Then they told what had happened on the road, and how he had been made known to them in the breaking of the bread. While they were talking about this, Jesus himself stood among them and said to them, "Peace be with you." They were startled and terrified, and thought that they were seeing a ghost. He said to them, "Why are you frightened, and why do doubts arise in your hearts? Look at my hands and my feet; see that it is I myself. Touch me and see; for a ghost does not have flesh and bones as you see that I have." And when he had said this, he showed them his hands and his feet. While in their joy they were disbelieving and still wondering, he said to them, "Have you anything here to eat?" They gave him a piece of broiled fish, and he took it and ate in their presence. Then he said to them, "These are my words that I spoke to you while I was still with you—that everything written about me in the law of Moses, the prophets, and the psalms must be fulfilled." Then he opened their minds to understand the scriptures, and he said to them, "Thus it is written, that the Messiah is to suffer and to rise from the dead on the third day, and that repentance and forgiveness of sins is to be proclaimed in his name to all nations, beginning from Jerusalem. You are witnesses of these things."

- Lord, you wish me to leave the safety of my private upper room and meet you as you come to me daily in the streets. But first let me be with you in prayer, waiting for the power of your Holy Spirit.

- The Greeks thought that only the soul survived after death. But Luke emphasizes that the risen Jesus is the same as the man who walked our earth. His wounds are still showing. The real Jesus is indeed back with his friends and doing all he can to help them to believe. Help my belief today, Lord.

Friday 17th April

John 21:1–14

After these things Jesus showed himself again to the disciples by the Sea of Tiberias; and he showed himself in this way. Gathered there together were Simon Peter, Thomas called the Twin, Nathanael of Cana in Galilee, the sons of Zebedee, and two others of his disciples. Simon Peter said to them, "I am going fishing." They said to him, "We will go with you." They went out and got into the boat, but that night they caught nothing. Just after daybreak, Jesus stood on the beach; but the disciples did not know that it was Jesus. Jesus said to them, "Children, you have no fish, have you?" They answered him, "No." He said to them, "Cast the net to the right side of the boat, and you will find some." So they cast it, and now they were not able to haul it in because there were so many fish. That disciple whom Jesus loved said to Peter, "It is the Lord!" When

Simon Peter heard that it was the Lord, he put on some clothes, for he was naked, and jumped into the sea. But the other disciples came in the boat, dragging the net full of fish, for they were not far from the land, only about a hundred yards off. When they had gone ashore, they saw a charcoal fire there, with fish on it, and bread. Jesus said to them, "Bring some of the fish that you have just caught." So Simon Peter went aboard and hauled the net ashore, full of large fish, a hundred and fifty-three of them; and though there were so many, the net was not torn. Jesus said to them, "Come and have breakfast." Now none of the disciples dared to ask him, "Who are you?" because they knew it was the Lord. Jesus came and took the bread and gave it to them, and did the same with the fish. This was now the third time that Jesus appeared to the disciples after he was raised from the dead.

- Peter is lost and struggling. He feels that he is a failure at what he usually does well. Can I identify with him sometimes? But Peter is open to another voice, which he dimly recognizes, but not quite. He does what is suggested to him, and wonderful results follow.

- It can be the same for me—if I am open to being surprised. Lord, let me accept you today as a God of good surprises.

Saturday 18th April
Mark 16:9–15

Now after he rose early on the first day of the week, he appeared first to Mary Magdalene, from whom he had cast out seven demons. She went out and told those who had been with him, while they were mourning and weeping. But when they heard that he was alive and had been seen by her, they would not believe it. After this he appeared in another form to two of them, as they were walking into the country. And they went back and told the rest, but they did not believe them. Later he appeared to the eleven themselves as they were sitting at the table; and he upbraided them for their lack of faith and stubbornness, because they had not believed those who saw him after he had risen. And he said to them, "Go into all the world and proclaim the Good News to the whole creation."

- Faith in the risen Christ came slowly to some if not all the disciples. Three times in this Gospel we are told that Jesus' witnesses were not believed. The disciples' lack of faith was a disappointment to Jesus, yet he sent them to proclaim the Good News.

- I am like the disciples: sometimes outwardly confident yet harboring doubts, at other times hesitant to proclaim what seems certain to me. Jesus invites me to a fullness of faith. He sees and understands my stubbornness and reluctance, yet trusts me. Calmly and gently he sends me to the whole world.

Second Week of Easter
April 19—April 25

Something to think and pray about each day this week:

A saying attributed to Pedro Arrupe, SJ, begins: "Nothing is more practical than finding God, that is, than falling in love in a quite absolute, final way." It's what Arrupe said next that strikes me.

> What you are in love with, what seizes your imagination, will affect everything. It will decide what will get you out of bed in the morning, what you will do with your evenings, how you will spend your weekends, what you read, who you know, what breaks your heart, and what amazes you with joy and gratitude. Fall in love, stay in love and it will decide everything.

I don't know a better description of what Ignatius of Loyola intended when he put the Spiritual Exercises together. He wants us to fall in love. He's interested in those deep currents of feeling that shape what we want, which in turn influences what we do. Psychologists talk about the three parts of the mind: the cognitive (reason and other mental processes), the conative (the will), and the affective (feelings and emotions). Ignatius zeroed in on the "affect." Understanding is important, and the will is vital, but what gets you out of bed in the morning is what you love. This is what Ignatius wanted the Spiritual Exercises to influence.

—Jim Manney, *God Finds Us*

The Presence of God

At any time of the day or night we can call on Jesus.
He is always waiting, listening for our call.
What a wonderful blessing.
No phone needed, no e-mails, just a whisper.

Freedom

Lord, grant me the grace to have freedom of the spirit. Cleanse my heart and soul so that I may live joyously in your love.

Consciousness

Knowing that God loves me unconditionally, I look honestly over the past day, its events, and my feelings. Do I have something to be grateful for? Then I give thanks. Is there something I am sorry for? Then I ask forgiveness.

The Word

The word of God comes down to us through the Scriptures.
May the Holy Spirit enlighten my mind and my heart
to respond to the Gospel teachings:
to love my neighbor as myself,
to care for my sisters and brothers in Christ.
(Please turn to the Scripture on the following pages. Inspiration points are there, should you need them. When you are ready, return here to continue.)

Conversation

I know with certainty that there were times when you carried me, Lord. There were times when it was through your strength that I got through the dark times in my life.

Conclusion

Glory be to the Father, and to the Son, and to the Holy Spirit,
As it was in the beginning, is now and ever shall be,
World without end. Amen.

Sunday 19th April
Second Sunday of Easter or Sunday of Divine Mercy
John 20:19–31

When it was evening on that day, the first day of the week, and the doors of the house where the disciples had met were locked for fear of the Jews, Jesus came and stood among them and said, "Peace be with you." After he said this, he showed them his hands and his side. Then the disciples rejoiced when they saw the Lord. Jesus said to them again, "Peace be with you. As the Father has sent me, so I send you." When he had said this, he breathed on them and said to them, "Receive the Holy Spirit. If you forgive the sins of any, they are forgiven them; if you retain the sins of any, they are retained." But Thomas (who was called the Twin), one of the twelve, was not with them when Jesus came. So the other disciples told him, "We have seen the Lord." But he said to them, "Unless I see the mark of the nails in his hands, and put my finger in the mark of the nails and my hand in his side, I will not believe." A week later his disciples were again in the house, and Thomas was with them. Although the doors were shut, Jesus came and stood among them and said, "Peace be with you." Then he said to Thomas, "Put your finger here and see my hands. Reach out your hand and put it in my side. Do not doubt but believe." Thomas answered him, "My Lord and my God!" Jesus said to him, "Have you believed because you have seen me? Blessed are those who have not seen and yet have come to believe." Now Jesus did many other signs in the presence of his disciples, which are not written in this book. But these are written so that you may come to believe that Jesus is the Messiah, the Son of God, and that through believing you may have life in his name.

- Are the doors of my heart locked? Do I not expect Jesus to show up and visit me? Am I afraid—afraid that my well-ordered ways of thinking and doing things might be turned upside down if I let Jesus in?

- Brave, honest Thomas had gone off to grieve on his own, so he missed that meeting with the Lord. I have suffered in this way when I isolated myself from the community of faith. It is when I am stunned by sorrow that I most need the company of friends and the support of faith.

Monday 20th April

John 3:1–8

Now there was a Pharisee named Nicodemus, a leader of the Jews. He came to Jesus by night and said to him, "Rabbi, we know that you are a teacher who has come from God; for no one can do these signs that you do apart from the presence of God." Jesus answered him, "Very truly, I tell you, no one can see the kingdom of God without being born from above." Nicodemus said to him, "How can anyone be born after having grown old? Can one enter a second time into the mother's womb and be born?" Jesus answered, "Very truly, I tell you, no one can enter the kingdom of God without being born of water and Spirit. What is born of the flesh is flesh, and what is born of the Spirit is spirit. Do not be astonished that I said to you, 'You must be born from above.' The wind blows where it chooses, and you hear the sound of it, but you do not know where it comes from or where it goes. So it is with everyone who is born of the Spirit."

- Cautious Nicodemus is spiritually as well as physically in the dark. Christ's words light a slow burning wick that will blaze into light at the most unlikely time. After the Crucifixion, when everything seemed over, Nicodemus declared himself by coming to the garden tomb bearing myrrh and aloes.

- The Spirit of God is everywhere—let's allow ourselves to be surprised by her! She is the gift of God, and wherever we find joy, peace, compassion, justice, and anything of life, there we find her. Prayer is our opening to this Spirit at prayer time and afterwards.

Tuesday 21st April

John 3:7b–15

[Jesus said,] "'You must be born from above.' The wind blows where it chooses, and you hear the sound of it, but you do not know where it comes from or where it goes. So it is with everyone who is born of the Spirit." Nicodemus said to him, "How can these things be?" Jesus answered him, "Are you a teacher of Israel, and yet you do not understand these things? Very truly, I tell you, we speak of what we know and testify to what we have seen; yet you do not receive our testimony. If I have told you about earthly things and you do not believe, how can you believe if I tell you about heavenly things? No one has ascended into heaven except the one who descended from heaven, the Son of Man. And just as Moses lifted up the serpent in the wilderness, so must the Son of Man be lifted up, that whoever believes in him may have eternal life."

- Nicodemus was a clever teacher but lacked a certain wisdom. Used to citing authorities, he was unable to recognize the authority of Jesus, who spoke of what he knew. Before God I recognize my habits, my preferences, and my inclinations; I ask God to give me the freedom I need to be touched by Jesus' words, to awaken to his imagination, and to want for myself the freedom that he desires for me.

- There is a divine dimension to each person. There is a depth in our hearts where God dwells. It is our most sacred space. God works there. Our DNA is divine.

Wednesday 22nd April
John 3:16–21

"For God so loved the world that he gave his only Son, so that everyone who believes in him may not perish but may have eternal life. Indeed, God did not send the Son into the world to condemn the world, but in order that the world might be saved through him. Those who believe in him are not condemned; but those who do not believe are condemned already, because they have not believed in the name of the only Son of God. And this is the judgment, that the light has come into the world, and people loved darkness rather than light because their deeds were evil. For all who do evil hate the light and do not come to the light, so that their deeds may not be exposed. But those who do what is true come to the light, so that it may be clearly seen that their deeds have been done in God."

- God gave his Son, only-begotten, the only Son of the eternal father. The words *Father*, *Son*, and *begotten* are human metaphors for the mysterious dynamic of the Blessed Trinity. We believe that God intervened in human history and gave his only Son to show that his attitude toward us is that of a loving parent.

- Prayer may be compared to a time of opening ourselves to the light of God, like sunning ourselves in the warmth of the sun, the gentle and bright light that illuminates us completely. In prayer, the light of God enters a person in a way that lightens the burdens of life and that encourages us to share light with others. It can help in prayer to imagine the light surrounding us and to be reminded that this light surrounds us outside prayer as well.

Thursday 23rd April

John 3:31–36

"The one who comes from above is above all; the one who is of the earth belongs to the earth and speaks about earthly things. The one who comes from heaven is above all. He testifies to what he has seen and heard, yet no one accepts his testimony. Whoever has accepted his testimony has certified this, that God is true. He whom God has sent speaks the words of God, for he gives the Spirit without measure. The Father loves the Son and has placed all things in his hands. Whoever believes in the Son has eternal life; whoever disobeys the Son will not see life, but must endure God's wrath."

- God "gives the Spirit without measure." We do not decide to be born. Nor can we force our rebirth in the Spirit. However, that rebirth is offered every day of this life. We must learn to receive what God offers without measure.

- God's Word is spoken unceasingly in my soul. There is never an instant when God is not present—within me and all around me. With God, I co-create my soul every day of my earthly life. I need have no fear of birth or rebirth, change or life or death. Instead, I see them for what they are: thrilling stages along a transcendent journey home.

Friday 24th April

John 6:1–15

After this Jesus went to the other side of the Sea of Galilee, also called the Sea of Tiberias. A large crowd kept following him, because they saw the signs that he was doing for the sick. Jesus went up the mountain and sat down there with his disciples. Now the Passover, the festival of the Jews, was near. When he looked up and saw a large crowd coming toward him, Jesus said to Philip, "Where are we to buy bread for these people to eat?" He said this to test him, for he himself knew what he was going to do.

Philip answered him, "Six months' wages would not buy enough bread for each of them to get a little." One of his disciples, Andrew, Simon Peter's brother, said to him, "There is a boy here who has five barley loaves and two fish. But what are they among so many people?" Jesus said, "Make the people sit down." Now there was a great deal of grass in the place; so they sat down, about five thousand in all. Then Jesus took the loaves, and when he had given thanks, he distributed them to those who were seated; so also the fish, as much as they wanted. When they were satisfied, he told his disciples, "Gather up the fragments left over, so that nothing may be lost." So they gathered them up, and from the fragments of the five barley loaves, left by those who had eaten, they filled twelve baskets. When the people saw the sign that he had done, they began to say, "This is indeed the prophet who is to come into the world." When Jesus realized that they were about to come and take him by force to make him king, he withdrew again to the mountain by himself.

- In this miracle, Jesus works with the little food the apostles have to feed the multitude. Through his actions he reveals God's action toward us: nourishing, caring, lavish, and concerned for all our needs.

- God also expects us to come to the aid of one another and to share what little we have. Saint Teresa of Calcutta said about Jesus: "He uses us to be his love and compassion in the world in spite of our weaknesses and frailties." I pray for the courage I need to risk giving even the little that I have.

Saturday 25th April
Saint Mark, Evangelist
Mark 16:15–20

And he said to them, "Go into all the world and proclaim the Good News to the whole creation. The one who believes and is baptized will be saved; but the one who does not believe will be condemned. And these signs will accompany those who believe: by using my name they will cast out demons; they will speak in new tongues; they will pick up snakes in their hands, and if they drink any deadly thing, it will not hurt them; they will lay their hands on the sick, and they will recover." So then the Lord Jesus, after he had spoken to them, was taken up into heaven and sat down at the right hand of God. And they went out and proclaimed the Good

News everywhere, while the Lord worked with them and confirmed the message by the signs that accompanied it.

- The words of Jesus at the end of his Easter appearances link heaven and earth. From his place in heaven, the Lord works with us and is a companion in the work of proclaiming Good News. His friendship with each of us is Good News for us. We are to share that in different situations. Prayer deepens in us the sense that the message of Jesus is Good News in our own lives and, through us, in the lives of others. Each of us is called into the ministry of Jesus in some way.

- We are called to be "other Christs," to be people who make known the love of God and his care for his people in the world. We may never know how much we have done this; it is sufficient that we do what we can. God has some work to do that can be done only through each person. In a time of prayer, we ask that we use our gifts and talents as best we can in God's service.

Third Week of Easter
April 26—May 2

Something to think and pray about each day this week:

The more honest we are able to be, the more mindful we are about why we are laughing and what we are laughing at, and the more transformative comedy is. Comedy doesn't happen in a vacuum; there is no such thing as something being funny for the sake of funny. We laugh at the guy slipping on the banana peel because he is human, and by definition that means that he is limited in his capacity to know what is going on around him. He would like to know everything that is going on around him and have total control, but he does not, and so he doesn't see the banana peel in front of him. The rest, as they say, is comedy gold.

—Jake Martin, SJ, *What's So Funny about Faith?*

The Presence of God

I remind myself that, as I sit here now,
God is gazing on me with love and holding me in being.
I pause for a moment and think of this.

Freedom

"There are very few people who realize what God would make of them
if they abandoned themselves into his hands, and let themselves be
formed by his grace" (Saint Ignatius). I ask for the grace to trust myself
totally to God's love.

Consciousness

Where do I sense hope, encouragement, and growth in my life? By looking back over the past few months, I may be able to see which activities
and occasions have produced rich fruit. If I do notice such areas, I will
determine to give those areas both time and space in the future.

The Word

Lord Jesus, you became human to communicate with me.
You walked and worked on this earth.
You endured the heat and struggled with the cold.
All your time on this earth was spent in caring for humanity.
You healed the sick, you raised the dead.
Most important of all, you saved me from death.
(Please turn to the Scripture on the following pages. Inspiration points
are there, should you need them. When you are ready, return here to
continue.)

Conversation

What is stirring in me as I pray? Am I consoled, troubled, left cold? I
imagine Jesus standing or sitting at my side, and I share my feelings with
him.

Conclusion

Glory be to the Father, and to the Son, and to the Holy Spirit,
As it was in the beginning, is now and ever shall be,
World without end. Amen.

Sunday 26th April
Third Sunday of Easter
Luke 24:13–35

Now on that same day two of them were going to a village called Emmaus, about seven miles from Jerusalem, and talking with each other about all these things that had happened. While they were talking and discussing, Jesus himself came near and went with them, but their eyes were kept from recognizing him. And he said to them, "What are you discussing with each other while you walk along?" They stood still, looking sad. Then one of them, whose name was Cleopas, answered him, "Are you the only stranger in Jerusalem who does not know the things that have taken place there in these days?" He asked them, "What things?" They replied, "The things about Jesus of Nazareth, who was a prophet mighty in deed and word before God and all the people, and how our chief priests and leaders handed him over to be condemned to death and crucified him. But we had hoped that he was the one to redeem Israel. Yes, and besides all this, it is now the third day since these things took place. Moreover, some women of our group astounded us. They were at the tomb early this morning, and when they did not find his body there, they came back and told us that they had indeed seen a vision of angels who said that he was alive. Some of those who were with us went to the tomb and found it just as the women had said; but they did not see him." Then he said to them, "Oh, how foolish you are, and how slow of heart to believe all that the prophets have declared! Was it not necessary that the Messiah should suffer these things and then enter into his glory?" Then beginning with Moses and all the prophets, he interpreted to them the things about himself in all the scriptures. As they came near the village to which they were going, he walked ahead as if he were going on. But they urged him strongly, saying, "Stay with us, because it is almost evening and the day is now nearly over." So he went in to stay with them. When he was at the table with them, he took bread, blessed and broke it, and gave it to them. Then their eyes were opened, and they recognized him; and he vanished from their sight. They said to each other, "Were not our hearts burning within us while he was talking to us on the road, while he was opening the scriptures to us?" That same hour they got up and returned to Jerusalem; and they found the eleven and their companions gathered together. They were saying, "The Lord has risen indeed, and he has appeared to Simon!" Then they told what had happened on the road, and how he had been made known to them in the breaking of the bread.

- Join the two disciples on their journey from Jerusalem to Emmaus. Sense their disappointment, despondency, disorientation. Listen as Jesus explains the meaning of the Scriptures to them. Be aware of their hearts burning within them. What a change of mood—from desolation to consolation! Is Jesus warming your heart? Are you seeing anything in a new light?

- Jesus, in times of disillusionment and faded dreams you stand at the door, waiting for me to invite you in. May the experience of your risen presence bring about a transformation in my daily engagement with others.

Monday 27th April
John 6:22–29

The next day the crowd that had stayed on the other side of the sea saw that there had been only one boat there. They also saw that Jesus had not got into the boat with his disciples, but that his disciples had gone away alone. Then some boats from Tiberias came near the place where they had eaten the bread after the Lord had given thanks. So when the crowd saw that neither Jesus nor his disciples were there, they themselves got into the boats and went to Capernaum looking for Jesus. When they found him on the other side of the sea, they said to him, "Rabbi, when did you come here?" Jesus answered them, "Very truly, I tell you, you are looking for me, not because you saw signs, but because you ate your fill of the loaves. Do not work for the food that perishes, but for the food that endures for eternal life, which the Son of Man will give you. For it is on him that God the Father has set his seal." Then they said to him, "What must we do to perform the works of God?" Jesus answered them, "This is the work of God, that you believe in him whom he has sent."

- The crowds search energetically for Jesus. They borrow some boats and row across the sea in search of him. At last they find him and are happy. Jesus, inflame my heart with a strong desire to keep in touch with you. In searching for you, I find happiness.

- The crowd is hungry again and pursues Jesus. They believe he will meet their needs. He tries to deepen their fragile faith in himself. Food for the body is necessary, but the food of eternal life meets a deeper need. Lord, I can be like the crowd, seeking only to satisfy my immediate hungers. Forgive the times when I have used you to serve my interests.

Tuesday 28th April
John 6:30–35

So they said to him, "What sign are you going to give us then, so that we may see it and believe you? What work are you performing? Our ancestors ate the manna in the wilderness; as it is written, 'He gave them bread from heaven to eat.'" Then Jesus said to them, "Very truly, I tell you, it was not Moses who gave you the bread from heaven, but it is my Father who gives you the true bread from heaven. For the bread of God is that which comes down from heaven and gives life to the world." They said to him, "Sir, give us this bread always." Jesus said to them, "I am the bread of life. Whoever comes to me will never be hungry, and whoever believes in me will never be thirsty."

- Notice how some of the Jews have conditions for Jesus to fulfill before they will accept him—for example, he must produce spectacular miracles as Moses did. Setting conditions prevents them from seeing and experiencing that God is revealing Godself directly and immediately in the person of Jesus.

- What preconditions do we lay down before we encounter Jesus? If we accept Jesus and allow ourselves to grow in relationship to him, we will find that he is the bread of life for which we hunger. What prevents us from experiencing Jesus as the bread of life?

Wednesday 29th April
Saint Catherine of Siena, Virgin and Doctor of the Church
John 6:35–40

Jesus said to them, "I am the bread of life. Whoever comes to me will never be hungry, and whoever believes in me will never be thirsty. But I said to you that you have seen me and yet do not believe. Everything that the Father gives me will come to me, and anyone who comes to me I will never drive away; for I have come down from heaven, not to do my own will, but the will of him who sent me. And this is the will of him who sent me, that I should lose nothing of all that he has given me, but raise it up on the last day. This is indeed the will of my Father, that all who see the Son and believe in him may have eternal life; and I will raise them up on the last day."

- The whole life of Jesus is a response to the magnetic attraction of the Father's will. Remaining completely faithful to the Father is what nourishes and sustains him. When we pray, we seek to find and do the Father's will ourselves, not to bring God around to doing ours. Jesus has come to draw each one of us to the Father. Everything he says and does is for this purpose.

- Our prayer helps us know what we really need and to recognize God as our source. We look beyond our preferences and selections, our comforts and wants, and, learning what we really need, trust in God to feed us and to lead us into life.

Thursday 30th April
John 6:44–51

[Jesus said to the people,] "No one can come to me unless drawn by the Father who sent me; and I will raise that person up on the last day. It is written in the prophets, 'And they shall all be taught by God.' Everyone who has heard and learned from the Father comes to me. Not that anyone has seen the Father except the one who is from God; he has seen the Father. Very truly, I tell you, whoever believes has eternal life. I am the bread of life. Your ancestors ate the manna in the wilderness, and they died. This is the bread that comes down from heaven, so that one may eat of it and not die. I am the living bread that came down from heaven. Whoever eats of this bread will live forever; and the bread that I will give for the life of the world is my flesh."

- We are drawn to the Father; we have a built-in GPS that guides us toward God. Saint Ignatius expressed this being drawn in a different way: "God taught me directly like a schoolmaster."

- All our practices of prayer—our liturgies, disciplines, and habits—are like school buses: they bring us to where a special kind of learning happens. We need to be present, ready, eager to go to receive truth. Jesus tells us that God wants to be the teacher of each person, and desires to speak heart to heart.

Friday 1st May
John 6:52–59

The Jews then disputed among themselves, saying, "How can this man give us his flesh to eat?" So Jesus said to them, "Very truly, I tell you, unless you eat the flesh of the Son of Man and drink his blood, you have no life in you. Those who eat my flesh and drink my blood have eternal life, and I will raise them up on the last day; for my flesh is true food and my blood is true drink. Those who eat my flesh and drink my blood abide in me, and I in them. Just as the living Father sent me, and I live because of the Father, so whoever eats me will live because of me. This is the bread that came down from heaven, not like that which your ancestors ate, and they died. But the one who eats this bread will live for ever." He said these things while he was teaching in the synagogue at Capernaum.

- We've heard the expression, "I love you so much I could eat you" or "your company is food and drink to me." Jesus is not advocating cannibalism any more than lovers are. Today's Gospel is saying, "My love for you is real and not mere words." We can take this love into our hearts and be nourished by Jesus. He really is food for our being.

- What is stopping you from taking in this love, from allowing Jesus to feed you with his presence and dwell in your heart?

Saturday 2nd May
Saint Athanasius, Bishop and Doctor of the Church
John 6:60–69

When many of his disciples heard it, they said, "This teaching is difficult; who can accept it?" But Jesus, being aware that his disciples were complaining about it, said to them, "Does this offend you? Then what if you were to see the Son of Man ascending to where he was before? It is the spirit that gives life; the flesh is useless. The words that I have spoken to you are spirit and life. But among you there are some who do not believe." For Jesus knew from the first who were the ones that did not believe, and who was the one that would betray him. And he said, "For this reason

I have told you that no one can come to me unless it is granted by the Father." Because of this many of his disciples turned back and no longer went about with him. So Jesus asked the twelve, "Do you also wish to go away?" Simon Peter answered him, "Lord, to whom can we go? You have the words of eternal life. We have come to believe and know that you are the Holy One of God."

- Jesus turns to those closest to him, and we wonder if he asks this question with some trepidation: "Do you also wish to go away?" It must have been a great relief to hear their response: "Lord, to whom can we go? You have the words of eternal life."

- Lord, to whom can we go? In my fainthearted moments I hear both Jesus' gentle voice, giving me the freedom to choose, and the strength of Peter's reply: You have the words of eternal life. Maybe Peter repeated these words often to himself. It can be a mantra of prayer for us, as can other favorite lines from the Gospels.

Something to think and pray about each day this week:

When you are with a friend and are riddled with fear, what else do you have to talk about that's important? If you don't talk about what's uppermost in your mind—the fear—you probably have little of substance to say. Also, you won't be fully attentive to what your friend is saying to you. This is just one more way that honesty—or the lack of it—affects our relationships.

If you open up about your fears, chances are, your friend will listen and sympathize. Once this happens, you feel a great change. Now you're not so alone. And you're relieved to have spoken aloud about the fear. Often it feels as if a burden has been lifted—and this happens when we're honest about our fears to another human being! It has been my experience—and I have witnessed this in other people, too—that opening up to God about our fears leads to great relief.

—William A. Barry, SJ, *Praying the Truth*

The Presence of God

"Be still, and know that I am God!" Lord, your words lead us to the calmness and greatness of your presence.

Freedom

"In these days, God taught me as a schoolteacher teaches a pupil" (Saint Ignatius). I remind myself that there are things God has to teach me yet, and I ask for the grace to hear them and let them change me.

Consciousness

How am I really feeling? Lighthearted? Heavyhearted? I may be very much at peace, happy to be here.
Equally, I may be frustrated, worried, or angry.
I acknowledge how I really am. It is the real me whom the Lord loves.

The Word

God speaks to each of us individually. I listen attentively to hear what he is saying to me. Read the text a few times, then listen. (Please turn to the Scripture on the following pages. Inspiration points are there, should you need them. When you are ready, return here to continue.)

Conversation

Do I notice myself reacting as I pray with the word of God? Do I feel challenged, comforted, angry? Imagining Jesus sitting or standing by me, I speak out my feelings, as one trusted friend to another.

Conclusion

I thank God for these moments we have spent together and for any insights I have been given concerning the text.

Sunday 3rd May
Fourth Sunday of Easter
John 10:1–10

"Very truly, I tell you, anyone who does not enter the sheepfold by the gate but climbs in by another way is a thief and a bandit. The one who enters by the gate is the shepherd of the sheep. The gatekeeper opens the gate for him, and the sheep hear his voice. He calls his own sheep by name and leads them out. When he has brought out all his own, he goes ahead of them, and the sheep follow him because they know his voice. They will not follow a stranger, but they will run from him because they do not know the voice of strangers." Jesus used this figure of speech with them, but they did not understand what he was saying to them. So again Jesus said to them, "Very truly, I tell you, I am the gate for the sheep. All who came before me are thieves and bandits; but the sheep did not listen to them. I am the gate. Whoever enters by me will be saved, and will come in and go out and find pasture. The thief comes only to steal and kill and destroy. I came that they may have life, and have it abundantly."

- Jesus used rich images from daily life to illustrate the depth of his desired relationship with us. He spoke of shepherd and sheep, gatekeeper and gate, pasture and life, recognition and salvation. How do these words relate to my life in this place and time?

- Jesus refers to strangers, thieves and bandits, killing and stealing, running away in fear instead of following, climbing in rather than walking through the open gate. Can I identify the thieves, those intent on destroying me rather than caring for me?

Monday 4th May
John 10:11–18

"I am the good shepherd. The good shepherd lays down his life for the sheep. The hired hand, who is not the shepherd and does not own the sheep, sees the wolf coming and leaves the sheep and runs away—and the wolf snatches them and scatters them. The hired hand runs away because a hired hand does not care for the sheep. I am the good shepherd. I know my own and my own know me, just as the Father knows me and I know the Father. And I lay down my life for the sheep. I have other sheep that do not belong to this fold. I must bring them also, and they will listen to my voice. So there will be one flock, one shepherd. For this reason the Father loves me, because I lay down my life in order to take it up again. No one takes it from me, but I lay it down of my own accord. I have power to lay it down, and I have power to take it up again. I have received this command from my Father."

- Jesus' death was not just a consequence of being in the wrong place at the wrong time, an unlucky outcome of his confrontation with the Pharisees. Rather, it was a result of Jesus freely choosing to be a light in the world, an exponent of the truth, and the embodiment of God's unconditional love and mercy.

- For Jesus, the keeping of the law was a consequence of being loved by God rather than the cause of being loved by God. Do you experience God's love as pure gift, or do you believe that you have to earn it?

Tuesday 5th May
John 10:22–30

At that time the festival of the Dedication took place in Jerusalem. It was winter, and Jesus was walking in the temple, in the portico of Solomon. So the Jews gathered around him and said to him, "How long will you keep us in suspense? If you are the Messiah, tell us plainly." Jesus answered, "I have told you, and you do not believe. The works that I do in my Father's name testify to me; but you do not believe, because you do not belong to my sheep. My sheep hear my voice. I know them, and they follow me. I give them eternal life, and they will never perish. No one will snatch them out of my hand. What my Father has given me is greater than all else, and no one can snatch it out of the Father's hand. The Father and I are one."

- Jesus comes across as being quite committed to those he has been given to save; he's very protective and vigilant about keeping them in relationship with him. He appreciates their being receptive to his voice: they "hear my voice . . . and they follow me."

- Picture a little bird in a nest, opening its beak to be fed by its mother. Do you imagine that, in your relationship with Jesus, most of the work is up to you? Or can you see yourself as a baby bird with beak (heart) open—and Jesus watching over you like a mother bird who waits for every opportunity to feed you?

Wednesday 6th May
John 12:44–50

Then Jesus cried aloud: "Whoever believes in me believes not in me but in him who sent me. And whoever sees me sees him who sent me. I have come as light into the world, so that everyone who believes in me should not remain in the darkness. I do not judge anyone who hears my words and does not keep them, for I came not to judge the world, but to save the world. The one who rejects me and does not receive my word has a judge; on the last day the word that I have spoken will serve as judge, for I have not spoken on my own, but the Father who sent me has himself given me a commandment about what to say and what to speak. And I know that his commandment is eternal life. What I speak, therefore, I speak just as the Father has told me."

- Jesus is claiming to be much more than an upright moral teacher. He is so attuned to God that there is nothing Jesus says that he did not already hear from God the Father. "The Father" is the source of existence expressing Godself in and through Jesus. To entrust yourself to Jesus is to entrust yourself to the Father.

- Jesus' will and mission are to save all people and usher them into their full potential, which is to be like Jesus: sons and daughters of God. Who are you really? How awake are you to seeing yourself with Jesus as a son or daughter of God, expressing Godself in a unique irreplaceable way?

Thursday 7th May
John 13:16–20

Jesus said, "Very truly, I tell you, servants are not greater than their master, nor are messengers greater than the one who sent them. If you know these things, you are blessed if you do them. I am not speaking of all of you; I know whom I have chosen. But it is to fulfill the scripture, 'The one who ate my bread has lifted his heel against me.' I tell you this now, before it occurs, so that when it does occur, you may believe that I am he. Very truly, I tell you, whoever receives one whom I send receives me; and whoever receives me receives him who sent me."

- Saint Ignatius reminds us that love is shown more in deeds than in words. I ask God for the help I need to allow the words in my mind and heart to become evident in my feet and hands, that I might recognize where God wants me to be and do what God wants me to do.

- I consider what it means to be servant or messenger. I am known, chosen, trusted, and sent. Jesus allows that there is a difference between knowing and doing. I take this time to let my knowing deepen, to become part of me.

Friday 8th May
John 14:1–6

Jesus said to his disciples: "Do not let your hearts be troubled. Believe in God, believe also in me. In my Father's house there are many dwelling places. If it were not so, would I have told you that I go to prepare a place for you? And if I go and prepare a place for you, I will come again and will take you to myself, so that where I am, there you may be also. And you know the way to the place where I am going." Thomas said to him, "Lord, we do not know where you are going. How can we know the way?" Jesus said to him, "I am the way, and the truth, and the life. No one comes to the Father except through me."

- Step into the scene of today's Scripture. See Jesus with his closest friends as he breaks the news to them that he has only hours to live. See their shock and bewilderment and their anticipatory grief. Jesus tries to console them, stressing that the loss of his physical presence is not the end of life; he will be with them in a different form.

- Though all sorts of things go wrong for us, we are not abandoned. We are destined for a blessed future, because he will come again and take us to himself. Lord, I often wonder what way to go in life. May I always turn to you for guidance, and whatever way I choose, may I try to live out of your commandment to love.

Saturday 9th May
John 14:7–14

"If you know me, you will know my Father also. From now on you do know him and have seen him." Philip said to him, "Lord, show us the Father, and we will be satisfied." Jesus said to him, "Have I been with you all this time, Philip, and you still do not know me? Whoever has seen me has seen the Father. How can you say, 'Show us the Father'? Do you not believe that I am in the Father and the Father is in me? The words that I say to you I do not speak on my own; but the Father who dwells in me does his works. Believe me that I am in the Father and the Father is in me; but if you do not, then believe me because of the works themselves. Very truly, I tell you, the one who believes in me will also do the works that I do and, in fact, will do greater works than these, because I am going to the Father. I will do whatever you ask in my name, so that the Father may be glorified in the Son. If in my name you ask me for anything, I will do it."

- As we receive Jesus and take him and his message to heart (a lifelong journey), we become more and more his presence in the world—so much so that to receive us is to receive Jesus, and to receive Jesus is to receive the Father. We need to be humble and patient about embodying the presence of Jesus in the world because we have so much false conditioning to shed. We are in constant need of purification, always a work in progress.

- We could start each day with the following morning offering and then in the evening go back over the day to see how we have lived out our offering and how much more we need to grow into it. "Lord Jesus, I give you my hands to do your work. I give you my feet to go your way. I give you my tongue to speak your words. I give you my mind that you may think in me. I give you my spirit that you may pray in me. Above all, I give you my heart that you may love in me your Father and all humankind. I give you my whole self that you may grow in me, so that it is you, Lord Jesus, who live and work and pray in me" (The Grail Prayer).

Something to think and pray about each day this week:

I use a straightforward dictionary definition of leadership when I conduct workshops: Leadership is the ability "to point out a way, direction or goal . . . and to influence others toward it." Isn't it true that each of us is leading in one way or another all the time? Parents are "pointing out a way" for their children when they model virtues such as patience, discipline, or fairness—or, unfortunately, when they model racism or greed or self-centeredness. We can lead for good or for ill. Students point out a way when they model hard work and a commitment to personal growth. As the great humanitarian Albert Schweitzer put it, "Example is not the main thing in influencing others. It is the only thing."

—Chris Lowney, *Make Today Matter*

The Presence of God
"Be still, and know that I am God!" Lord, your words lead us to the calmness and greatness of your presence.

Freedom
Everything has the potential to draw forth from me a fuller love and life. Yet my desires are often fixed, caught, on illusions of fulfillment. I ask that God, through my freedom, may orchestrate my desires in a vibrant loving melody rich in harmony.

Consciousness
I exist in a web of relationships: links to nature, people, God.
I trace out these links, giving thanks for the life that flows through them.
Some links are twisted or broken; I may feel regret, anger, disappointment.
I pray for the gift of acceptance and forgiveness.

The Word
I read the word of God slowly, a few times over, and I listen to what God is saying to me. (Please turn to the Scripture on the following pages. Inspiration points are there, should you need them. When you are ready, return here to continue.)

Conversation
Jesus, you speak to me through the words of the Gospels. May I respond to your call today. Teach me to recognize your hand at work in my daily living.

Conclusion
I thank God for these moments we have spent together and for any insights I have been given concerning the text.

Sunday 10th May
Fifth Sunday of Easter

John 14:1–12

Jesus said "Do not let your hearts be troubled. Believe in God, believe also in me. In my Father's house there are many dwelling-places. If it were not so, would I have told you that I go to prepare a place for you? And if I go and prepare a place for you, I will come again and will take you to myself, so that where I am, there you may be also. And you know the way to the place where I am going." Thomas said to him, "Lord, we do not know where you are going. How can we know the way?" Jesus said to him, "I am the way, and the truth, and the life. No one comes to the Father except through me. If you know me, you will know my Father also. From now on you do know him and have seen him." Philip said to him, "Lord, show us the Father, and we will be satisfied." Jesus said to him, "Have I been with you all this time, Philip, and you still do not know me? Whoever has seen me has seen the Father. How can you say, 'Show us the Father'? Do you not believe that I am in the Father and the Father is in me? The words that I say to you I do not speak on my own; but the Father who dwells in me does his works. Believe me that I am in the Father and the Father is in me; but if you do not, then believe me because of the works themselves. Very truly, I tell you, the one who believes in me will also do the works that I do and, in fact, will do greater works than these, because I am going to the Father."

- Everything Jesus did was through the power of the Holy Spirit. It is astounding that the Father gives us this same Holy Spirit so that we can do the works Jesus did. As Saint Paul said, "I can do all things through him who strengthens me" (Philippians 4:13).

- Jesus is the firstborn of the new creation: the Holy Spirit–inspired community. Through surrendering to the gift of his Spirit, we are called to become his body and are destined to do great things. "Come Holy Spirit, fill the hearts of your faithful and kindle in them the fire of your love. Send forth your Spirit and they shall be created. And You shall renew the face of the earth."

Monday 11th May
John 14:21–26

[Jesus said,] "They who have my commandments and keep them are those who love me; and those who love me will be loved by my Father, and I will love them and reveal myself to them." Judas (not Iscariot) said to him, "Lord, how is it that you will reveal yourself to us, and not to the world?" Jesus answered him, "Those who love me will keep my word, and my Father will love them, and we will come to them and make our home with them. Whoever does not love me does not keep my words; and the word that you hear is not mine, but is from the Father who sent me. I have said these things to you while I am still with you. But the Advocate, the Holy Spirit, whom the Father will send in my name, will teach you everything, and remind you of all that I have said to you."

- Lord, I often feel my life is shapeless and going nowhere. Thank you for the gift of the great Spirit of God, who is by my side, defending me, consoling me, and teaching me the ways of love. "Come, Holy Spirit, enkindle in me the fire of your love."

- I imagine the Father and the Son deciding to come to me. Why do they do this? What do they think and say about me as they travel? What gifts do they choose for me? What do they find when they arrive? I am the focus of a great love.

Tuesday 12th May
John 14:27–31a

"Peace I leave with you; my peace I give to you. I do not give to you as the world gives. Do not let your hearts be troubled, and do not let them be afraid. You heard me say to you, 'I am going away, and I am coming to you.' If you loved me, you would rejoice that I am going to the Father, because the Father is greater than I. And now I have told you this before it occurs, so that when it does occur, you may believe. I will no longer talk much with you, for the ruler of this world is coming. He has no power over me; but I do as the Father has commanded me, so that the world may know that I love the Father."

- Knowing and loving God brings us peace and joy that nothing else can give. Once we know God as source of being, we love all of creation as expressions of this love and goodness. Creation, including all our beloved, are not rivals for God's love but expressions of God's love.

- If you love someone, you want the greatest good of all for that person: that he or she would know the peace that the world cannot give on its own. This peace comes only from knowing and loving God and God's presence in creation. I thank you, Lord, for your being and the miracle of your presence in my life.

Wednesday 13th May
John 15:1–8

"I am the true vine, and my Father is the vinegrower. He removes every branch in me that bears no fruit. Every branch that bears fruit he prunes to make it bear more fruit. You have already been cleansed by the word that I have spoken to you. Abide in me as I abide in you. Just as the branch cannot bear fruit by itself unless it abides in the vine, neither can you unless you abide in me. I am the vine, you are the branches. Those who abide in me and I in them bear much fruit, because apart from me you can do nothing. Whoever does not abide in me is thrown away like a branch and withers; such branches are gathered, thrown into the fire, and burned. If you abide in me, and my words abide in you, ask for whatever you wish, and it will be done for you. My Father is glorified by this, that you bear much fruit and become my disciples."

- The term "to abide" was music to the Hebrews, who had been nomads and exiles. They longed for a place in which they could rest permanently. Jesus offers, not a country, but his very self, for this abiding. Relationship, not place, is what matters. I thank God that even though my life is always changing, Jesus is my home, my permanent resting place.

- How do I abide in the Lord? Above all by prayer, raising my heart and mind to God each morning. There is a worldwide community that prays along with me, as we all abide in Jesus and draw strength from him.

Thursday 14th May
Saint Matthias, Apostle
John 15:9–17

"As the Father has loved me, so I have loved you; abide in my love. If you keep my commandments, you will abide in my love, just as I have kept my Father's commandments and abide in his love. I have said these things to you so that my joy may be in you, and that your joy may be complete. This is my commandment, that you love one another as I have loved you. No one has greater love than this, to lay down one's life for one's friends. You are my friends if you do what I command you. I do not call you servants any longer, because the servant does not know what the master is doing; but I have called you friends, because I have made known to you everything that I have heard from my Father. You did not choose me but I chose you. And I appointed you to go and bear fruit, fruit that will last, so that the Father will give you whatever you ask him in my name. I am giving you these commands so that you may love one another."

- "You did not choose me but I chose you." Jesus' choosing of me gives me a sense of my place in the world, a sense of purpose. What fruit am I called on to bear?

- To love one another as Jesus has loved us, we need first to allow ourselves to experience Jesus' love. I can love myself because I am the beloved of God (Romans 1:7)!

Friday 15th May
John 15:12–17

"This is my commandment, that you love one another as I have loved you. No one has greater love than this, to lay down one's life for one's friends. You are my friends if you do what I command you. I do not call you servants any longer, because the servant does not know what the master is doing; but I have called you friends, because I have made known to you everything that I have heard from my Father. You did not choose me but I chose you. And I appointed you to go and bear fruit, fruit that will last, so that the Father will give you whatever you ask him in my name. I am giving you these commands so that you may love one another."

- Lord, you are inviting me, choosing me, to be your intimate friend, to go out in your name, and to make an impact on this precious world, and bear lasting fruit. Is there any reason I should hold back?

- My well-being is intertwined with the well-being of every other human being. Jesus understood this and thus said again and again how we must care for one another. I try to imagine my life connected to others, here and everywhere.

Saturday 16th May
John 15:18–21

"If the world hates you, be aware that it hated me before it hated you. If you belonged to the world, the world would love you as its own. Because you do not belong to the world, but I have chosen you out of the world— therefore the world hates you. Remember the word that I said to you, 'Servants are not greater than their master.' If they persecuted me, they will persecute you; if they kept my word, they will keep yours also. But they will do all these things to you on account of my name, because they do not know him who sent me."

- Can we be true Christians if we don't challenge and encounter violence from those who exploit everything and everyone for their own benefit alone? The Good News isn't Good News initially for them, and yet God embraces them in God's desire to save all men and women. "Repent, and believe in the Good News" (Mark 1:15).

- This talk about hatred is distasteful stuff, Lord, politically incorrect. But I have to admit that it rings true. It happens that good Christians are slandered and hated, for whatever reason. Then I need to remember how you were hated, and kept your peace, and did not let your heart flame up in resentment.

Sixth Week of Easter
May 17—May 23

Something to think and pray about each day this week:

Don't treat your life as a race to be won. Don't focus on getting to the top of the heap, because every peak you reach will yield a clearer view of the next summit, already occupied by another competitor in the game of life. Run every race as if it's your last, but decide first why you're running. Instead of competing against me or anyone else, why not contribute your energies to making us better people, through your coaching, love, inspiring example, or noble mission? Instead of trying to win the race, why not make it your mission to contribute to the race, the *human* race—by making your corner of the world more just, more loving, and more happy.
—Chris Lowney, *Make Today Matter*

The Presence of God

I pause for a moment
and reflect on God's life-giving presence
in every part of my body,
in everything around me,
in the whole of my life.

Freedom

Many countries are at this moment suffering the agonies of war. I bow my head in thanksgiving for my freedom. I pray for all prisoners and captives.

Consciousness

Knowing that God loves me unconditionally, I look honestly over the past day, its events, and my feelings. Do I have something to be grateful for? Then I give thanks. Is there something I am sorry for? Then I ask forgiveness.

The Word

Now I turn to the Scripture set out for me this day. I read slowly over the words and see if any sentence or sentiment appeals to me. (Please turn to the Scripture on the following pages. Inspiration points are there, should you need them. When you are ready, return here to continue.)

Conversation

I know with certainty that there were times when you carried me, Lord. There were times when it was through your strength that I got through the dark times in my life.

Conclusion

Glory be to the Father, and to the Son, and to the Holy Spirit,
As it was in the beginning, is now and ever shall be,
World without end. Amen.

Sunday 17th May
Sixth Sunday of Easter
John 14:15–21

"If you love me, you will keep my commandments. And I will ask the Father, and he will give you another Advocate, to be with you for ever. This is the Spirit of truth, whom the world cannot receive, because it neither sees him nor knows him. You know him, because he abides with you, and he will be in you. I will not leave you orphaned; I am coming to you. In a little while the world will no longer see me, but you will see me; because I live, you also will live. On that day you will know that I am in my Father, and you in me, and I in you. They who have my commandments and keep them are those who love me; and those who love me will be loved by my Father, and I will love them and reveal myself to them."

- Jesus is aware that the imminent loss of his physical presence will be a blow for his disciples. He reassures them, "I will not leave you orphaned." The loss of his physical presence will be made up to them by the sending of the Holy Spirit, who will be with them permanently. In our changing and increasingly secularized society, one can easily feel a sense of loss and abandonment. But the Holy Spirit continues to guide and inspire us into new and creative forms of communicating the Good News in ways that are relevant to today's world.

- I do not need to rely on my own resources but turn to God, who promises to help me, and who sends the Holy Spirit. To be open to the spirit, I must quiet first my body, then my heart. In this time of quiet, God teaches me to see my world differently; I don't act in it alone but am accompanied by God's ever-present Spirit.

Monday 18th May
John 15:26—16:4a

Jesus said, "When the Advocate comes, whom I will send to you from the Father, the Spirit of truth who comes from the Father, he will testify on my behalf. You also are to testify because you have been with me from the beginning. I have said these things to you to keep you from stumbling. They will put you out of the synagogues. Indeed, an hour is coming when those who kill you will think that by doing so they are offering worship to God. And they will do this because they have not known the Father or me. But I have said these things to you so that when their hour comes you may remember that I told you about them. I did not say these things to you from the beginning, because I was with you."

- Terrible things have been done in God's name. But God's way is love, and Jesus assures us that those who do such things are misled. We ask to know him more closely so that we will not make the same mistakes.

- There's an atmosphere in these chapters of John's Gospel that Jesus wants to be with us, that he likes being with us, and cares about his friendships with us. Prayer is first of all God's invitation to us to be present before we take action. We pray because God is God, because God exists, and because God is love. Prayer time is "handing-over time"—handing over cares, joys, and sorrows into the care of the loving God.

Tuesday 19th May

John 16:5–11

Jesus said, "Now I am going to him who sent me; yet none of you asks me, 'Where are you going?' But because I have said these things to you, sorrow has filled your hearts. Nevertheless, I tell you the truth: it is to your advantage that I go away, for if I do not go away, the Advocate will not come to you; but if I go, I will send him to you. And when he comes, he will prove the world wrong about sin and righteousness and judgment: about sin, because they do not believe in me; about righteousness, because I am going to the Father and you will see me no longer; about judgment, because the ruler of this world has been condemned."

- The whole purpose of Jesus was to awaken in us the realization that we are sons and daughters of God (by grace); coheirs to God's kingdom with him. "We are children of God, and if children, then heirs, heirs of God and joint heirs with Christ" (Romans 8:16–17).

- I am not alone. The Holy Spirit can help me in everything, no matter how weak and helpless I feel. Bidden or unbidden, the Spirit is present everywhere, challenging false values so that truth and goodness may prevail. I am meant to be a spokesperson for the Spirit. Can the Spirit count on me?

Wednesday 20th May

John 16:12–15

"I still have many things to say to you, but you cannot bear them now. When the Spirit of truth comes, he will guide you into all the truth; for he will not speak on his own, but will speak whatever he hears, and he will declare to you the things that are to come. He will glorify me, because he will take what is mine and declare it to you. All that the Father has is mine. For this reason I said that he will take what is mine and declare it to you."

- Jesus presents the Trinity in terms of a divine relationship, a community of love. It is to be the model of all human society. Saint Ignatius spoke of the Trinity in terms of three notes that combine to make one musical chord—each makes a profound contribution to the whole. This may or may not help us to understand the Trinity. But what is more important is that the three divine Persons understand and love us!

- Jesus is sensitive to his followers' limited understanding. By telling them he has more to tell them, he is, in a gentle way, preparing them! I ask his wisdom to know when it is good to speak and when it is better to wait and be silent. Jesus knows how anxious we can be both to let go of the past and to trust what the future will bring. Can I speak to him about my anxieties?

Thursday 21st May

John 16:16–20

[Jesus said to his disciples,] "A little while, and you will no longer see me, and again a little while, and you will see me." Then some of his disciples said to one another, "What does he mean by saying to us, 'A little while, and you will no longer see me, and again a little while, and you will see me'; and 'Because I am going to the Father'?" They said, "What does he mean by this 'a little while'? We do not know what he is talking about." Jesus knew that they wanted to ask him, so he said to them, "Are you discussing among yourselves what I meant when I said, 'A little while, and you will no longer see me, and again a little while, and you will see me'? Very truly, I tell you, you will weep and mourn, but the world will rejoice; you will have pain, but your pain will turn into joy."

- Jesus tries to prepare the disciples for what will soon occur. He gives them information and anticipates their questions. Notice that he does not give details about what will happen or instructions about what they must do or how to prepare; he describes what they will feel. He anticipates the impact events will have on those who are close to him. I take comfort in Jesus' attention to what I go through and will go through.

- After all the time the disciples have spent with Jesus, they still hesitate to ask him questions sometimes. I suffer a similar hesitance. Why do I shy away from direct questions in my prayer? Do I think God will not listen, or will not answer? Do I fear the answer itself?

Friday 22nd May
John 16:20–23

"Very truly, I tell you, you will weep and mourn, but the world will rejoice; you will have pain, but your pain will turn into joy. When a woman is in labor, she has pain, because her hour has come. But when her child is born, she no longer remembers the anguish because of the joy of having brought a human being into the world. So you have pain now; but I will see you again, and your hearts will rejoice, and no one will take your joy from you. On that day you will ask nothing of me. Very truly, I tell you, if you ask anything of the Father in my name, he will give it to you."

- Every woman who has given birth can bear witness to the truth of what Jesus says here, that once the child is born, relatively all the pain of giving birth is forgotten, so great is the joy of bringing a child into the world. And yet this joy pales in comparison with the joy of finally falling into the everlasting arms of God's love, a joy that can never be taken from us.

- Do you trust that God is silently planning for you in love? Speak to God in your heart, noticing how Jesus says, "If you ask anything of the Father in my name, he will give it to you."

Saturday 23rd May
John 16:23b–28

[Jesus said to his disciples,] "Very truly, I tell you, if you ask anything of the Father in my name, he will give it to you. Until now you have not asked for anything in my name. Ask and you will receive, so that your joy may be complete. I have said these things to you in figures of speech. The hour is coming when I will no longer speak to you in figures, but will tell you plainly of the Father. On that day you will ask in my name. I do not say to you that I will ask the Father on your behalf; for the Father himself loves you, because you have loved me and have believed that I came from God. I came from the Father and have come into the world; again, I am leaving the world and am going to the Father."

- Jesus endeavors to get across to us that God is so loving that there is nothing God will not grant us if it is for our good and the good of humanity. There is nothing more that God wants for us than our true happiness: the fullness of joy. Jesus reassures us that he mirrors the Father exactly in this way, and that there is nothing that would please the Father more than for us to trust in his unconditional love. Jesus' whole person is coming into the world to mirror this love of the Father for us, and now that his mission is about to be fulfilled, he returns to the Father.

- Imagine God asking you this question: "Would you be willing to trust that I love you with an everlasting love?" Notice how you respond.

May 24—May 30

Something to think and pray about each day this week:

Psychologists have discovered that human resilience, the capacity to persevere, is like an emotional muscle. That is, we build stronger resilience through the right "exercises," particularly these three: showing gratitude, being altruistic, and exhibiting a strong sense of life purpose. . . .

Do you want to make today matter? If so, you will need to persevere. Some of your plans won't work out; people will disappoint you; you'll disappoint yourself. You'll transcend setbacks only by building your resilience, by learning to put one foot in front of the other, up the hills and down the hills of your life journey.

You'll build the needed resilience by acquiring the habits championed throughout these pages: living for a purpose that matters greatly to you, for example, and becoming an altruistic person dedicated to giving away your sneakers, and being grateful always.

In good times, this "virtuous circle" of mutually reinforcing habits will make life feel like riding a bicycle on level ground: Momentum keeps building, and each crank of the pedal comes more easily than the previous one.

And on life's bad, uphill days? Your good habits will generate the fierce willpower needed just to stay on the bike, to keep going.

—Chris Lowney, *Make Today Matter*

The Presence of God

I remind myself that I am in the presence of God, who is my strength in times of weakness and my comforter in times of sorrow.

Freedom

Saint Ignatius thought that a thick and shapeless tree trunk would never believe that it could become a statue, admired as a miracle of sculpture, and would never submit itself to the chisel of the sculptor, who sees by her genius what she can make of it. I ask for the grace to let myself be shaped by my loving Creator.

Consciousness

Dear Lord, help me to remember that you gave me life. Teach me to slow down, to be still and enjoy the pleasures created for me. To be aware of the beauty that surrounds me: the marvel of mountains, the calmness of lakes, the fragility of a flower petal. I need to remember that all these things come from you.

The Word

In this expectant state of mind, please turn to the text for the day with confidence. Believe that the Holy Spirit is present and may reveal whatever the passage has to say to you. Read reflectively, listening with a third ear to what may be going on in your heart. (Please turn to the Scripture on the following pages. Inspiration points are there, should you need them. When you are ready, return here to continue.)

Conversation

What feelings are rising in me as I pray and reflect on God's word? I imagine Jesus himself sitting or standing near me, and I open my heart to him.

Conclusion

I thank God for these moments we have spent together and for any insights I have been given concerning the text.

Sunday 24th May
The Ascension of the Lord
Matthew 28:16–20

Now the eleven disciples went to Galilee, to the mountain to which Jesus had directed them. When they saw him, they worshiped him; but some doubted. And Jesus came and said to them, "All authority in heaven and on earth has been given to me. Go therefore and make disciples of all nations, baptizing them in the name of the Father and of the Son and of the Holy Spirit, and teaching them to obey everything that I have commanded you. And remember, I am with you always, to the end of the age."

- Each person of the Blessed Trinity is fulfilled by fully giving self lovingly to the other two persons, and fully receiving the love of the other two persons. It is an everlasting circle of love between three divine persons: Father, Son, and Holy Spirit. We are made in the image and likeness of God, and we are fulfilled only by giving ourselves to others out of love and fully receiving God's love for us.

- I hear Jesus' commission to invite others to become disciples of love: "Go therefore and make disciples of all nations." Where do I start? Instead of focusing on my reluctance, I think of God's eagerness to be in fuller relationship with me. For only by fully giving and receiving do we become our true selves. God will always be with us in this work because it is God's work.

Monday 25th May
John 16:29–33

His disciples said, "Yes, now you are speaking plainly, not in any figure of speech! Now we know that you know all things, and do not need to have anyone question you; by this we believe that you came from God." Jesus answered them, "Do you now believe? The hour is coming, indeed it has come, when you will be scattered, each one to his home, and you will leave me alone. Yet I am not alone because the Father is with me. I have said this to you, so that in me you may have peace. In the world you face persecution. But take courage; I have conquered the world!"

- Jesus could see his disciples' doubts—that they wouldn't be able to cope with the challenges to come, and that they would be scattered in all directions. He tells them not to be discouraged but to stand with him. He reassures them that God will strengthen them and encourages them to be at peace, that he will overcome the world and in time they would overcome the world too.

- Do you become discouraged by your failures? Do you trust that with God you can overcome obstacles and challenges, that you can become a unique beneficial presence of God's love in the world?

Tuesday 26th May
Saint Philip Neri, Priest
John 17:1–11a

After Jesus had spoken these words, he looked up to heaven and said, "Father, the hour has come; glorify your Son so that the Son may glorify you, since you have given him authority over all people, to give eternal life to all whom you have given him. And this is eternal life, that they may know you, the only true God, and Jesus Christ whom you have sent. I glorified you on earth by finishing the work that you gave me to do. So now, Father, glorify me in your own presence with the glory that I had in your presence before the world existed. I have made your name known to those whom you gave me from the world. They were yours, and you gave them to me, and they have kept your word. Now they know that everything you have given me is from you; for the words that you gave to me I have given to them, and they have received them and know in truth that I came from you; and they have believed that you sent me. I am asking on their behalf; I am not asking on behalf of the world, but on behalf of those whom you gave me, because they are yours. All mine are yours, and yours are mine; and I have been glorified in them. And now I am no longer in the world, but they are in the world, and I am coming to you. Holy Father, protect them in your name that you have given me, so that they may be one, as we are one."

- To be enveloped by intimacy with God is to experience something of what eternal life will be like. God, protect me and those I love. Keep me in the hollow of your hand, and draw me ever more deeply into your friendship.

- As I grow in knowledge of God, I begin to taste the eternal life Jesus promises. I thank God for the light I have, for the quiet revelations, and for the personal inspirations that have been given to me.

Wednesday 27th May

John 17:11b–19

[Jesus looked up to heaven and said,] "And now I am no longer in the world, but they are in the world, and I am coming to you. Holy Father, protect them in your name that you have given me, so that they may be one, as we are one. While I was with them, I protected them in your name that you have given me. I guarded them, and not one of them was lost except the one destined to be lost, so that the scripture might be fulfilled. But now I am coming to you, and I speak these things in the world so that they may have my joy made complete in themselves. I have given them your word, and the world has hated them because they do not belong to the world, just as I do not belong to the world. I am not asking you to take them out of the world, but I ask you to protect them from the evil one. They do not belong to the world, just as I do not belong to the world. Sanctify them in the truth; your word is truth. As you have sent me into the world, so I have sent them into the world. And for their sakes I sanctify myself, so that they also may be sanctified in truth."

- Jesus' love for his disciples does not fade. It endures eternally. He asks the Father to protect and guide them. He entrusts us, his friends and companions, to the loving care of his Father.

- Parents and guardians spend their best years guiding children in life and in faith. Then there is a gradual letting go as they grow into adulthood. Like Jesus we should pray for those who move beyond our active care. The Father's arms are a safe place for them.

Thursday 28th May

John 17:20–26

[Jesus looked up to heaven and said,] "I ask not only on behalf of these, but also on behalf of those who will believe in me through their word, that they may all be one. As you, Father, are in me and I am in you, may they also be in us, so that the world may believe that you have sent me. The glory that you have given me I have given them, so that they may be one, as we are one, I in them and you in me, that they may become completely one, so that the world may know that you have sent me and have loved them even as you have loved me. Father, I desire that those also, whom you have given me, may be with me where I am, to see my glory, which you have given me because you loved me before the foundation of the world. Righteous Father, the world does not know you, but I know you; and these know that you have sent me. I made your name known to them, and I will make it known, so that the love with which you have loved me may be in them, and I in them."

- Jesus prayed for the apostles and for all who would believe. That is us! Try to imagine Jesus praying somewhere, maybe on the hillside or among his followers. He is praying for you. What might you think he would be asking his Father for you? Can you make this prayer for yourself? He prays because he loves each of us. How do I pray for people I love? He prays for everyone I know. I can join my prayer with his today.

- What Jesus asks for us is what he sought for himself: unity with God. As I am invited into this relationship, I consider what it might cost me, and I ask for the freedom I need. Jesus wants his disciples to live in such a way that the work of God is evident in them. I think of how I live, and I name the help I need.

Friday 29th May
John 21:15–19

When they had finished breakfast, Jesus said to Simon Peter, "Simon son of John, do you love me more than these?" He said to him, "Yes, Lord; you know that I love you." Jesus said to him, "Feed my lambs." A second time he said to him, "Simon son of John, do you love me?" He said to him, "Yes, Lord; you know that I love you." Jesus said to him, "Tend my sheep." He said to him the third time, "Simon son of John, do you love me?" Peter felt hurt because he said to him the third time, "Do you love me?" And he said to him, "Lord, you know everything; you know that I love you." Jesus said to him, "Feed my sheep. Very truly, I tell you, when you were younger, you used to fasten your own belt and to go wherever you wished. But when you grow old, you will stretch out your hands, and someone else will fasten a belt around you and take you where you do not wish to go." (He said this to indicate the kind of death by which he would glorify God.) After this he said to him, "Follow me."

- Peter must have wondered, *Where do I stand now?* But Jesus shows him amazing courtesy and kindness, and all doubts are dispelled. Peter becomes a new creation: a fisherman-turned-shepherd.

- Guided by Saint Ignatius, I might ask, "What have I done for Christ? What am I doing for Christ? What will I do?" Peter realizes that he is being given increasing responsibility for the flock. How graciously do I accept growing responsibility?

Saturday 30th May
John 21:20–25

Peter turned and saw the disciple whom Jesus loved following them; he was the one who had reclined next to Jesus at the supper and had said, "Lord, who is it that is going to betray you?" When Peter saw him, he said to Jesus, "Lord, what about him?" Jesus said to him, "If it is my will that he remain until I come, what is that to you? Follow me!" So the rumor spread in the community that this disciple would not die. Yet Jesus did not say to him that he would not die, but, "If it is my will that he remain until I come, what is that to you?" This is the disciple who is testifying to these things and has written them, and we know that his testimony is true. But there are also many other things that Jesus did; if every one of them were written down, I suppose that the world itself could not contain the books that would be written.

- "What about him?" asked Peter. Is there a hint here of sibling rivalry, jealous curiosity? There is reproach in Jesus' comment: "What is that to you?" Lord, will I ever outgrow this sense of rivalry, wanting to be the center of attention? Let your love flow through me in an unselfish way.

- Before God, I consider the works of Jesus in my life, giving thanks for both the hidden and the evident ways in which I have come to life. I think of myself as a Gospel, a testament to God's loving presence and action.

Something to think and pray about each day this week:

Our hurting world is plagued by challenges that can't be overcome unless we bring big heart and our best selves to confront the world's ills. You didn't ask for that burden and opportunity, but you're here on the playing field at this moment in history, and that's how "calling" often emerges in life. Sometimes you get to choose your moments, causes, and vocation. But, other times, you don't get to choose the opportunity. The moment chooses you: A troubled colleague or student walks into your office; a loved one takes ill; a refugee family is resettled in the neighborhood; a natural disaster befalls your hometown; or politicians float proposals that would unjustly disadvantage the community's poor or marginalized.

Righting the world's injustices is a grueling struggle that won't end in our lifetimes. We need a few million more happy warriors. And the world needs you to be one of them.

—Chris Lowney, *Make Today Matter*

The Presence of God
Dear Jesus, I come to you today longing for your presence. I desire to love you as you love me. May nothing ever separate me from you.

Freedom
Lord, grant me the grace to be free from the excesses of this life. Let me not get caught up with the desire for wealth. Keep my heart and mind free to love and serve you.

Consciousness
Where do I sense hope, encouragement, and growth in my life? By looking back over the past few months, I may be able to see which activities and occasions have produced rich fruit. If I do notice such areas, I will determine to give those areas both time and space in the future.

The Word
God speaks to each of us individually. I listen attentively, to hear what he is saying to me. Read the text a few times, then listen. (Please turn to the Scripture on the following pages. Inspiration points are there should you need them. When you are ready, return here to continue.)

Conversation
What is stirring in me as I pray? Am I consoled, troubled, left cold? I imagine Jesus standing or sitting at my side, and I share my feelings with him.

Conclusion
Glory be to the Father, and to the Son, and to the Holy Spirit,
As it was in the beginning, is now and ever shall be,
World without end. Amen.

Sunday 31st May
Pentecost Sunday
John 20:19–23

When it was evening on that day, the first day of the week, and the doors of the house where the disciples had met were locked for fear of the Jews, Jesus came and stood among them and said, "Peace be with you." After he said this, he showed them his hands and his side. Then the disciples rejoiced when they saw the Lord. Jesus said to them again, "Peace be with you. As the Father has sent me, so I send you." When he had said this, he breathed on them and said to them, "Receive the Holy Spirit. If you forgive the sins of any, they are forgiven them; if you retain the sins of any, they are retained."

- Take time today and allow the word *Peace* to echo in your mind and heart. Let the word and all it may mean fill your body and remain within you. It is the constant promise of Jesus to his followers. It is a gift nobody can take from us. Give time each day to receive this gift of God's Spirit. He gives it without even being asked.

- As you receive peace from God, send this peace in a prayer to those close to you or those who may sorely need prayer today.

Monday 1st June
The Blessed Virgin Mary, Mother of the Church (Ninth Week in Ordinary Time)
John 19:25–34

Meanwhile, standing near the cross of Jesus were his mother, and his mother's sister, Mary the wife of Clopas, and Mary Magdalene. When Jesus saw his mother and the disciple whom he loved standing beside her, he said to his mother, "Woman, here is your son." Then he said to the disciple, "Here is your mother." And from that hour the disciple took her into his own home. After this, when Jesus knew that all was now finished, he said (in order to fulfill the scripture), "I am thirsty." A jar full of sour wine was standing there. So they put a sponge full of the wine on a branch of hyssop and held it to his mouth. When Jesus had received the wine, he said, "It is finished." Then he bowed his head and gave up his spirit. Since it was the day of Preparation, the Jews did not want the bodies left on the cross during the sabbath, especially because that sabbath was a day of great solemnity. So they asked Pilate to have the legs of the crucified men broken and the bodies removed. Then the soldiers came and broke the legs of the first and of the other who had been crucified with him. But when they came to Jesus and saw that he was already dead, they did not break his legs. Instead, one of the soldiers pierced his side with a spear, and at once blood and water came out.

- The early Jesuit priest Peter Claver spent much of his life in the holds of slave ships with African victims who had no hope in this world. Out of that experience he used to say, "The only book people should read is the story of the Passion." A time comes to all of us to stretch out our hands as Jesus did, in passivity, unable to do anything with them: a time when God takes over, and our resistance folds. This is the hardest meditation; it touches a reality that in the long run we cannot escape.

- Can you look at the cross and allow Jesus to die for you? Notice how you feel and what you would like to say. Maybe the questions of Saint Ignatius of Loyola in looking at the crucified Christ come to mind: "What have I done for Christ? What am I doing for Christ? What ought I to do for Christ?"

Tuesday 2nd June
Mark 12:13–17

Then they sent to him some Pharisees and some Herodians to trap him in what he said. And they came and said to him, "Teacher, we know that you are sincere, and show deference to no one; for you do not regard people with partiality, but teach the way of God in accordance with truth. Is it lawful to pay taxes to the emperor, or not? Should we pay them, or should we not?" But knowing their hypocrisy, he said to them, "Why are you putting me to the test? Bring me a denarius and let me see it." And they brought one. Then he said to them, "Whose head is this, and whose title?" They answered, "The emperor's." Jesus said to them, "Give to the emperor the things that are the emperor's, and to God the things that are God's." And they were utterly amazed at him.

- Jesus lived in constant danger of how religious and political authorities would react to his words and actions. He was willing to accept, but not to choose, suffering and death. In this Gospel passage he deflects questions that might put him in danger. Later he will not be able to do this and will go to where the love and call of his Father will lead him.

- Jesus advised us to pray that we would not be put to the test or led into temptation. Jesus made decisions from the wisdom of his relationship with the Father. Although the approach of the Pharisees was flattering and courteous, Jesus recognized that he was being tested. I pray that I may have the presence of mind not to be distracted by empty conversations.

Wednesday 3rd June
Saint Charles Lwanga and Companions, Martyrs
Mark 12:18–27

Some Sadducees, who say there is no resurrection, came to him and asked him a question, saying, "Teacher, Moses wrote for us that if a man's brother dies, leaving a wife but no child, the man shall marry the widow and raise up children for his brother. There were seven brothers; the first married and, when he died, left no children; and the second married her and died, leaving no children; and the third likewise; none of the seven left children. Last of all the woman herself died. In the resurrection whose wife will she be? For the seven had married her." Jesus said to them, "Is not this the reason you are wrong, that you know neither the scriptures nor the power of God? For when they rise from the dead, they neither marry nor are given in marriage, but are like angels in heaven. And as for the dead being raised, have you not read in the book of Moses, in the story about the bush, how God said to him, 'I am the God of Abraham, the God of Isaac, and the God of Jacob'? He is God not of the dead, but of the living; you are quite wrong."

- Again Jesus deflects a question that might endanger him. Whatever we may think of death, we still believe in God of the living, who loves life and sends his Son to bring us life to the full. Jesus enters our humanity to assure us that everything alive in us is from the God of the living and brings us in touch with the life-giving God, now and in eternity.

- Jesus invokes the story of Moses at the burning bush to underline that the God revealed there is God of the living, not of the dead. How strong is my belief in the resurrection? What difference does this belief make to the way I live here and now?

Thursday 4th June
Mark 12:28–34

One of the scribes came near and heard them disputing with one another, and seeing that he answered them well, he asked him, "Which commandment is the first of all?" Jesus answered, "The first is, 'Hear, O Israel: the Lord our God, the Lord is one; you shall love the Lord your God with all your heart, and with all your soul, and with all your mind, and with all your strength.' The second is this, 'You shall love your neighbor as yourself.' There is no other commandment greater than these." Then the scribe said to him, "You are right, Teacher; you have truly said that 'he is one, and besides him there is no other'; and 'to love him with all the heart, and with all the understanding, and with all the strength,' and 'to love one's neighbor as oneself,'—this is much more important than all whole burnt offerings and sacrifices." When Jesus saw that he answered wisely, he said to him, "You are not far from the kingdom of God." After that no one dared to ask him any question.

- Jesus teaches that adherence to religious rituals is less important than love of God and love of neighbor. But do I sometimes find religious practices easier than engaging with others?

- The Jewish lawyers were blamed for multiplying regulations, but they also liked to seek out the essentials of the law, to give the whole of their religion in one sound bite. Jesus takes the lawyer's question seriously and points to an interior religion, one of the heart, not of rule keeping or ritual. What question might I bring to Jesus today in my prayer?

Friday 5th June
Saint Boniface, Bishop and Martyr
Mark 12:35–37

While Jesus was teaching in the temple, he said, "How can the scribes say that the Messiah is the son of David? David himself, by the Holy Spirit, declared, 'The Lord said to my Lord, "Sit at my right hand, until I put your enemies under your feet."' David himself calls him Lord; so how can he be his son?" And the large crowd was listening to him with delight.

- Jesus is more than the son of David. In prayer I express my faith that Jesus is Lord, the beloved Son in whom the Father was well pleased. He is Son of God, human and divine. In his love and to him we pray.

- They listened with delight. Lord, may I listen to you in this way, relish your goodness and insight, and nourish myself daily on your words.

Saturday 6th June
Mark 12:38–44

As he taught, he said, "Beware of the scribes, who like to walk around in long robes, and to be greeted with respect in the marketplaces, and to have the best seats in the synagogues and places of honor at banquets! They devour widows' houses and for the sake of appearance say long prayers. They will receive the greater condemnation." He sat down opposite the treasury, and watched the crowd putting money into the treasury. Many rich people put in large sums. A poor widow came and put in two small copper coins, which are worth a penny. Then he called his disciples and said to them, "Truly I tell you, this poor widow has put in more than all those who are contributing to the treasury. For all of them have contributed out of their abundance; but she out of her poverty has put in everything she had, all she had to live on."

- We think of love as spontaneous, so a commandment to love seems strange at first. Being made in the image of God who is love, with hearts of love, we have the desire and capacity to develop that gift. But we are frail, with selfish tendencies to go our own way. True love is a decision to respond generously even when we do not feel like it.

- "Love God!" This seems easy. "Love your neighbor!" This is harder. "Love yourself!" This seems alien to the gospel, but there is a healthy self-love that acknowledges God's creative love in ourselves. God sees all that is made, including me, and says it is very good. Can I accept this gift happily?

June 7—June 13

Something to think and pray about each day this week:

Mercy in the family is a sign that relationships matter more than being right, more than money or possessions, and more than hanging on to our hurts. "Seven times seventy times" is just about the right number of opportunities that family members are given to forgive one another over the years. Mercy and forgiveness require lots of prayer. We are not capable of forgiving big hurts by ourselves because our love is too small. But God is invincible. He can forgive the gravest of harm when we cannot. Some say that praying to God to forgive our loved one is the path to being able to forgive that person ourselves.

—Jane Knuth, *The Prayer List*

The Presence of God

Lord, help me to be fully alive to your holy presence. Enfold me in your love. Let my heart become one with yours.

My soul longs for your presence, Lord. When I turn my thoughts to you, I find peace and contentment.

Freedom

Your death on the cross has set me free. I can live joyously and freely without fear of death. Your mercy knows no bounds.

Consciousness

At this moment, Lord, I turn my thoughts to you.

I will leave aside my chores and preoccupations.

I will take rest and refreshment in your presence.

The Word

The word of God comes down to us through the Scriptures.

May the Holy Spirit enlighten my mind and my heart

to respond to the Gospel teachings:

to love my neighbor as myself,

to care for my sisters and brothers in Christ.

(Please turn to the Scripture on the following pages. Inspiration points are there, should you need them. When you are ready, return here to continue.)

Conversation

Begin to talk to Jesus about the Scripture you have just read. What part of it strikes a chord in you? Perhaps the words of a friend—or some story you have heard recently—will slowly rise to the surface of your consciousness. If so, does the story throw light on what the Scripture passage may be saying to you?

Conclusion

I thank God for these moments we have spent together and for any insights I have been given concerning the text.

Sunday 7th June
The Most Holy Trinity
John 3:16–18

"For God so loved the world that he gave his only Son, so that everyone who believes in him may not perish but may have eternal life. Indeed, God did not send the Son into the world to condemn the world, but in order that the world might be saved through him. Those who believe in him are not condemned; but those who do not believe are condemned already, because they have not believed in the name of the only Son of God."

- God sent Jesus into the world to save it, not to condemn it. How might this truth affect the way I look at the world and at myself?

- "God so loved the world" is the whole message of Jesus, expressed in his words and embodied, directly or indirectly, in the whole of his life. As one theologian has said about his message, "There just isn't anything else." Am I convinced of this myself? In love for me, God desires my salvation, my being made whole.

Monday 8th June
Matthew 5:1–12

When Jesus saw the crowds, he went up the mountain; and after he sat down, his disciples came to him. Then he began to speak, and taught them, saying: "Blessed are the poor in spirit, for theirs is the kingdom of heaven. Blessed are those who mourn, for they will be comforted. Blessed are the meek, for they will inherit the earth. Blessed are those who hunger and thirst for righteousness, for they will be filled. Blessed are the merciful, for they will receive mercy. Blessed are the pure in heart, for they will see God. Blessed are the peacemakers, for they will be called children of God. Blessed are those who are persecuted for righteousness' sake, for theirs is the kingdom of heaven. Blessed are you when people revile you and persecute you and utter all kinds of evil against you falsely on my account. Rejoice and be glad, for your reward is great in heaven, for in the same way they persecuted the prophets who were before you."

- Jesus lists the attitudes that will make us truly happy. Then he elaborates on what it means to learn from him: "Take my yoke upon you, and learn from me; for I am gentle and humble in heart, and you will find rest for your souls" (Matthew 11:29). Jesus wants us to face two realities. One is that we are limited and sinful, and the other is that we are by nature gifted and we share in the divine life.

- For a period of prayer, spend time in Jesus' presence and let him accept a side of yourself that you are not content with. Then let him appreciate something about you. Tell him how you feel about this.

Tuesday 9th June
Matthew 5:13–16

"You are the salt of the earth; but if salt has lost its taste, how can its saltiness be restored? It is no longer good for anything, but is thrown out and trampled under foot. You are the light of the world. A city built on a hill cannot be hidden. No one after lighting a lamp puts it under the bushel basket, but on the lampstand, and it gives light to all in the house. In the same way, let your light shine before others, so that they may see your good works and give glory to your Father in heaven."

- Salt purifies, seasons, and preserves. Jesus wants us, by our gospel-centered lives, to be a distinctive seasoning in our communities.
- I am to let the message of Jesus shine out through my words and actions. Goodness lights up both the giver and the recipient. I stand up for the just rights of God's little ones. I work for a world of kindness, peace, and love.

Wednesday 10th June
Matthew 5:17–19

Jesus said to the crowds, "Do not think that I have come to abolish the law or the prophets; I have come not to abolish but to fulfill. For truly I tell you, until heaven and earth pass away, not one letter, not one stroke of a letter, will pass from the law until all is accomplished. Therefore, whoever breaks one of the least of these commandments, and teaches others to do the same, will be called least in the kingdom of heaven; but whoever does them and teaches them will be called great in the kingdom of heaven."

- In what ways do we sometimes minimize God's law and wisdom for us? In what ways do we encourage others to do the same? I pray to see clearly when I am guilty of this.

- I end my prayer with the writer of the Psalms: "Make me to know your ways, O LORD; teach me your paths. Lead me in your truth, and teach me, for you are the God of my salvation" (Psalm 25:4–5).

Thursday 11th June
Saint Barnabas, Apostle
Matthew 5:20–26

"For I tell you, unless your righteousness exceeds that of the scribes and Pharisees, you will never enter the kingdom of heaven. You have heard that it was said to those of ancient times, 'You shall not murder'; and 'whoever murders shall be liable to judgment.' But I say to you that if you are angry with a brother or sister, you will be liable to judgment; and if you insult a brother or sister, you will be liable to the council; and if you say, 'You fool,' you will be liable to the hell of fire. So when you are offering your gift at the altar, if you remember that your brother or sister has something against you, leave your gift there before the altar and go; first be reconciled to your brother or sister, and then come and offer your gift. Come to terms quickly with your accuser while you are on the way to court with him, or your accuser may hand you over to the judge, and the judge to the guard, and you will be thrown into prison. Truly I tell you, you will never get out until you have paid the last penny."

- Jesus speaks to the heart that lies below words and actions. Hating someone is not the same as killing that person, but it has the power to damage me as well as the person I hate. I must be the same inside—in my attitudes and beliefs—as I am in my physical actions.

- Is there anybody I need to forgive? I pray for the grace to forgive that person in my heart and to let go fully of any feelings of anger or resentment. I ask the Lord for the grace to go to that person and be reconciled.

Friday 12th June
Matthew 5:27–32

"You have heard that it was said, 'You shall not commit adultery.' But I say to you that everyone who looks at a woman with lust has already committed adultery with her in his heart. If your right eye causes you to sin, tear it out and throw it away; it is better for you to lose one of your members than for your whole body to be thrown into hell. And if your right hand causes you to sin, cut it off and throw it away; it is better for you to lose one of your members than for your whole body to go into hell. It was also said, 'Whoever divorces his wife, let him give her a certificate of divorce.' But I say to you that anyone who divorces his wife, except on the ground of unchastity, causes her to commit adultery; and whoever marries a divorced woman commits adultery."

- The word translated here as "unchastity" probably refers to incestuous unions that were never valid and need to be dissolved.

- Lord, what is the core that you're getting at with these strict statements? What do you want me to hear today?

Saturday 13th June
Saint Anthony of Padua, Priest and Doctor of the Church
Matthew 5:33–37

"Again, you have heard that it was said to those of ancient times, 'You shall not swear falsely, but carry out the vows you have made to the Lord.' But I say to you, Do not swear at all, either by heaven, for it is the throne of God, or by the earth, for it is his footstool, or by Jerusalem, for it is the city of the great King. And do not swear by your head, for you cannot make one hair white or black. Let your word be 'Yes, Yes' or 'No, No'; anything more than this comes from the evil one."

- An honest, trustworthy person should never need to take an oath to establish the truth of any statement. My word is my bond.

- My actions show the sincerity of my words. I ask God's help to live as I profess. I know that I have made promises in the past and admit that I may not always have fulfilled these promises. I place myself before God who loves me, recognizes my desire to do good, and forgives me.

June 14—June 20

Something to think and pray about each day this week:

Family prayers can be for complete strangers. When I was a child in school, if a siren sounded, the nuns who taught us would stop class and have the entire class pray together for whoever needed the siren. I still do this, and I taught my daughters to do it. We typically say, "Lord, please help whoever is part of that siren." This includes the person in need—who could be experiencing the worst day of his or her life—the family members, and the rescue personnel. Include a person or group of people on your prayer list who are in need, even if you don't know them.

—Jane Knuth, *The Prayer List*

The Presence of God

I pause for a moment and think of the love and the grace that God showers on me. I am created in the image and likeness of God; I am God's dwelling place.

Freedom

Lord, you granted me the great gift of freedom. In these times, O Lord, grant that I may be free from any form of racism or intolerance. Remind me that we are all equal in your loving eyes.

Consciousness

Knowing that God loves me unconditionally, I can afford to be honest about how I am.
How has the day been, and how do I feel now? I share my feelings openly with the Lord.

The Word

I take my time to read the word of God slowly, a few times, allowing myself to dwell on anything that strikes me. (Please turn to the Scripture on the following pages. Inspiration points are there, should you need them. When you are ready, return here to continue.)

Conversation

Sometimes I wonder what I might say if I were to meet you in person, Lord.
I think I might say, "Thank you" because you are always there for me.

Conclusion

I thank God for these moments we have spent together and for any insights I have been given concerning the text.

Sunday 14th June
The Most Holy Body and Blood of Christ
John 6:51–58

[Jesus said,] "I am the living bread that came down from heaven. Whoever eats of this bread will live for ever; and the bread that I will give for the life of the world is my flesh." The Jews then disputed among themselves, saying, "How can this man give us his flesh to eat?" So Jesus said to them, "Very truly, I tell you, unless you eat the flesh of the Son of Man and drink his blood, you have no life in you. Those who eat my flesh and drink my blood have eternal life, and I will raise them up on the last day; for my flesh is true food and my blood is true drink. Those who eat my flesh and drink my blood abide in me, and I in them. Just as the living Father sent me, and I live because of the Father, so whoever eats me will live because of me. This is the bread that came down from heaven, not like that which your ancestors ate, and they died. But the one who eats this bread will live forever."

- The day before this, on the far shore of the sea, Jesus had fed over five thousand people by multiplying five loaves and two fish. They now gather round him again, looking for more. He tells them that such food cannot last, just like the manna from heaven that Moses gave their ancestors in the desert. The true bread he now offers is his own flesh and blood. His words challenge the people to consider hunger beyond the physical needs of food and water. How do I react to his statements here?

- The twelve disciples will be with Jesus at the Last Supper, when he will take some bread, bless it, and give it to them, saying, "Take, eat, this is my body . . ." When I next partake of the Eucharist, I will take with me this story of the people Jesus fed and the story of the Last Supper. I ask God to use these scenes to deepen my understanding of the bread and wine.

Monday 15th June
Matthew 5:38–42

"You have heard that it was said, 'An eye for an eye and a tooth for a tooth.' But I say to you, Do not resist an evildoer. But if anyone strikes you on the right cheek, turn the other also; and if anyone wants to sue you and take your coat, give your cloak as well; and if anyone forces you to go one mile, go also the second mile. Give to everyone who begs from you, and do not refuse anyone who wants to borrow from you."

- Jesus puts the highest ideals before us. We waive our rights for the benefit of others. No revenge! No retaliation! When Jesus was struck on the face at his trial by one of the police, he calmly asked the culprit, "Why do you strike me?" (John 18:23).

- Jesus calls for generosity: Give! Share! Lend! When somebody is looking for help, do we pass by on the other side, as did the priest in the parable of the Good Samaritan? Pope Francis calls on us not to ignore anybody begging on the street, and he says that the way one reaches out to people looking for help must be done by looking them in the eyes and touching their hands.

Tuesday 16th June
Matthew 5:43–48

"You have heard that it was said, 'You shall love your neighbor and hate your enemy.' But I say to you, Love your enemies and pray for those who persecute you, so that you may be children of your Father in heaven; for he makes his sun rise on the evil and on the good, and sends rain on the righteous and on the unrighteous. For if you love those who love you, what reward do you have? Do not even the tax collectors do the same? And if you greet only your brothers and sisters, what more are you doing than others? Do not even the Gentiles do the same? Be perfect, therefore, as your heavenly Father is perfect."

- Is it possible for hate and love to dwell in the same person? It seems that, eventually, one or the other will become the prominent trait. I pray that my spiritual practices will help love to grow and cause hate to starve.

- I think of a person who is hard to love, someone I am tempted to hate, someone I perceive to be an enemy. And I pray for that person. In fact, I commit to pray for this person every day for a week. Then I will reflect on how this prayer influenced my own feelings.

Wednesday 17th June

Matthew 6:1–6, 16–18

"Beware of practicing your piety before others in order to be seen by them; for then you have no reward from your Father in heaven. So whenever you give alms, do not sound a trumpet before you, as the hypocrites do in the synagogues and in the streets, so that they may be praised by others. Truly I tell you, they have received their reward. But when you give alms, do not let your left hand know what your right hand is doing, so that your alms may be done in secret; and your Father who sees in secret will reward you. And whenever you pray, do not be like the hypocrites; for they love to stand and pray in the synagogues and at the street corners, so that they may be seen by others. Truly I tell you, they have received their reward. But whenever you pray, go into your room and shut the door and pray to your Father who is in secret; and your Father who sees in secret will reward you. And whenever you fast, do not look dismal, like the hypocrites, for they disfigure their faces so as to show others that they are fasting. Truly I tell you, they have received their reward. But when you fast, put oil on your head and wash your face, so that your fasting may be seen not by others but by your Father who is in secret; and your Father who sees in secret will reward you."

- It is remarkable how strongly Jesus feels about hypocrisy. He hammers home his disapproval through a series of examples: Hypocrisy can undermine the virtue in almsgiving, in prayer, and in fasting. This list is not exhaustive. Maybe you can add to it. Ask Jesus to sensitize you to any hypocrisy that may have crept into your own life.

- Do I sometimes set out to get praise and admiration? We are asked to carry out almsgiving, prayer, and fasting in secret. Whatever is done with sincere love will last eternally. I ask for a heart that is free, that enables me to live with sincere love.

Thursday 18th June

Matthew 6:7–15

[Jesus said,] "When you are praying, do not heap up empty phrases as the Gentiles do; for they think that they will be heard because of their many words. Do not be like them, for your Father knows what you need before you ask him. Pray then in this way: Our Father in heaven, hallowed be your name. Your kingdom come. Your will be done, on earth as it is in heaven. Give us this day our daily bread. And forgive us our debts, as we also have forgiven our debtors. And do not bring us to the time of trial, but rescue us from the evil one. For if you forgive others their trespasses, your heavenly Father will also forgive you; but if you do not forgive others, neither will your Father forgive your trespasses."

- Many of us are guilty of heaping up words and calling them prayer. Sometimes our multiplied words are aimed at justifying what we think and do. Sometimes we talk on and on to distract us from the important issues we should be talking with God about. I ask the Holy Spirit to alert me to times when I use words to avoid true encounter with God.

- Jesus instructed us to pray that God would not lead us into trial and would protect us from the evil one. How often do I pray for protection? How often do I ask God to guide me away from trial and trouble?

Friday 19th June
The Most Sacred Heart of Jesus
Matthew 11:25–30

At that time Jesus said, "I thank you, Father, Lord of heaven and earth, because you have hidden these things from the wise and the intelligent and have revealed them to infants; yes, Father, for such was your gracious will. All things have been handed over to me by my Father; and no one knows the Son except the Father, and no one knows the Father except the Son and anyone to whom the Son chooses to reveal him. Come to me, all you that are weary and are carrying heavy burdens, and I will give you rest. Take my yoke upon you, and learn from me; for I am gentle and humble in heart, and you will find rest for your souls. For my yoke is easy, and my burden is light."

- Do you sometimes find yourself weary—from struggles, pains, disappointments? Jesus' invitation, "Come to me," is always open, especially when you need the peace, rest, protection, and God's love.

- Inside you there is a space for the divine. You can ask God to come into your poor heart and fill it with divine love and wisdom. In that secret place, heart can speak to heart. Ask today for what you want and be open to what God sees best to give you.

Saturday 20th June
The Immaculate Heart of the Blessed Virgin Mary
Luke 2:41–51

Now every year his parents went to Jerusalem for the festival of the Passover. And when [Jesus] was twelve years old, they went up as usual for the festival. When the festival was ended and they started to return, the boy Jesus stayed behind in Jerusalem, but his parents did not know it. Assuming that he was in the group of travelers, they went a day's journey. Then they started to look for him among their relatives and friends. When they did not find him, they returned to Jerusalem to search for him. After three days they found him in the temple, sitting among the teachers, listening to them and asking them questions. And all who heard him were amazed at his understanding and his answers. When his parents saw him they were astonished; and his mother said to him, "Child, why have you treated us like this? Look, your father and I have been searching for you in great anxiety." He said to them, "Why were you searching for me? Did you not know that I must be in my Father's house?" But they did not understand what he said to them. Then he went down with them and came to Nazareth, and was obedient to them. His mother treasured all these things in her heart.

- A missing child is a parent's worst nightmare, panic leading to a frantic search. It would have been the same for Mary and Joseph as they searched for twelve-year-old Jesus. Then the exasperation of discovering him in the temple. His mother knows there's something special about this boy, just as the teachers in the temple knew.

- And he was to become a teacher too in the temple: Rabbi Jesus who noticed the poor woman put two small coins in the basket . . . worth more than all the rich people's offerings. Eventually Rabbi Jesus threw the shopkeepers out, and this was too much. The temple personnel began to plot his death.

Something to think and pray about each day this week:

God can do anything. This is true. But God doesn't do "just anything"; he's too wise for that. I think it all depends on the relationship. A father does anything that is good for his children, but sometimes children don't know what is good for them. When prayers on my list aren't answered the way I want them to be, I no longer scratch them out. Perhaps the answer will come with a man riding a scooter, or in a baby stronger than anyone could imagine.

—Jane Knuth, *The Prayer List*

The Presence of God

I pause for a moment and think of the love and the grace that God showers on me. I am created in the image and likeness of God; I am God's dwelling place.

Freedom

I am free. When I look at these words in writing, they seem to create in me a feeling of awe. Yes, a wonderful feeling of freedom. Thank you, God.

Consciousness

In the presence of my loving Creator, I look honestly at my feelings over the past day: the highs, the lows, and the level ground. Can I see where the Lord has been present?

The Word

I read the word of God slowly, a few times over, and I listen to what God is saying to me. (Please turn to the Scripture on the following pages. Inspiration points are there, should you need them. When you are ready, return here to continue.)

Conversation

Remembering that I am still in God's presence,
I imagine Jesus standing or sitting beside me,
and I say whatever is on my mind, whatever is in my heart,
speaking as one friend to another.

Conclusion

Glory be to the Father, and to the Son, and to the Holy Spirit,
As it was in the beginning, is now and ever shall be,
World without end. Amen.

Sunday 21st June
Twelfth Sunday in Ordinary Time
Matthew 10:26–33

"So have no fear of them; for nothing is covered up that will not be un-covered, and nothing secret that will not become known. What I say to you in the dark, tell in the light; and what you hear whispered, proclaim from the housetops. Do not fear those who kill the body but cannot kill the soul; rather fear him who can destroy both soul and body in hell. Are not two sparrows sold for a penny? Yet not one of them will fall to the ground unperceived by your Father. And even the hairs of your head are all counted. So do not be afraid; you are of more value than many spar-rows. Everyone therefore who acknowledges me before others, I also will acknowledge before my Father in heaven; but whoever denies me before others, I also will deny before my Father in heaven."

• Jesus reminds me that I do not have to have all the answers or convince everyone of the truth. In God's time, not mine, all will be made clear.

• But Jesus mentions fear five times here. Does fear sometimes make me betray the truth? Perhaps I may know what to do in a situation, but I do nothing for fear of the reactions of others. I ask to believe that God knows me fully and values me limitlessly, so I need not fear.

Monday 22nd June
Matthew 7:1–5

"Do not judge, so that you may not be judged. For with the judgment you make you will be judged, and the measure you give will be the measure you get. Why do you see the speck in your neighbor's eye, but do not no-tice the log in your own eye? Or how can you say to your neighbor, 'Let me take the speck out of your eye,' while the log is in your own eye? You hypocrite, first take the log out of your own eye, and then you will see clearly to take the speck out of your neighbor's eye."

• I can ask God to judge me favorably, and God does this. But in turn God wants me to look lovingly on others and to judge them favorably! We are to act toward others as God acts toward us. We are to enhance the dignity of others and never despise or devalue them. It is said that we judge ourselves by our intentions but judge others only by their actions!

- A few lines from the poet Patrick Kavanagh: "He had the knack of making men feel / As small as they really were / Which meant as great as God had made them."

Tuesday 23rd June
Matthew 7:6, 12–14

"Do not give what is holy to dogs; and do not throw your pearls before swine, or they will trample them under foot and turn and maul you. . . . In everything do to others as you would have them do to you; for this is the law and the prophets. Enter through the narrow gate; for the gate is wide and the road is easy that leads to destruction, and there are many who take it. For the gate is narrow and the road is hard that leads to life, and there are few who find it."

- It is easy to drift, to follow the broad and easy route, but that does not lead to life. Jesus is the way to life, and he is the entry point. "Very truly, I tell you, I am the gate for the sheep. . . . Whoever enters by me will be saved, and will come in and go out and find pasture" (John 10:7–9). Lord, help me to be a good follower of you.

- "Pearls before swine"—the phrase seems harsh, yet it reflects life experience. All communication must be geared to the listener's ability to take it in. Good news may not make sense to listeners whose world is far removed from such messages.

Wednesday 24th June
The Nativity of Saint John the Baptist
Luke 1:57–66, 80

Now the time came for Elizabeth to give birth, and she bore a son. Her neighbors and relatives heard that the Lord had shown his great mercy to her, and they rejoiced with her. On the eighth day they came to circumcise the child, and they were going to name him Zechariah after his father. But his mother said, "No; he is to be called John." They said to her, "None of your relatives has this name." Then they began motioning to his father to find out what name he wanted to give him. He asked for a writing tablet and wrote, "His name is John." And all of them were amazed. Immediately his mouth was opened and his tongue freed, and he began to speak, praising God. Fear came over all their neighbors, and all these things were talked about throughout the entire hill country of Judea. All who heard them pondered them and said, "What then will this child become?" For, indeed, the hand of the Lord was with him. . . . The child grew and became strong in spirit, and he was in the wilderness until the day he appeared publicly to Israel.

- The birth of a long-awaited child is an occasion of great joy. The unexpected has happened! To highlight this, the child is given a new name to show that God has a special mission for him.

- But you, too, have a new name: your baptismal name. God has something special for you to do: you are to reveal God's love where you find yourself, through your gifts and talents. Ask for the grace to carry out your mission as faithfully as John did his, even though the cost may be great.

Thursday 25th June
Matthew 7:21–29

"Not everyone who says to me, 'Lord, Lord,' will enter the kingdom of heaven, but only the one who does the will of my Father in heaven. On that day many will say to me, 'Lord, Lord, did we not prophesy in your name, and cast out demons in your name, and do many deeds of power in your name?' Then I will declare to them, 'I never knew you; go away from me, you evildoers.' Everyone then who hears these words of mine and acts on them will be like a wise man who built his house on rock. The rain fell, the floods came, and the winds blew and beat on that house, but it did not fall, because it had been founded on rock. And everyone who hears these words of mine and does not act on them will be like a foolish man who built his house on sand. The rain fell, and the floods came, and the winds blew and beat against that house, and it fell—and great was its fall!" Now when Jesus had finished saying these things, the crowds were astounded at his teaching, for he taught them as one having authority, and not as their scribes.

- Jesus hits hard at every form of pretense. He has no time for it. Does he see any traces of pretense in me? Do I tell small lies? I ask him to remove my deceptiveness.

- The humble people begin to discern the source of Jesus' authority, and see his teachings as a benchmark for their own beliefs and practices.

Lord, may you be the rock that supports my faith and my actions, so that I fear neither wind nor flood.

Friday 26th June
Matthew 8:1–4

When Jesus had come down from the mountain, great crowds followed him; and there was a leper who came to him and knelt before him, saying, "Lord, if you choose, you can make me clean." He stretched out his hand and touched him, saying, "I do choose. Be made clean!" Immediately his leprosy was cleansed. Then Jesus said to him, "See that you say nothing to anyone; but go, show yourself to the priest, and offer the gift that Moses commanded, as a testimony to them."

- The marvel of Jesus' heart is revealed here. He should be tending to the great crowds, but instead he focuses on a leper! The leper is despised, feared, shunned, a nobody: but he becomes the object of divine attention.

- Let me be the leper now: for a few moments let me relax into the blessed mystery of being loved and healed. And later let me reach out to someone who is a nobody and show that person my love and care. Thus, today's miracle is reenacted in my time and place.

Saturday 27th June
Matthew 8:5–17

When he entered Capernaum, a centurion came to him, appealing to him and saying, "Lord, my servant is lying at home paralyzed, in terrible distress." And he said to him, "I will come and cure him." The centurion answered, "Lord, I am not worthy to have you come under my roof; but only speak the word, and my servant will be healed. For I also am a man under authority, with soldiers under me; and I say to one, 'Go,' and he goes, and to another, 'Come,' and he comes, and to my slave, 'Do this,' and the slave does it." When Jesus heard him, he was amazed and said to those who followed him, "Truly I tell you, in no one in Israel have I found such faith. I tell you, many will come from east and west and will eat with Abraham and Isaac and Jacob in the kingdom of heaven, while the heirs of the kingdom will be thrown into the outer darkness, where there will be weeping and gnashing of teeth." And to the centurion Jesus said, "Go; let it be done for you according to your faith." And the servant was healed in that hour. When Jesus entered Peter's house, he saw his mother-in-law lying in bed with a fever; he touched her hand, and the fever left her, and she got up and began to serve him. That evening they brought to him many who were possessed by demons; and he cast out the spirits with a word, and cured all who were sick. This was to fulfill what had been spoken through the prophet Isaiah, "He took our infirmities and bore our diseases."

- Can we capture the attitude of the centurion, a Roman officer, commander in an occupying force, who with the utmost politeness asks this Jewish teacher for help? His sensitivity (he felt an observant Jew might be reluctant to enter the house of a Gentile) and humility so astonished early Christians that they incorporated his words into the liturgy of the Eucharist: *Lord, I am not worthy to receive you under my roof.*

- Lord, I can receive you in Holy Communion day by day. May I welcome you with the same reverence as the Roman centurion, and with the same expectation that you will bring healing.

Something to think and pray about each day this week:

Jesus also told his friends to "follow me." So, it seems clear that it is fine to talk to people who have gone on ahead of us. We can even have a conversation with them if they initiate it. Even though it isn't recommended that we ask them to do things for us—we should ask only God—it's long been a tradition to ask them to pray for us. They are, after all, our loved ones who prayed for us while in the flesh. And since prayer is talking with God, our loved ones are as capable of praying for us after death as they were before. Why would we not pray for them in return? Death is not a reason to stop praying for people. In the Catholic tradition, the Hail Mary is a prayer that specifically asks Jesus' mother to "pray for us now and at the hour of our death."

—Jane Knuth, The Prayer List

The Presence of God

"Come to me, all you who are weary and are carrying heavy burdens, and I will give you rest." Here I am, Lord. I come to seek your presence. I long for your healing power.

Freedom

By God's grace I was born to live in freedom. Free to enjoy the pleasures he created for me. Dear Lord, grant that I may live as you intended, with complete confidence in your loving care.

Consciousness

Knowing that God loves me unconditionally, I look honestly over the past day, its events, and my feelings. Do I have something to be grateful for? Then I give thanks. Is there something I am sorry for? Then I ask forgiveness.

The Word

God speaks to each of us individually. I listen attentively to hear what he is saying to me. Read the text a few times, then listen. (Please turn to the Scripture on the following pages. Inspiration points are there, should you need them. When you are ready, return here to continue.)

Conversation

I know with certainty that there were times when you carried me, Lord. There were times when it was through your strength that I got through the dark times in my life.

Conclusion

Glory be to the Father, and to the Son, and to the Holy Spirit,
As it was in the beginning, is now and ever shall be,
World without end. Amen.

Sunday 28th June
Thirteenth Sunday in Ordinary Time
Matthew 10:37–42

"Whoever loves father or mother more than me is not worthy of me; and whoever loves son or daughter more than me is not worthy of me; and whoever does not take up the cross and follow me is not worthy of me. Those who find their life will lose it, and those who lose their life for my sake will find it. Whoever welcomes you welcomes me, and whoever welcomes me welcomes the one who sent me. Whoever welcomes a prophet in the name of a prophet will receive a prophet's reward; and whoever welcomes a righteous person in the name of a righteous person will receive the reward of the righteous; and whoever gives even a cup of cold water to one of these little ones in the name of a disciple—truly I tell you, none of these will lose their reward."

- The gospel of Jesus is not simply about a way of life founded on love and mercy; above all, it is about the person of Jesus himself. Today he claims a special place in our lives, more important than our dearest ones. Being a disciple is not a marginal aspect of my life, it is central. I ask for the grace to be a real disciple of Jesus, capable of taking up my cross and following him.

- At the same time, Jesus assures us that even the smallest gesture of mercy to those in need will not go unnoticed. I reflect for a few moments on the many such gestures that fill my life.

Monday 29th June
Saints Peter and Paul, Apostles
Matthew 16:13–19

Now when Jesus came into the district of Caesarea Philippi, he asked his disciples, "Who do people say that the Son of Man is?" And they said, "Some say John the Baptist, but others Elijah, and still others Jeremiah or one of the prophets." He said to them, "But who do you say that I am?" Simon Peter answered, "You are the Messiah, the Son of the living God." And Jesus answered him, "Blessed are you, Simon son of Jonah! For flesh and blood has not revealed this to you, but my Father in heaven. And I tell you, you are Peter, and on this rock I will build my church, and the gates of Hades will not prevail against it. I will give you the keys of the kingdom of heaven, and whatever you bind on earth will be bound in heaven, and whatever you loose on earth will be loosed in heaven."

- We are not, as is sometimes phrased, "followers of the church." We *are* the church, served by bishops and others, but with our own wisdom. Lord, you did not leave us orphans. We are the people of God, with a leader, and the support of the Holy Spirit. I am not alone.

- "But who do you say that I am?" It is not enough to quote the Catechism of the Catholic Church or the views of one or another theologian. Try to answer not only from the head but from the heart. You might helpfully rephrase the question as: Who is Jesus for me?

Tuesday 30th June
Matthew 8:23–27

And when he got into the boat, his disciples followed him. A windstorm arose on the sea, so great that the boat was being swamped by the waves; but he was asleep. And they went and woke him up, saying, "Lord, save us! We are perishing!" And he said to them, "Why are you afraid, you of little faith?" Then he got up and rebuked the winds and the sea; and there was a dead calm. They were amazed, saying, "What sort of man is this, that even the winds and the sea obey him?"

- "Lord, save us! We are perishing!" I may find that today this simple prayer resonates in my heart as I look at my family, my community, my country, our world. I stay with these words, pleading for Jesus' help.

- And he said to them, "Why are you afraid, you of little faith?" I acknowledge my weak faith, my fear that Jesus is asleep while the gale threatens to overwhelm me. I ask for simple trust and share in the apostles' wonder at the power present in the person of Jesus.

Wednesday 1st July
Matthew 8:28–34

When he came to the other side, to the country of the Gadarenes, two demoniacs coming out of the tombs met him. They were so fierce that no one could pass that way. Suddenly they shouted, "What have you to do with us, Son of God? Have you come here to torment us before the time?" Now a large herd of swine was feeding at some distance from them. The demons begged him, "If you cast us out, send us into the herd of swine." And he said to them, "Go!" So they came out and entered the swine; and suddenly, the whole herd rushed down the steep bank into the sea and perished in the water. The swineherds ran off, and on going into the town, they told the whole story about what had happened to the demoniacs. Then the whole town came out to meet Jesus; and when they saw him, they begged him to leave their neighborhood.

- Jesus' word is astonishingly powerful: it can defeat a huge crowd of demons. Sometimes I feel overwhelmed by the power of evil in the world—in politics, at work, or in my heart. I turn to Jesus and beg him to increase my faith in the power of his word, to believe that no evil, however strong and deep-rooted, can resist his power.

- Both the demoniacs and the inhabitants of the town ask Jesus to leave them alone. His presence is too disconcerting for them; they prefer to remain in their suffering rather than have the balance of their lives upset by Jesus' power. I ask myself if I find this contradiction in my heart, and I ask for greater inner freedom to open my life to Jesus.

Thursday 2nd July
Matthew 9:1–8

And after getting into a boat [Jesus] crossed the sea and came to his own town. And just then some people were carrying a paralyzed man lying on a bed. When Jesus saw their faith, he said to the paralytic, "Take heart, son; your sins are forgiven." Then some of the scribes said to themselves, "This man is blaspheming." But Jesus, perceiving their thoughts, said, "Why do you think evil in your hearts? For which is easier, to say, 'Your sins are forgiven,' or to say, 'Stand up and walk'? But so that you may know that the Son of Man has authority on earth to forgive sins"— he then said to the paralytic—"Stand up, take your bed and go to your home." And he stood up and went to his home. When the crowds saw it, they were filled with awe, and they glorified God, who had given such authority to human beings.

- When Jesus saw their faith, he said to the paralytic, "Take heart, son; your sins are forgiven." This is indeed the Good News brought to us by Jesus, the news that he asked the apostles to take to the whole world. I ask myself whether God's mercy is at the center of my understanding of the gospel, of God himself. Does my faith enable me to take heart? Am I discouraged at the sin present around me and within me?

- "When the crowds saw it, they were filled with awe, and they glorified God, who had given such authority to human beings." By the time the Gospel of Matthew was written, the early church was certain of its God-given power to forgive sins. It is certainly an awesome power, perhaps too big not to scandalize us. Especially because the human beings to whom this power is given are themselves in need of forgiveness. I give glory to God for his goodness to us.

Friday 3rd July
Saint Thomas, Apostle
John 20:24–29

But Thomas (who was called the Twin), one of the twelve, was not with them when Jesus came. So the other disciples told him, "We have seen the Lord." But he said to them, "Unless I see the mark of the nails in his hands, and put my finger in the mark of the nails and my hand in his side, I will not believe." A week later his disciples were again in the house, and Thomas was with them. Although the doors were shut, Jesus came and stood among them and said, "Peace be with you." Then he said to Thomas, "Put your finger here and see my hands. Reach out your hand and put it in my side. Do not doubt but believe." Thomas answered him, "My Lord and my God!" Jesus said to him, "Have you believed because you have seen me? Blessed are those who have not seen and yet have come to believe."

- We can only imagine how ashamed and angry at themselves the apostles must have been after their desertion of Jesus. To miss Jesus' apparition must have been the last straw for Thomas. Yet Jesus has no words of reproach but of peace. He accepts Thomas's emotional reaction and gently leads him to one of the finest expressions of faith in the whole of the gospel: "My Lord and my God." The risen Jesus brings peace to troubled hearts, he heals us and leads us to faith. I imagine him taking me gently by the hand and letting me physically feel his presence at my side. What words well up from my grateful heart?

- Thomas's anger led him to discover the deep faith he had in Jesus. Sometimes I am unaware of how helpful my strong emotions may be in my growth as a person and a believer. I ask to hear the risen Jesus' favorite greeting: "Peace be with you," words that enable me to look deep into my heart.

Saturday 4th July
Matthew 9:14–17

Then the disciples of John came to Jesus, saying, "Why do we and the Pharisees fast often, but your disciples do not fast?" And Jesus said to them, "The wedding guests cannot mourn as long as the bridegroom is with them, can they? The days will come when the bridegroom is taken away from them, and then they will fast. No one sews a piece of unshrunk cloth on an old cloak, for the patch pulls away from the cloak, and a worse tear is made. Neither is new wine put into old wineskins; otherwise, the skins burst, and the wine is spilled, and the skins are destroyed; but new wine is put into fresh wineskins, and so both are preserved."

- "New wine is put into new wineskins." What a challenge to our freedom and to our wisdom! Jesus is calling us to accept the radical novelty of the kingdom he has come to inaugurate, and to be ready to give up what is now old to be able to embrace it fully. So many opportunities are lost because we, as individuals and as communities, are not ready to leave behind what is no longer valid and useful, and instead, we look for painless change. In doing so, we lose both the wine and the wineskins.

- Yet we also need the wisdom to distinguish between what is new and what is old and useless. Some things are always new, they never grow old, especially love and the new commandment to love as Jesus loved us. Like good wine, they even improve with age.

Something to think and pray about each day this week:

Jesus calls people to be merciful like the Father: to love others indiscriminately, even irresponsibly, without regard for any personal gain. He calls them to downward mobility, to embrace the graces of exclusion in order that they might develop selves free from social pressures and unhealthy desires. What many would call poverty Jesus calls freedom. For vessels that have been emptied of all pride are wide open and ready to receive love, and equally ready to pour it out in the love of others. They become persons who show the face of God. And they become capable of authentic friendship.

—Tim Muldoon, *Living against the Grain*

The Presence of God
"Be still, and know that I am God!" Lord, your words lead us to the calmness and greatness of your presence.

Freedom
God is not foreign to my freedom. The Spirit breathes life into my most intimate desires, gently nudging me toward all that is good. I ask for the grace to let myself be enfolded by the Spirit.

Consciousness
Where do I sense hope, encouragement, and growth in my life? By looking back over the past few months, I may be able to see which activities and occasions have produced rich fruit. If I do notice such areas, I will determine to give those areas both time and space in the future.

The Word
The word of God comes down to us through the Scriptures. May the Holy Spirit enlighten my mind and my heart to respond to the Gospel teachings. (Please turn to the Scripture on the following pages. Inspiration points are there, should you need them. When you are ready, return here to continue.)

Conversation
What is stirring in me as I pray? Am I consoled, troubled, left cold? I imagine Jesus standing or sitting at my side, and I share my feelings with him.

Conclusion
Glory be to the Father, and to the Son, and to the Holy Spirit,
As it was in the beginning, is now and ever shall be,
World without end. Amen.

Sunday 5th July
Fourteenth Sunday in Ordinary Time
Matthew 11:25–30

At that time Jesus said, "I thank you, Father, Lord of heaven and earth, because you have hidden these things from the wise and the intelligent and have revealed them to infants; yes, Father, for such was your gracious will. All things have been handed over to me by my Father; and no one knows the Son except the Father, and no one knows the Father except the Son and anyone to whom the Son chooses to reveal him. Come to me, all you that are weary and are carrying heavy burdens, and I will give you rest. Take my yoke upon you, and learn from me; for I am gentle and humble in heart, and you will find rest for your souls. For my yoke is easy, and my burden is light."

• When am I most willing to come to Jesus with all my labors and burdens? When do I most resist going to him?

• Jesus, I can know God the Father because of my friendship with you. Remind me to rely on the resources of your love and wisdom as I learn how to live as a child of God.

Monday 6th July
Matthew 9:18–26

While he was saying these things to them, suddenly a leader of the synagogue came in and knelt before him, saying, "My daughter has just died; but come and lay your hand on her, and she will live." And Jesus got up and followed him, with his disciples. Then suddenly a woman who had been suffering from hemorrhages for twelve years came up behind him and touched the fringe of his cloak, for she said to herself, "If I only touch his cloak, I will be made well." Jesus turned, and seeing her he said, "Take heart, daughter; your faith has made you well." And instantly the woman was made well. When Jesus came to the leader's house and saw the flute players and the crowd making a commotion, he said, "Go away; for the girl is not dead but sleeping." And they laughed at him. But when the crowd had been put outside, he went in and took her by the hand, and the girl got up. And the report of this spread throughout that district.

- Like the woman in today's text I may be suffering from some malady, physical or spiritual, that has become a permanent feature of my life, holding me back from being my true self. Like her I might feel the urge to seek healing, to touch Jesus discreetly but believing in his power to heal me. I listen to Jesus' reply, affirming my move.

- Jesus came for us to have life, and life in abundance. He raises this girl back to life, and his own story ends in his triumph over death and sin. I pray that I, too, can believe firmly in life and in all that enhances it, on all levels.

Tuesday 7th July
Matthew 9:32–38

After they had gone away, a demoniac who was mute was brought to him. And when the demon had been cast out, the one who had been mute spoke; and the crowds were amazed and said, "Never has anything like this been seen in Israel." But the Pharisees said, "By the ruler of the demons he casts out the demons." Then Jesus went about all the cities and villages, teaching in their synagogues, and proclaiming the Good News of the kingdom, and curing every disease and every sickness. When he saw the crowds, he had compassion for them, because they were harassed and helpless, like sheep without a shepherd. Then he said to his disciples, "The harvest is plentiful, but the laborers are few; therefore ask the Lord of the harvest to send out laborers into his harvest."

- Sometimes we are like the mute demoniac. We find it difficult to speak about what we believe in; we are too embarrassed to speak to others about God and our faith. I ask Jesus to set me free from this fear.

- What do I feel when I look around and see so much confusion and loneliness: is it anger or moral superiority, fear perhaps, or is it compassion and a desire to bring the Good News of salvation? I ask the Lord to send laborers to his abundant harvest, and I ask to be one of them.

Wednesday 8th July
Matthew 10:1–7

Then Jesus summoned his twelve disciples and gave them authority over unclean spirits, to cast them out, and to cure every disease and every sickness. These are the names of the twelve apostles: first, Simon, also known as Peter, and his brother Andrew; James son of Zebedee, and his brother John; Philip and Bartholomew; Thomas and Matthew the tax collector; James son of Alphaeus, and Thaddaeus; Simon the Cananaean, and Judas Iscariot, the one who betrayed him. These twelve Jesus sent out with the following instructions: "Go nowhere among the Gentiles, and enter no town of the Samaritans, but go rather to the lost sheep of the house of Israel. As you go, proclaim the Good News, 'The kingdom of heaven has come near.'"

- Jesus' choice of the Twelve is perhaps his most baffling decision. Could he not have made a better choice? Yet, at the end they were ready to obey his more daring commission to take the gospel to the whole world. He did make the right choice! The Gospel shows us the care he took to prepare them well for their mission.

- He called them to him and sent them to others. We cannot be real disciples of Jesus without also being apostles to others. The mission is the same that Jesus received from the Father: Go and tell everyone the Good News that the kingdom of heaven is near; bring healing to all who need it and get involved in the struggle against evil. I ask for the grace not to be deaf to the call to be a disciple and apostle.

Thursday 9th July
Matthew 10:7–15

Jesus said, "As you go, proclaim the Good News, 'The kingdom of heaven has come near.' Cure the sick, raise the dead, cleanse the lepers, cast out demons. You received without payment; give without payment. Take no gold, or silver, or copper in your belts, no bag for your journey, or two tunics, or sandals, or a staff; for laborers deserve their food. Whatever town or village you enter, find out who in it is worthy, and stay there until you leave. As you enter the house, greet it. If the house is worthy, let your peace come upon it; but if it is not worthy, let your peace return to you. If anyone will not welcome you or listen to your words, shake off the dust from your feet as you leave that house or town. Truly I tell you, it will be more tolerable for the land of Sodom and Gomorrah on the day of judgment than for that town."

- "You received without payment; give without payment." This is the call of the disciple: to acknowledge with gratitude all that I have received so that I can give freely. This purifies me from any pride or self-righteousness, as I realize that we are all recipients of God's mercy, and I can look at those to whom I am sent with respect and gratitude. As I listen to Jesus instructing his disciples, I ask for the grace to let his words make me a better disciple.

- Jesus' word, like Jesus himself, always carries judgment with it, for those who accept it, as for those who reject it. I pray for the conversion of those who are closed to the Good News of Jesus, and for a deeper conversion of my own heart.

Friday 10th July
Matthew 10:16–23

"See, I am sending you out like sheep into the midst of wolves; so be wise as serpents and innocent as doves. Beware of them, for they will hand you over to councils and flog you in their synagogues; and you will be dragged before governors and kings because of me, as a testimony to them and the Gentiles. When they hand you over, do not worry about how you are to speak or what you are to say; for what you are to say will be given to you at that time; for it is not you who speak, but the Spirit of your Father speaking through you. Brother will betray brother to death, and a father his child, and children will rise against parents and have them put to death; and you will be hated by all because of my name. But the one who endures to the end will be saved. When they persecute you in one town, flee to the next; for truly I tell you, you will not have gone through all the towns of Israel before the Son of Man comes."

- Often we struggle with the opposition we face when we try to live an honest Christian life, and with the increasing duplicity that seems to surround us. So, we do well to listen to Jesus' words about sheep among wolves and the need to know how to be both wise and transparent. Jesus knows all this, yet he still sends us to take the gospel to this difficult world. But he also promises us his assistance: he asks us not to worry!

- This makes sense only if we are doing it because of Jesus. We are being his disciples, following him along the path he has already trod. I ask for the grace of fortitude until the end, for myself and for those who suffer for being witnesses to Jesus. I think especially of the Christians in the Middle East.

Saturday 11th July
Saint Benedict, Abbot
Matthew 10:24–33

"A disciple is not above the teacher, nor a slave above the master; it is enough for the disciple to be like the teacher, and the slave like the master. If they have called the master of the house Beelzebul, how much more will they malign those of his household! So have no fear of them; for nothing is covered up that will not be uncovered, and nothing secret that will not become known. What I say to you in the dark, tell in the light; and what you hear whispered, proclaim from the housetops. Do not fear those who kill the body but cannot kill the soul; rather fear him who can destroy both soul and body in hell. Are not two sparrows sold for a penny? Yet not one of them will fall to the ground unperceived by your Father. And even the hairs of your head are all counted. So do not be afraid; you are of more value than many sparrows. Everyone therefore who acknowledges me before others, I also will acknowledge before my Father in heaven; but whoever denies me before others, I also will deny before my Father in heaven."

- When we feel the heat of persecution, we do well to look at the incredible accusations leveled at Jesus himself, especially that he was the master of the house of Beelzebul!

- "Do not be afraid." This is an invitation we encounter so often in the Bible. God is reminding us all the time that we can face our difficult choices without fear, trusting in his aid and protection. We meet these words so often because we do need to hear them repeatedly. Let me ask for the grace to trust God, as I hear him telling me not to be afraid.

Fifteenth Week in Ordinary Time
July 12—July 18

Something to think and pray about each day this week:

I am convinced that we who are joyful are so precisely because we know who we are in the eyes of the Father. We are *always* beloved sons and daughters! This knowledge enables each of us to move along with the path, always *adapting to change* in our surroundings because we recognize that nothing human is foreign. We are always in the midst of companionship with other sisters and brothers along the way. Joy, it seems to me, is essentially the knowledge of the heart and mind that no matter what happens in our journey, God is always with us as we move along, revealing himself often through the kindness and gentleness of our fellow sojourners.

—Casey Beaumier, SJ, *A Purposeful Path*

The Presence of God

Dear Jesus, as I call on you today, I realize that often I come asking for favors. Today I'd like just to be in your presence. Draw my heart in response to your love.

Freedom

It is so easy to get caught up
with the trappings of wealth in this life.
Grant, O Lord, that I may be free
from greed and selfishness.
Remind me that the best things in life are free:
Love, laughter, caring, and sharing.

Consciousness

How am I really feeling? Lighthearted? Heavyhearted? I may be very much at peace, happy to be here.
Equally, I may be frustrated, worried, or angry.
I acknowledge how I really am. It is the real me whom the Lord loves.

The Word

Lord Jesus, you became human to communicate with me.
You walked and worked on this earth.
You endured the heat and struggled with the cold.
All your time on this earth was spent in caring for humanity.
You healed the sick, you raised the dead.
Most important of all, you saved me from death.
(Please turn to the Scripture on the following pages. Inspiration points are there, should you need them. When you are ready, return here to continue.)

Conversation

Do I notice myself reacting as I pray with the word of God? Do I feel challenged, comforted, angry? Imagining Jesus sitting or standing by me, I speak out my feelings, as one trusted friend to another.

Conclusion

Glory be to the Father, and to the Son, and to the Holy Spirit,
As it was in the beginning, is now and ever shall be,
World without end. Amen.

Sunday 12th July
Fifteenth Sunday in Ordinary Time
Matthew 13:1–9

That same day Jesus went out of the house and sat beside the sea. Such great crowds gathered around him that he got into a boat and sat there, while the whole crowd stood on the beach. And he told them many things in parables, saying: "Listen! A sower went out to sow. And as he sowed, some seeds fell on the path, and the birds came and ate them up. Other seeds fell on rocky ground, where they did not have much soil, and they sprang up quickly, since they had no depth of soil. But when the sun rose, they were scorched; and since they had no root, they withered away. Other seeds fell among thorns, and the thorns grew up and choked them. Other seeds fell on good soil and brought forth grain, some a hundred-fold, some sixty, some thirty. Let anyone with ears listen!"

- We can think of the seed as the word and the sower as God, whose will can never be stopped. The seed falls on different types of ground, but the great majority certainly falls on good ground, and its fruit more than makes up for the seeds that fall on more difficult ground. This is the parable of optimism, something that is often lacking in followers of the gospel.

- Jesus was speaking to people who knew all about seeds and different types of soil—many of them grew their own food or grew crops to sell. When Jesus described the various situations that affected growth, his hearers could imagine exactly what prevented full growth and fruition. May I pay attention to what helps or hinders the growth of God's word in my own life.

Monday 13th July
Matthew 10:34—11:1

"Do not think that I have come to bring peace to the earth; I have not come to bring peace, but a sword. For I have come to set a man against his father, and a daughter against her mother, and a daughter-in-law against her mother-in-law; and one's foes will be members of one's own household. Whoever loves father or mother more than me is not worthy of me; and whoever loves son or daughter more than me is not worthy of me; and whoever does not take up the cross and follow me is not worthy of me.

Those who find their life will lose it, and those who lose their life for my sake will find it. Whoever welcomes you welcomes me, and whoever welcomes me welcomes the one who sent me. Whoever welcomes a prophet in the name of a prophet will receive a prophet's reward; and whoever welcomes a righteous person in the name of a righteous person will receive the reward of the righteous; and whoever gives even a cup of cold water to one of these little ones in the name of a disciple—truly I tell you, none of these will lose their reward." Now when Jesus had finished instructing his twelve disciples, he went on from there to teach and proclaim his message in their cities.

- These hard words of Jesus can be understood only in the light of our life experience, the times we face the dramatic choices Jesus speaks of. We know there are moments when stark choices need to be made to ensure we can still call ourselves disciples of Jesus, moments when we wield the sword of division or separation.

- Do I want to save my life or lose it? Am I ready to lose it, or do I cling for fear of losing it? This is perhaps the basic condition for discipleship, and no moralistic or perfect obedience to any law or system of rules can replace it. I ask insistently for the grace of real interior freedom and for courage to be true to myself and to my calling.

Tuesday 14th July
Saint Kateri Tekakwitha, Virgin
Matthew 11:20–24

Then Jesus began to reproach the cities in which most of his deeds of power had been done, because they did not repent. "Woe to you, Chorazin! Woe to you, Bethsaida! For if the deeds of power done in you had been done in Tyre and Sidon, they would have repented long ago in sackcloth and ashes. But I tell you, on the day of judgment it will be more tolerable for Tyre and Sidon than for you. And you, Capernaum, will you be exalted to heaven? No, you will be brought down to Hades. For if the deeds of power done in you had been done in Sodom, it would have remained until this day. But I tell you that on the day of judgment it will be more tolerable for the land of Sodom than for you."

- We might not feel very comfortable with the idea of Jesus as our judge, who thunders terrible threats on big and powerful cities. We might prefer the nice sayings about love and universal fraternity because these hard words unsettle us from our self-righteousness. I try to listen to these words as directed to me and my society's way of life. I also ask for the adequate response to this call for conversion.

- Not only individuals but our whole societies are urgently called to conversion. There are too many innocent victims of our self-centered way of life, in economics and in our life together, not to make us ask some very painful questions about the way we are organized. I pray for my society and for its conversion from what I consider the most obnoxious elements in God's eyes. I ask for light to see what part I can play as a responsible citizen.

Wednesday 15th July
Saint Bonaventure, Bishop and Doctor of the Church
Matthew 11:25–27

At that time Jesus said, "I thank you, Father, Lord of heaven and earth, because you have hidden these things from the wise and the intelligent and have revealed them to infants; yes, Father, for such was your gracious will. All things have been handed over to me by my Father; and no one knows the Son except the Father, and no one knows the Father except the Son and anyone to whom the Son chooses to reveal him."

- I share Jesus' joy and gratitude for the great gift of the Father's showing himself to us, especially to those who are small. I ask for the grace not to consider myself wise and intelligent before God's greatness but to become like a little child, willing to listen and learn, to be surprised by how and what God tells me about himself.

- In deep wonder I adore God's greatness, his sovereignty, his love for us in becoming one of us so that we can understand better who he is.

Thursday 16th July
Matthew 11:28–30

Jesus said, "Come to me, all you that are weary and are carrying heavy burdens, and I will give you rest. Take my yoke upon you, and learn from me; for I am gentle and humble in heart, and you will find rest for your souls. For my yoke is easy, and my burden is light."

- The reign of the coming savior king will not just bring security and welcome to any persons who feel lost and abandoned. Jesus' kingdom also promises relief and support to those who simply feel that life has become too much for them. Jesus understands each of us better than we understand ourselves, and his gentle heart goes out to us.

- Jesus' rest—a sense of having been accepted—banishes weariness and renews our energy. No surprise here: the Savior and Lord himself is the energy center of the universe, the creator, the one who names each star.

Friday 17th July
Matthew 12:1–8

At that time Jesus went through the grainfields on the sabbath; his disciples were hungry, and they began to pluck heads of grain and to eat. When the Pharisees saw it, they said to him, "Look, your disciples are doing what is not lawful to do on the sabbath." He said to them, "Have you not read what David did when he and his companions were hungry? He entered the house of God and ate the bread of the Presence, which it was not lawful for him or his companions to eat, but only for the priests. Or have you not read in the law that on the sabbath the priests in the temple break the sabbath and yet are guiltless? I tell you, something greater than the temple is here. But if you had known what this means, 'I desire mercy and not sacrifice,' you would not have condemned the guiltless. For the Son of Man is lord of the sabbath."

- Jesus' internal freedom, built on his self-awareness as someone wholly unique, must have confused and irritated his critics. He always referred to a rule of behavior that was higher and purer than the observances his hearers were used to. Sometimes this seemed too much for them. Are we still capable of being shocked by Jesus' words and actions?

- Jesus proclaims himself as greater than the temple, even Lord of the Sabbath itself, two of the most sacred Jewish institutions. I pray that I can allow myself to be challenged by Jesus' presence and demands, especially regarding how I understand Christianity and the church.

Saturday 18th July

Matthew 12:14–21

But the Pharisees went out and conspired against him, how to destroy him. When Jesus became aware of this, he departed. Many crowds followed him, and he cured all of them, and he ordered them not to make him known. This was to fulfill what had been spoken through the prophet Isaiah: "Here is my servant, whom I have chosen, my beloved, with whom my soul is well pleased. I will put my Spirit upon him, and he will proclaim justice to the Gentiles. He will not wrangle or cry aloud, nor will anyone hear his voice in the streets. He will not break a bruised reed or quench a smoldering wick until he brings justice to victory. And in his name the Gentiles will hope."

• Jesus was an advocate of justice who quietly proclaimed a message of love that set his people free. When he encountered hostility as the Pharisees conspired against him, he did not want his followers to make him known. This was to fulfill the prophecy of Isaiah about the suffering servant, who was full of gentleness and compassion, which Jesus applies to himself.

• I pray the words of Isaiah and give thanks. God has chosen me; I am his beloved son or daughter, and he is pleased with me. He has given me his Spirit, and he wants to bless me as I draw closer to him.

July 19—July 25

Something to think and pray about each day this week:

Jerome Nadal, a leader of the early Jesuits, applauded "the conversational disciple." This person would "quietly and slowly win over his neighbor, to deal with him gently and light the flame of charity in his heart." Nadal said that Ignatius was a master of conversation. "Even though the person in question was a hardened sinner, he found something in him to love," Nadal said. Ignatius would start a conversation and look for an opportunity to give it a spiritual turn. Ignatius called this method "entering by their door so as to come out by our door."

Ignatius cared about the way Jesuits talked. He told Jesuits participating in the Council of Trent to adjust their tone: "In discussions and arguments it is well to be brief; in order, however, to get men to follow virtue and to flee from vice, your speech should be long, and full of charity and kindness." Centuries before hacked e-mails, he warned his men to be prudent in conversation.

—Jim Manney, *Ignatius Spirituality A to Z*

The Presence of God

As I sit here, the beating of my heart,
the ebb and flow of my breathing, the movements of my mind
are all signs of God's ongoing creation of me.
I pause for a moment and become aware
of this presence of God within me.

Freedom

I will ask God's help
to be free from my own preoccupations,
to be open to God in this time of prayer,
to come to know, love, and serve God more.

Consciousness

At this moment, Lord, I turn my thoughts to you.
I will leave aside my chores and preoccupations.
I will take rest and refreshment in your presence.

The Word

Now I turn to the Scripture set out for me this day. I read slowly over the words and see if any sentence or sentiment appeals to me. (Please turn to the Scripture on the following pages. Inspiration points are there, should you need them. When you are ready, return here to continue.)

Conversation

Begin to talk to Jesus about the Scripture you have just read. What part of it strikes a chord in you? Perhaps the words of a friend—or some story you have heard recently—will slowly rise to the surface of your consciousness. If so, does the story throw light on what the Scripture passage may be saying to you?

Conclusion

Glory be to the Father, and to the Son, and to the Holy Spirit,
As it was in the beginning, is now and ever shall be,
World without end. Amen.

Sunday 19th July
Sixteenth Sunday in Ordinary Time
Matthew 13:24–30

Jesus put before them another parable: "The kingdom of heaven may be compared to someone who sowed good seed in his field; but while everybody was asleep, an enemy came and sowed weeds among the wheat, and then went away. So when the plants came up and bore grain, then the weeds appeared as well. And the slaves of the householder came and said to him, 'Master, did you not sow good seed in your field? Where, then, did these weeds come from?' He answered, 'An enemy has done this.' The slaves said to him, 'Then do you want us to go and gather them?' But he replied, 'No; for in gathering the weeds you would uproot the wheat along with them. Let both of them grow together until the harvest; and at harvest time I will tell the reapers, Collect the weeds first and bind them in bundles to be burned, but gather the wheat into my barn.'"

• The farmer discovers the malicious act but avoids a hasty response. He is prepared to wait until the proper time, knowing that, while the seedlings are indistinguishable, the plants will be evidently different from one another. As I lay my life before God, I remind myself that the task of judgment is not mine, nor is it for now.

• Good and evil coexist in human life and in the world. Nothing and no one is perfect. We are all in need of forgiveness and redemption. Lord Jesus, you know my strengths and my weaknesses. Help me to produce a rich harvest of good works to the greater glory of the Father.

Monday 20th July
Matthew 12:38–42

Then some of the scribes and Pharisees said to him, "Teacher, we wish to see a sign from you." But he answered them, "An evil and adulterous generation asks for a sign, but no sign will be given to it except the sign of the prophet Jonah. For just as Jonah was three days and three nights in the belly of the sea monster, so for three days and three nights the Son of Man will be in the heart of the earth. The people of Nineveh will rise up at the judgment with this generation and condemn it, because they repented at the proclamation of Jonah, and see, something greater than

Jonah is here! The queen of the South will rise up at the judgment with this generation and condemn it, because she came from the ends of the earth to listen to the wisdom of Solomon, and see, something greater than Solomon is here!"

- Like the scribes and the Pharisees, we would love to have a sign that would remove the need to believe and trust that God is speaking to us in and through Jesus. Yet, as elsewhere in the Gospels, Jesus has only one sign to give us: himself after the Resurrection. That is the supreme sign of the Father's confirmation of his words and of all he stands for. How important is the Resurrection in the way I understand and follow Jesus?

- Jesus compares himself to Jonah, the prophet who preached conversion. Moreover, he claims he is even greater than Jonah, than the wise Solomon, so that our resistance to conversion will be our condemnation. Elsewhere, Jesus says that he will sit in judgment on the nations at the end. I ask not to be deaf to his call to change what I need to change.

Tuesday 21st July

Matthew 12:46–50

While he was still speaking to the crowds, his mother and his brothers were standing outside, wanting to speak to him. Someone told him, "Look, your mother and your brothers are standing outside, wanting to speak to you." But to the one who had told him this, Jesus replied, "Who is my mother, and who are my brothers?" And pointing to his disciples, he said, "Here are my mother and my brothers! For whoever does the will of my Father in heaven is my brother and sister and mother."

- Mary added the assurance that Jesus gave to what she already valued in her heart and was given greater cause to rejoice; she knew her own value in her being and in her doing. I ask God to affirm me in who I am and in what I do.

- Jesus always speaks of the invitation to God's reign as being broad and inclusive. I give thanks for the generosity of God that sees me included in God's loving plan.

Wednesday 22nd July
Saint Mary Magdalene
John 20:1–2, 11–18

Early on the first day of the week, while it was still dark, Mary Magdalene came to the tomb and saw that the stone had been removed from the tomb. So she ran and went to Simon Peter and the other disciple, the one whom Jesus loved, and said to them, "They have taken the Lord out of the tomb, and we do not know where they have laid him." . . . But Mary stood weeping outside the tomb. As she wept, she bent over to look into the tomb; and she saw two angels in white, sitting where the body of Jesus had been lying, one at the head and the other at the feet. They said to her, "Woman, why are you weeping?" She said to them, "They have taken away my Lord, and I do not know where they have laid him." When she had said this, she turned around and saw Jesus standing there, but she did not know that it was Jesus. Jesus said to her, "Woman, why are you weeping? For whom are you looking?" Supposing him to be the gardener, she said to him, "Sir, if you have carried him away, tell me where you have laid him, and I will take him away." Jesus said to her, "Mary!" She turned and said to him in Hebrew, "Rabbouni!" (which means Teacher). Jesus said to her, "Do not hold on to me, because I have not yet ascended to the Father. But go to my brothers and say to them, 'I am ascending to my Father and your Father, to my God and your God.'" Mary Magdalene went and announced to the disciples, "I have seen the Lord"; and she told them that he had said these things to her.

• Mary is one of the first witnesses of the Resurrection; she was the one who brought the news of the empty tomb to Peter and John, and later she announced to the disciples, "I have seen the Lord!" I thank God for these witnesses, and I ask for the grace to be a joyful and enthusiastic witness to the presence of the risen Jesus in the world and to the joy and freedom that he radiates.

• The risen Jesus does not let Mary cling to him but sends her on a mission, telling others he is risen. What do I feel Jesus sending me to do, after my personal encounter with him after his resurrection? I pray for the grace not to be deaf to this call but ready to respond to it with generosity.

Thursday 23rd July
Matthew 13:10–17

The disciples came to Jesus and asked him, "Why do you speak to them in parables?" He answered, "To you it has been given to know the secrets of the kingdom of heaven, but to them it has not been given. For to those who have, more will be given, and they will have an abundance; but from those who have nothing, even what they have will be taken away. The reason I speak to them in parables is that 'seeing they do not perceive, and hearing they do not listen, nor do they understand.' With them indeed is fulfilled the prophecy of Isaiah that says: 'You will indeed listen, but never understand, and you will indeed look, but never perceive. For this people's heart has grown dull, and their ears are hard of hearing, and they have shut their eyes; so that they might not look with their eyes, and listen with their ears, and understand with their heart and turn—and I would heal them.' But blessed are your eyes, for they see, and your ears, for they hear. Truly I tell you, many prophets and righteous people longed to see what you see, but did not see it, and to hear what you hear, but did not hear it."

- Am I one of those who look without seeing, or hear without understanding? Jesus speaks in parables to challenge us out of our laziness, seeking the deeper meaning of things. How easy to be distracted, especially nowadays when we feel overwhelmed by too much information and images without any insight.

- Jesus calls me blessed and happy, for I am a witness of his presence, unlike many prophets and holier persons who were living in expectation. I ask for a greater awareness of this presence and for a deep joy in being a member of the kingdom.

Friday 24th July
Matthew 13:18–23

"Hear then the parable of the sower. When anyone hears the word of the kingdom and does not understand it, the evil one comes and snatches away what is sown in the heart; this is what was sown on the path. As for what was sown on rocky ground, this is the one who hears the word and immediately receives it with joy; yet such a person has no root, but endures only for a while, and when trouble or persecution arises on account of the word, that person immediately falls away. As for what was sown among thorns, this is the one who hears the word, but the cares of the world and the lure of wealth choke the word, and it yields nothing. But as for what was sown on good soil, this is the one who hears the word and understands it, who indeed bears fruit and yields, in one case a hundredfold, in another sixty, and in another thirty."

- I look at my life in gratitude for the abundant fruit that the word sown in my heart has produced in my relationships, in my freedom and openness to God and others, and in my sensibility to suffering around me. Especially to the place Jesus has in my life.

- I also look at the margins of my heart, those areas where the word finds it difficult to bear lasting fruit, and I ask for light and freedom to remove these obstacles and distractions.

Saturday 25th July
Saint James, Apostle
Matthew 20:20–28

Then the mother of the sons of Zebedee came to him with her sons, and kneeling before him, she asked a favor of him. And he said to her, "What do you want?" She said to him, "Declare that these two sons of mine will sit, one at your right hand and one at your left, in your kingdom." But Jesus answered, "You do not know what you are asking. Are you able to drink the cup that I am about to drink?" They said to him, "We are able." He said to them, "You will indeed drink my cup, but to sit at my right hand and at my left, this is not mine to grant, but it is for those for whom it has been prepared by my Father." When the ten heard it, they were angry with the two brothers. But Jesus called them to him and said, "You know that the rulers of the Gentiles lord it over them, and their great ones are tyrants over them. It will not be so among you; but whoever wishes to be great among you must be your servant, and whoever wishes to be first among you must be your slave; just as the Son of Man came not to be served but to serve, and to give his life a ransom for many."

- On the feast of James, one of Jesus' inner circle, I rejoice in the faithfulness of these men. They were ready to let the Spirit enable them to overcome their many shortcomings, transforming them into the first apostles of the Good News of the kingdom. Thanks to them and their love for Jesus and their readiness to drink the cup he was about to drink, the faith has come to us and to billions of others throughout the world. I ask for gratitude, and for their sense of urgency in spreading the gospel to the whole world.

- How often the gospel portrays even those closest to Jesus struggling with questions of power and service. I look into my own heart and dwell on Jesus' words about the Christian's attitude to such an important aspect of our life together. I ask for the grace to grow in my imitation of him who came to serve and not to be served.

Seventeenth Week in Ordinary Time
July 26—August 1

Something to think and pray about each day this week:

Spiritual detachment requires accepting my true feelings and ideas but wanting to follow them only insofar as they lead me toward God. The more we are aware of the things and people and experiences that we are passionate about, the better we can discern where the Holy Spirit is inviting us in the welter of our affections and the tangle of our minds. For one thing, the Holy Spirit often inspires in us a passionate desire for what God wants done next.

—Joseph A. Tetlow, SJ, *Always Discerning*

The Presence of God
At any time of the day or night we can call on Jesus.
He is always waiting, listening for our call.
What a wonderful blessing.
No phone needed, no e-mails, just a whisper.

Freedom
If God were trying to tell me something, would I know?
If God were reassuring me or challenging me, would I notice?
I ask for the grace to be free of my own preoccupations
and open to what God may be saying to me.

Consciousness
Help me, Lord, become more conscious of your presence. Teach me to recognize your presence in others. Fill my heart with gratitude for the times your love has been shown to me through the care of others.

The Word
In this expectant state of mind, please turn to the text for the day with confidence. Believe that the Holy Spirit is present and may reveal whatever the passage has to say to you. Read reflectively, listening with a third ear to what may be going on in your heart. (Please turn to the Scripture on the following pages. Inspiration points are there, should you need them. When you are ready, return here to continue.)

Conversation
Conversation requires talking and listening.
As I talk to Jesus, may I also learn to pause and listen.
I picture the gentleness in his eyes and the love in his smile.
I can be totally honest with Jesus as I tell him my worries and cares.
I will open my heart to Jesus as I tell him my fears and doubts.
I will ask him to help me place myself fully in his care, knowing that he always desires good for me.

Conclusion
I thank God for these moments we have spent together and for any insights I have been given concerning the text.

Sunday 26th July
Seventeenth Sunday in Ordinary Time
Matthew 13:44–52

Jesus said, "The kingdom of heaven is like treasure hidden in a field, which someone found and hid; then in his joy he goes and sells all that he has and buys that field. Again, the kingdom of heaven is like a merchant in search of fine pearls; on finding one pearl of great value, he went and sold all that he had and bought it. Again, the kingdom of heaven is like a net that was thrown into the sea and caught fish of every kind; when it was full, they drew it ashore, sat down, and put the good into baskets but threw out the bad. So it will be at the end of the age. The angels will come out and separate the evil from the righteous and throw them into the furnace of fire, where there will be weeping and gnashing of teeth. Have you understood all this?" They answered, "Yes." And he said to them, "Therefore every scribe who has been trained for the kingdom of heaven is like the master of a household who brings out of his treasure what is new and what is old."

- Have I found the pearl of great value, for which I am ready to sell all I have in order to buy it? Am I still looking for it, or am I resigned to a life of mediocrity in my relationships with others, with God in my prayer, in my work life? If I have found this pearl, am I ready to sell all that I have to obtain it? Jesus compares this pearl to the kingdom he came to proclaim and inaugurate, and this gives me joy and hope.

- The scribe who has been trained for the kingdom knows how to bring out of his treasure what is new and what is old. In our world, even in our churches, we are becoming more and more polarized between the liberals and the conservatives, as both claim to be the only ones to have all the truth. I ask for wisdom and freedom to seek the kingdom before all else.

Monday 27th July
Matthew 13:31–35

He put before them another parable: "The kingdom of heaven is like a mustard seed that someone took and sowed in his field; it is the smallest of all the seeds, but when it has grown it is the greatest of shrubs and becomes a tree, so that the birds of the air come and make nests in its branches." He told them another parable: "The kingdom of heaven is like yeast that a woman took and mixed in with three measures of flour until all of it was leavened." Jesus told the crowds all these things in parables; without a parable he told them nothing. This was to fulfill what had been spoken through the prophet: "I will open my mouth to speak in parables; I will proclaim what has been hidden from the foundation of the world."

- Like the Jews of Jesus' time, we would like to see the kingdom as something spectacular that cannot but convince everybody of its truth. Yet Jesus speaks of a tiny seed that will eventually grow into a tree that offers shelter to the small ones. I ask for light to see the many mustard seeds that inhabit my world so that I may grow in trust and in my readiness to commit myself more fully to the kingdom.

- Saint Ignatius of Loyola might not be the most popular saint, but the way he understood the Christian life still inspires many. I try to focus in thanksgiving on what today I find inspiring in his worldview: the priority to God's will, his optimism, his deep personal life for Jesus, understanding of discernment. I ask to grow in my ability to live for the greater glory of God.

Tuesday 28th July
Matthew 13:36–43

Then he left the crowds and went into the house. And his disciples approached him, saying, "Explain to us the parable of the weeds of the field." He answered, "The one who sows the good seed is the Son of Man; the field is the world, and the good seed are the children of the kingdom; the weeds are the children of the evil one, and the enemy who sowed them is the devil; the harvest is the end of the age, and the reapers are angels. Just as the weeds are collected and burned up with fire, so will it be at the end of the age. The Son of Man will send his angels, and they will collect out of his kingdom all causes of sin and all evildoers, and they will throw them into the furnace of fire, where there will be weeping and gnashing of teeth. Then the righteous will shine like the sun in the kingdom of their Father. Let anyone with ears listen!"

- The world and the individuals in it are a mixture of good and evil. We have within ourselves warring spirits. Am I aware of these spirits within myself? How do I distinguish one from another?

- I pray to gain knowledge of the true life in Christ and an understanding of the deceits of Satan.

Wednesday 29th July
Saint Martha
Luke 10:38–42

Now as they went on their way, Jesus entered a certain village, where a woman named Martha welcomed him into her home. She had a sister named Mary, who sat at the Lord's feet and listened to what he was saying. But Martha was distracted by her many tasks; so she came to him and asked, "Lord, do you not care that my sister has left me to do all the work by myself? Tell her then to help me." But the Lord answered her, "Martha, Martha, you are worried and distracted by many things; there is need of only one thing. Mary has chosen the better part, which will not be taken away from her."

- Today we celebrate the feast of Saint Martha, whom the Gospel describes as a friend of Jesus. Martha loved to welcome him into her home and felt free enough to complain that Jesus was not there when her brother died. I look at my relationship with Jesus and, through her intercession, ask for a greater familiarity and personal love for him.

- It is easy to be distracted and fragmented when many things call for attention—even what is good can lose its luster if we forget what busyness is about. Martha seems to have been distracted by the many things she had to do; she forgot whom she was doing them for.

Thursday 30th July
Matthew 13:47–53

"Again, the kingdom of heaven is like a net that was thrown into the sea and caught fish of every kind; when it was full, they drew it ashore, sat down, and put the good into baskets but threw out the bad. So it will be at the end of the age. The angels will come out and separate the evil from the righteous and throw them into the furnace of fire, where there will be weeping and gnashing of teeth. Have you understood all this?" They answered, "Yes." And he said to them, "Therefore every scribe who has been trained for the kingdom of heaven is like the master of a household who brings out of his treasure what is new and what is old." When Jesus had finished these parables, he left that place.

- Jesus speaks in parables, a form of storytelling, to help his words come to life for his followers in everyday language. Many of the disciples were fishermen who spent their lives casting out their nets to draw in the fish. They could understand the method of separating the "good" from the "bad."

- Will judgment be a final division of good and bad? The early church held the hope that somehow, by the goodness of God, we will all be saved. I must work and pray for this.

Friday 31st July
Saint Ignatius of Loyola, Priest
Matthew 13:54–58

He came to his hometown and began to teach the people in their synagogue, so that they were astounded and said, "Where did this man get this wisdom and these deeds of power? Is not this the carpenter's son? Is not his mother called Mary? And are not his brothers James and Joseph and Simon and Judas? And are not all his sisters with us? Where then did this man get all this?" And they took offense at him. But Jesus said to them, "Prophets are not without honor except in their own country and in their own house." And he did not do many deeds of power there, because of their unbelief.

- Familiarity is not the same as close relationship. The people that grew up around you may think they know you—know your gifts and talents, your wisdom and strength, or your faults and frailties. But who knows what is really happening within you as you grow in your relationship with God and come to know your true self better? We must not be held back by others' perceptions of us.

- The Nazarenes were jealous of Jesus; they couldn't cope with him being anything other than the carpenter's son. They wanted to take him down to their level. How do you respond to positive growth and change in people you knew in the past? Next time you meet someone from the past and notice how they have grown since you last met them, will you give generous acknowledgement, or will you take offense?

Saturday 1st August
Saint Alphonsus Liguori, Bishop and Doctor of the Church
Matthew 14:1–12

At that time Herod the ruler heard reports about Jesus; and he said to his servants, "This is John the Baptist; he has been raised from the dead, and for this reason these powers are at work in him." For Herod had arrested John, bound him, and put him in prison on account of Herodias, his brother Philip's wife, because John had been telling him, "It is not lawful for you to have her." Though Herod wanted to put him to death, he feared the crowd, because they regarded him as a prophet. But when Herod's birthday came, the daughter of Herodias danced before the company, and she pleased Herod so much that he promised on oath to grant her whatever she might ask. Prompted by her mother, she said, "Give me the head of John the Baptist here on a platter." The king was grieved, yet out of regard for his oaths and for the guests, he commanded it to be given; he sent and had John beheaded in the prison. The head was brought on a platter and given to the girl, who brought it to her mother. His disciples came and took the body and buried it; then they went and told Jesus.

- John's death led his disciples to Jesus. When all seemed lost, they risked their lives in a final act of love to reclaim John's body, and then they went and told Jesus. Let us realize that chaos and destruction often lead us into the next good thing.

- The vanity of Herod brought him into terrible situations. I think of how well I am able to back down, to change my mind, to admit that I am wrong. I ask God for the help I need.

August 2—August 8

Something to think and pray about each day this week:

The Ignatian charism is to hold opposing tendencies in balance. In the Ignatian view we must balance trust in God with confident use of our talents; enjoying our community with throwing ourselves into mission; revering sacred things with openness to the world; reflective inwardness with bold action; obedience to authority with hunger for change. One of Ignatius's favorite images was the "pointer of a balance." Think of a child's seesaw in a playground, perfectly level with equal weights on each side, poised in balance on the fulcrum.

—Jim Manney, *Ignatian Spirituality A to Z*

The Presence of God
Dear Lord, as I come to you today, fill my heart, my whole being, with the wonder of your presence. Help me remain receptive to you as I put aside the cares of this world. Fill my mind with your peace.

Freedom
Lord, grant me the grace to be free from the excesses of this life. Let me not get caught up with the desire for wealth. Keep my heart and mind free to love and serve you.

Consciousness
I exist in a web of relationships: links to nature, people, God.
I trace out these links, giving thanks for the life that flows through them.
Some links are twisted or broken; I may feel regret, anger, disappointment.
I pray for the gift of acceptance and forgiveness.

The Word
God speaks to each of us individually. I listen attentively to hear what he is saying to me. Read the text a few times, then listen. (Please turn to the Scripture on the following pages. Inspiration points are there, should you need them. When you are ready, return here to continue.)

Conversation
Jesus, you speak to me through the words of the Gospels. May I respond to your call today. Teach me to recognize your hand at work in my daily living.

Conclusion
I thank God for these moments we have spent together and for any insights I have been given concerning the text.

Sunday 2nd August
Eighteenth Sunday in Ordinary Time
Matthew 14:13–21

Now when Jesus heard this, he withdrew from there in a boat to a deserted place by himself. But when the crowds heard it, they followed him on foot from the towns. When he went ashore, he saw a great crowd; and he had compassion for them and cured their sick. When it was evening, the disciples came to him and said, "This is a deserted place, and the hour is now late; send the crowds away so that they may go into the villages and buy food for themselves." Jesus said to them, "They need not go away; you give them something to eat." They replied, "We have nothing here but five loaves and two fish." And he said, "Bring them here to me." Then he ordered the crowds to sit down on the grass. Taking the five loaves and the two fish, he looked up to heaven, and blessed and broke the loaves, and gave them to the disciples, and the disciples gave them to the crowds. And all ate and were filled; and they took up what was left over of the broken pieces, twelve baskets full. And those who ate were about five thousand men, besides women and children.

- Jesus does not produce food out of nowhere. He takes the little that the apostles have and multiplies it a thousandfold. I am reminded that Jesus can provide spiritual nourishment beyond my imagining. There is a mysterious disproportion between what I give and what the Lord makes of it.

- When Jesus had heard the news about John the Baptist's execution, he needed time alone, despite the expectations of the crowds. If I have ever heard myself say that I am too busy to pray, I think of what moves Jesus and ask that God's Spirit guide and direct me, too.

Monday 3rd August
Matthew 14:22–36

Immediately he made the disciples get into the boat and go on ahead to the other side, while he dismissed the crowds. And after he had dismissed the crowds, he went up the mountain by himself to pray. When evening came, he was there alone, but by this time the boat, battered by the waves, was far from the land, for the wind was against them. And early in the morning he came walking toward them on the sea. But when the disciples saw him walking on the sea, they were terrified, saying, "It is a ghost!" And they cried out in fear. But immediately Jesus spoke to them and said, "Take heart, it is I; do not be afraid." Peter answered him, "Lord, if it is you, command me to come to you on the water." He said, "Come." So Peter got out of the boat, started walking on the water, and came toward Jesus. But when he noticed the strong wind, he became frightened, and beginning to sink, he cried out, "Lord, save me!" Jesus immediately reached out his hand and caught him, saying to him, "You of little faith, why did you doubt?" When they got into the boat, the wind ceased. And those in the boat worshiped him, saying, "Truly you are the Son of God." When they had crossed over, they came to land at Gennesaret. After the people of that place recognized him, they sent word throughout the region and brought all who were sick to him, and begged him that they might touch even the fringe of his cloak; and all who touched it were healed.

- Having sent everybody away, Jesus went to pray. His prayer, however, did not distance him from the needs of others but prompted him to go to the aid of his friends. Show me, Jesus, how you come to me when I am battered by the waves. Let me, like Peter, reach out to you in faith and seek to be close to you in times of trouble.

- Jesus did not come immediately to rescue the struggling disciples. He let them battle through most of the night. We experience this, too: our faith is sometimes stretched almost to the breaking point. The humanity of Peter is reassuring. He jumps into the water without thinking. But once he takes his eyes off Jesus, he begins to sink. In our own troubled times, we must keep our focus on Jesus.

Tuesday 4th August
Saint John Vianney, Priest
Matthew 15:1–2, 10–14

Then Pharisees and scribes came to Jesus from Jerusalem and said, "Why do your disciples break the tradition of the elders? For they do not wash their hands before they eat." . . . Then he called the crowd to him and said to them, "Listen and understand: it is not what goes into the mouth that defiles a person, but it is what comes out of the mouth that defiles." Then the disciples approached and said to him, "Do you know that the Pharisees took offense when they heard what you said?" He answered,

"Every plant that my heavenly Father has not planted will be uprooted. Let them alone; they are blind guides of the blind. And if one blind person guides another, both will fall into a pit."

- The Pharisees were concerned with the rituals of their time and judged people who did not observe them. It can happen in our time, too, that people become focused on what they eat and look down on those who live differently. Jesus pays attention to words and works. He is less interested in how the body performs than in how the heart is formed.

- Traditions and rules can give us false security; as long as we know we are "doing it right," we need not worry about the complex workings of the soul. Jesus understood that a person speaks and acts out of that interior life. Lord, teach me to tend my soul with care and with faith in your help.

Wednesday 5th August
Matthew 15:21–28

Jesus left that place and went away to the district of Tyre and Sidon. Just then a Canaanite woman from that region came out and started shouting, "Have mercy on me, Lord, Son of David; my daughter is tormented by a demon." But he did not answer her at all. And his disciples came and urged him, saying, "Send her away, for she keeps shouting after us." He answered, "I was sent only to the lost sheep of the house of Israel." But she came and knelt before him, saying, "Lord, help me." He answered, "It is not fair to take the children's food and throw it to the dogs." She said, "Yes, Lord, yet even the dogs eat the crumbs that fall from their masters' table." Then Jesus answered her, "Woman, great is your faith! Let it be done for you as you wish." And her daughter was healed instantly.

- Like the woman in this story, I come before Jesus, bringing others in my prayer. As I pray for those I love, I grow in appreciation of their goodness and ask God's blessings for them. I think again of how they are blessings for me, and I give thanks.

- The Canaanite woman acknowledges Jesus as Son of David, a Messianic title. She kneels before him and calls him "Lord." She refuses to take offense at a seemingly rude insult. She knows the power and the mercy of this man. She believes in him. Her request is granted. What can I let this woman teach me?

Thursday 6th August
The Transfiguration of the Lord
Matthew 17:1–9

Six days later, Jesus took with him Peter and James and his brother John and led them up a high mountain, by themselves. And he was transfigured before them, and his face shone like the sun, and his clothes became dazzling white. Suddenly there appeared to them Moses and Elijah, talking with him. Then Peter said to Jesus, "Lord, it is good for us to be here; if you wish, I will make three dwellings here, one for you, one for Moses, and one for Elijah." While he was still speaking, suddenly a bright cloud overshadowed them, and from the cloud a voice said, "This is my Son, the Beloved; with him I am well pleased; listen to him!" When the disciples heard this, they fell to the ground and were overcome by fear. But Jesus came and touched them, saying, "Get up and do not be afraid." And when they looked up, they saw no one except Jesus himself alone. As they were coming down the mountain, Jesus ordered them, "Tell no one about the vision until after the Son of Man has been raised from the dead."

- The disciples see Jesus revealed in all his divine glory. It is a special moment for them, as Peter confirms. The voice of God the Father resounding from the cloud has an important message to convey to the disciples and us: "Listen to him." A listening heart is one warmed by the love of God and taught by his words. The one we listen to is the Son of God, Jesus, transfigured in his humanity.

- Prayer is better described as listening than speaking. Spend some time echoing Jesus' words, or just listening to the mood of love and peace in prayer.

Friday 7th August
Matthew 16:24–28

Then Jesus told his disciples, "If any want to become my followers, let them deny themselves and take up their cross and follow me. For those who want to save their life will lose it, and those who lose their life for my sake will find it. For what will it profit them if they gain the whole world but forfeit their life? Or what will they give in return for their life? For the Son of Man is to come with his angels in the glory of his Father, and then he will repay everyone for what has been done. Truly I tell you, there are some standing here who will not taste death before they see the Son of Man coming in his kingdom."

- We have to die so that we can live. We have to root out what is bad in order that the good within us can flourish. To share the glory of Christ, we have to share his suffering; this makes no sense except through faith in Christ.

- Comfort becomes a priority when the world is a rough place. Perhaps we need to be careful not to cushion ourselves too much, careful not to forget that the cross is always within sight of the Christian. We may not want to make life difficult for ourselves, but our prayer acknowledges the pain that is experienced by others in which Jesus still suffers.

Saturday 8th August
Saint Dominic, Priest
Matthew 17:14–20

When they came to the crowd, a man came to him, knelt before him, and said, "Lord, have mercy on my son, for he is an epileptic and he suffers terribly; he often falls into the fire and often into the water. And I brought him to your disciples, but they could not cure him." Jesus answered, "You faithless and perverse generation, how much longer must I be with you? How much longer must I put up with you? Bring him here to me." And Jesus rebuked the demon, and it came out of him, and the boy was cured instantly. Then the disciples came to Jesus privately and said, "Why could we not cast it out?" He said to them, "Because of your little faith. For truly I tell you, if you have faith the size of a mustard seed, you will say to this mountain, 'Move from here to there', and it will move; and nothing will be impossible for you."

- We can understand this story only through contemplation. In prayer see the people involved, hear what they are saying, and note what they are doing. Enter the scene and question the participants, the Lord included. Listen closely before asking your questions.

- What answers do you get? Jesus has no doubt that if we had enough faith we could move mountains. I pray for an increase in faith and a deeper love of Jesus. Lord, "I believe; help my unbelief" (Mark 9:24).

August 9—August 15

Something to think and pray about each day this week:

Ignatius says that people often make decisions backward. They say, "I want to do this. Now how can I do this and somehow praise, reverence, and serve God? How can I work the means around to the end?" Ignatius says that we should instead start with the end. The end is being a disciple of Jesus: "What does it mean for me to love as Jesus loved?" The most challenging line in all of Scripture is "Love one another as I have loved you." What could be more challenging? That makes the Golden Rule look like a piece of cake. This love of altruism and self-sacrifice is our goal. Ignatius wants us to reflect first on why we are here and what the purpose of our life is. Then in that context, we choose the best means to get there.

—Gerald M. Fagin, SJ, *Discovering Your Dream*

The Presence of God

To be present is to arrive as one is and open up to the other.
At this instant, as I arrive here, God is present waiting for me.
God always arrives before me, desiring to connect with me
even more than my most intimate friend.
I take a moment and greet my loving God.

Freedom

Leave me here freely all alone. / In cell where never sunlight shone. /
Should no one ever speak to me. / This golden silence makes me free!

—Part of a poem by Bl. Titus Brandsma, written while
he was a prisoner at Dachau concentration camp

Consciousness

Where am I with God? With others?
Do I have something to be grateful for? Then I give thanks.
Is there something I am sorry for? Then I ask forgiveness.

The Word

I take my time to read the word of God slowly, a few times, allowing myself to dwell on anything that strikes me. (Please turn to the Scripture on the following pages. Inspiration points are there, should you need them. When you are ready, return here to continue.)

Conversation

How has God's word moved me? Has it left me cold?
Has it consoled me or moved me to act in a new way?
I imagine Jesus standing or sitting beside me;
I turn and share my feelings with him.

Conclusion

Glory be to the Father, and to the Son, and to the Holy Spirit,
As it was in the beginning, is now and ever shall be,
World without end. Amen.

Sunday 9th August
Nineteenth Sunday in Ordinary Time
Matthew 14:22–33

Immediately he made the disciples get into the boat and go on ahead to the other side, while he dismissed the crowds. And after he had dismissed the crowds, he went up the mountain by himself to pray. When evening came, he was there alone, but by this time the boat, battered by the waves, was far from the land, for the wind was against them. And early in the morning he came walking toward them on the sea. But when the disciples saw him walking on the sea, they were terrified, saying, "It is a ghost!" And they cried out in fear. But immediately Jesus spoke to them and said, "Take heart, it is I; do not be afraid." Peter answered him, "Lord, if it is you, command me to come to you on the water." He said, "Come." So Peter got out of the boat, started walking on the water, and came toward Jesus. But when he noticed the strong wind, he became frightened, and beginning to sink, he cried out, "Lord, save me!" Jesus immediately reached out his hand and caught him, saying to him, "You of little faith, why did you doubt?" When they got into the boat, the wind ceased. And those in the boat worshiped him, saying, "Truly you are the Son of God."

• The apostles, despite living side by side with Jesus and seeing the wonders he worked, were still amazed when he calmed the storm. So many storms batter our lives: sin and temptation, anxiety, fear, and despair. And yet Jesus is no farther away from us than he was from the disciples in that small boat.

• When we're in the storm, we bring our troubles to Jesus. We sit with him in prayer and let him know how we are and just allow his calm to come over us. Our prayer gives us the courage and strength to deal with the weather as it comes.

Monday 10th August
Saint Lawrence, Deacon and Martyr
John 12:24–26

"Very truly, I tell you, unless a grain of wheat falls into the earth and dies, it remains just a single grain; but if it dies, it bears much fruit. Those who love their life lose it, and those who hate their life in this world will keep it for eternal life. Whoever serves me must follow me, and where I am, there will my servant be also. Whoever serves me, the Father will honor."

- Without the right conditions, a grain will lie dormant and never bear fruit. The grain needs sun, rain, and nutrients before it can begin to grow. Is my faith life dormant? Or am I nourishing it so that it will yield an abundant harvest? What needs to die in me that I may live more fully?

- The image Jesus presents is simple yet strong. He does not speak of "passing away" or "falling asleep" but of death and loss. Faith in Jesus strengthens me to look beyond death to the beginning of new life. Jesus speaks to me as friend and calls me into his family.

Tuesday 11th August
Saint Clare, Virgin
Matthew 18:1–5, 10, 12–14

At that time the disciples came to Jesus and asked, "Who is the greatest in the kingdom of heaven?" He called a child, whom he put among them, and said, "Truly I tell you, unless you change and become like children, you will never enter the kingdom of heaven. Whoever becomes humble like this child is the greatest in the kingdom of heaven. Whoever welcomes one such child in my name welcomes me. . . . Take care that you do not despise one of these little ones; for, I tell you, in heaven their angels continually see the face of my Father in heaven. . . . What do you think? If a shepherd has a hundred sheep, and one of them has gone astray, does he not leave the ninety-nine on the mountains and go in search of the one that went astray? And if he finds it, truly I tell you, he rejoices over it more than over the ninety-nine that never went astray? So it is not the will of your Father in heaven that one of these little ones should be lost."

- Jesus is telling us clearly that every life is precious in his eyes. Every person I meet is invaluable and irreplaceable. Jesus turns conventional attitudes upside down: the little ones, the people whom the world does not rate as important, are the most precious of all. Will my attitudes today reflect this?

- If I were the only person in the world needing salvation, Jesus would still die for me. Does that thrill me or terrify me? Why?

Wednesday 12th August
Matthew 18:15–20

"If another member of the church sins against you, go and point out the fault when the two of you are alone. If the member listens to you, you have regained that one. But if you are not listened to, take one or two others along with you, so that every word may be confirmed by the evidence of two or three witnesses. If the member refuses to listen to them, tell it to the church; and if the offender refuses to listen even to the church, let such a one be to you as a Gentile and a tax collector. Truly I tell you, whatever you bind on earth will be bound in heaven, and whatever you loose on earth will be loosed in heaven. Again, truly I tell you, if two of you agree on earth about anything you ask, it will be done for you by my Father in heaven. For where two or three are gathered in my name, I am there among them."

- Perhaps Jesus does not mean that the agreement disciples might reach in prayer is a guarantee of God's miraculous intervention but sees that the miracle lies in two people being fully of one mind and heart. When people trust one another and believe in God, the reign of God is brought into being.

- If I am upset with somebody, then the first person for me to approach is that person, with respect and kindness, whether it is a relative or an acquaintance, a parish priest or a coworker. So many people start by running to authority. Whatever I do when I am upset, Lord, help me do it in charity.

Thursday 13th August
Matthew 18:21—19:1

Then Peter came and said to him, "Lord, if another member of the church sins against me, how often should I forgive? As many as seven times?" Jesus said to him, "Not seven times, but, I tell you, seventy-seven times. For this reason the kingdom of heaven may be compared to a king who wished to settle accounts with his slaves. When he began the reckoning, one who owed him ten thousand talents was brought to him; and, as he could not pay, his lord ordered him to be sold, together with his wife and children and all his possessions, and payment to be made. So the slave fell on his knees before him, saying, 'Have patience with me, and I will pay you everything.' And out of pity for him, the lord of that slave released him and forgave him the debt. But that same slave, as he went out, came upon one of his fellow slaves who owed him a hundred denarii; and seizing him by the throat, he said, 'Pay what you owe.' Then his fellow slave fell down and pleaded with him, 'Have patience with me, and I will pay you.' But he refused; then he went and threw him into prison until he should pay the debt. When his fellow slaves saw what had happened, they were greatly distressed, and they went and reported to their lord all that had taken place. Then his lord summoned him and said to him, 'You wicked slave! I forgave you all that debt because you pleaded with me. Should you not have had mercy on your fellow slave, as I had mercy on you?' And in anger his lord handed him over to be tortured until he should pay his entire debt. So my heavenly Father will also do to every one of you, if you do not forgive your brother or sister from your heart." When Jesus had finished saying these things, he left Galilee and went to the region of Judea beyond the Jordan.

- Jesus points out that forgiveness knows no limit.
- The inability to forgive those who have offended us can be corrosive and the harboring of hurts destructive. Are there people you can't forgive? If so, devote time to pray for the ability to do so, and linger over the phrase in the Our Father: "forgive us our debts, as we also have forgiven our debtors" (Matthew 6:12).

Friday 14th August
Saint Maximilian Kolbe, Priest and Martyr
Matthew 19:3–12

Some Pharisees came to him, and to test him they asked, "Is it lawful for a man to divorce his wife for any cause?" He answered, "Have you not read that the one who made them at the beginning 'made them male and female,' and said, 'For this reason a man shall leave his father and mother and be joined to his wife, and the two shall become one flesh'? So they are no longer two, but one flesh. Therefore what God has joined together, let no one separate." They said to him, "Why then did Moses command us to give a certificate of dismissal and to divorce her?" He said to them, "It was because you were so hard-hearted that Moses allowed you to divorce your wives, but from the beginning it was not so. And I say to you, whoever divorces his wife, except for unchastity, and marries another commits adultery." His disciples said to him, "If such is the case of a man with his wife, it is better not to marry." But he said to them, "Not everyone can accept this teaching, but only those to whom it is given. For there are eunuchs who have been so from birth, and there are eunuchs who have been made eunuchs by others, and there are eunuchs who have made themselves eunuchs for the sake of the kingdom of heaven. Let anyone accept this who can."

- Whether we marry or remain single, we are called to live wholeheartedly. I pray with thanks for all the people I know who have been able to live out their desires and dreams. I pray with compassion for all who have been disappointed by the changing circumstances of their lives.

- God's desire is for man and woman to come together in body, mind, and soul. In the commitment of marriage, the two are deeply united. Jesus doesn't seem to give a last word on marriage and unfaithfulness here. He looks with compassion on our human faults and failings. His heart reaches out to all who are in any way connected with marital difficulties and breakup.

Saturday 15th August
The Assumption of the Blessed Virgin Mary
Luke 1:39–56

In those days Mary set out and went with haste to a Judean town in the hill country, where she entered the house of Zechariah and greeted Elizabeth. When Elizabeth heard Mary's greeting, the child leapt in her womb. And Elizabeth was filled with the Holy Spirit and exclaimed with a loud cry, "Blessed are you among women, and blessed is the fruit of your womb. And why has this happened to me, that the mother of my Lord comes to me? For as soon as I heard the sound of your greeting, the child in my womb leapt for joy. And blessed is she who believed that there would be a fulfillment of what was spoken to her by the Lord." And Mary said, "My soul magnifies the Lord, and my spirit rejoices in God my Savior, for he has looked with favor on the lowliness of his servant. Surely, from now on all generations will call me blessed; for the Mighty One has done great things for me, and holy is his name. His mercy is for those who fear him from generation to generation. He has shown strength with his arm; he has scattered the proud in the thoughts of their hearts. He has brought down the powerful from their thrones, and lifted up the lowly; he has filled the hungry with good things, and sent the rich away empty. He has helped his servant Israel, in remembrance of his mercy, according to the promise he made to our ancestors, to Abraham and to his descendants forever." And Mary remained with her for about three months and then returned to her home.

- There is no false humility in Mary's prayer. There is the true humility of knowing that all that is being accomplished in her is through God's action. Mary accepts the greatness of her mission fully, joyfully, and expectantly.

- Lord, help me do your will joyfully and fearlessly. I want to answer your call with an exultant "Yes!" secure in the knowledge that, as I move into the unknown, my journey will be made radiant by your transfiguring presence.

August 16—August 22

Something to think and pray about each day this week:

It takes, I think, a lot more humility than pride to try a lot of things: to be willing to make a fool of yourself for Christ, to give yourself totally and completely to some job that has never been tried before. It takes humility, I think, to put yourself in a position where others will take advantage of you and think you some sort of "easy mark," to do this so that others may love Christ more. Actually, many times the truly humble person will look very proud, for she isn't thinking of her own image or what others are thinking of her. She'll be out to give her total self to the job she has to do and to her whole life and not care what others think, or don't think, of her, or care whether others talk or don't talk. This looks like pride, but I think it takes a lot of real humility to act like this.

—Walter J. Ciszek, SJ, *With God in America*

The Presence of God
As I sit here, the beating of my heart,
the ebb and flow of my breathing, the movements of my mind
are all signs of God's ongoing creation of me.
I pause for a moment and become aware
of this presence of God within me.

Freedom
It is so easy to get caught up
with the trappings of wealth in this life.
Grant, O Lord, that I may be free
from greed and selfishness.
Remind me that the best things in life are free:
Love, laughter, caring, and sharing.

Consciousness
Knowing that God loves me unconditionally, I can afford to be honest
about how I am.
How has the day been, and how do I feel now? I share my feelings openly
with the Lord.

The Word
Lord Jesus, you became human to communicate with me.
You walked and worked on this earth.
You endured the heat and struggled with the cold.
All your time on this earth was spent in caring for humanity.
You healed the sick, you raised the dead.
Most important of all, you saved me from death.
(Please turn to the Scripture on the following pages. Inspiration points
are there, should you need them. When you are ready, return here to
continue.)

Conversation
Sometimes I wonder what I might say if I were to meet you in person, Lord.
I think I might say, "Thank you" because you are always there for me.

Conclusion
I thank God for these moments we have spent together and for any insights I have been given concerning the text.

Sunday 16th August
Twentieth Sunday in Ordinary Time
Matthew 15:21–28

Jesus left that place and went away to the district of Tyre and Sidon. Just then a Canaanite woman from that region came out and started shouting, "Have mercy on me, Lord, Son of David; my daughter is tormented by a demon." But he did not answer her at all. And his disciples came and urged him, saying, "Send her away, for she keeps shouting after us." He answered, "I was sent only to the lost sheep of the house of Israel." But she came and knelt before him, saying, "Lord, help me." He answered, "It is not fair to take the children's food and throw it to the dogs." She said, "Yes, Lord, yet even the dogs eat the crumbs that fall from their masters' table." Then Jesus answered her, "Woman, great is your faith! Let it be done for you as you wish." And her daughter was healed instantly.

- In the tradition preserved for us in the Scriptures, Jesus is presented to us as a formidable debater, but in this instance the Canaanite woman comfortably wins the debating point. Jesus praises the woman for her faith, but what was her faith? What did she believe about Jesus? One would love to know her subsequent history. Did this act of Jesus mark a turning point in her life? We do not know.

- In a way, this pagan woman can give us a lesson on prayer. We are not always happy with our lot or the lot of others, and we should express our real feelings to Christ, not just our sanitized ones. Jesus hears my prayer.

Monday 17th August
Matthew 19:16–22

Then someone came to him and said, "Teacher, what good deed must I do to have eternal life?" And he said to him, "Why do you ask me about what is good? There is only one who is good. If you wish to enter into life, keep the commandments." He said to him, "Which ones?" And Jesus said, "You shall not murder; You shall not commit adultery; You shall not steal; You shall not bear false witness; Honor your father and mother; also, You shall love your neighbor as yourself." The young man said to him, "I have kept all these; what do I still lack?" Jesus said to him, "If you wish to be perfect, go, sell your possessions, and give the money to the poor, and you will have treasure in heaven; then come, follow me." When the young man heard this word, he went away grieving, for he had many possessions.

- The parable invites us to consider what possessions might be holding us back from following Christ in some ways. I pray for the grace to see more clearly those things that get in the way of my giving myself fully to the service of Christ.

- Interestingly, the commandments Jesus recites to the rich young man do not include the first three, which all relate to our relationship with God. Instead, he lists those that address our relationships with one another. The message is clear: we do not live in isolation. Love for our neighbor is the door to eternal life. What attachments in my life are holding me back from a deeper relationship with my neighbor and with God?

Tuesday 18th August
Matthew 19:23–30

Then Jesus said to his disciples, "Truly I tell you, it will be hard for a rich person to enter the kingdom of heaven. Again I tell you, it is easier for a camel to go through the eye of a needle than for someone who is rich to enter the kingdom of God." When the disciples heard this, they were greatly astounded and said, "Then who can be saved?" But Jesus looked at them and said, "For mortals it is impossible, but for God all things are possible." Then Peter said in reply, "Look, we have left everything and followed you. What then will we have?" Jesus said to them, "Truly I tell you, at the renewal of all things, when the Son of Man is seated on the throne of his glory, you who have followed me will also sit on twelve thrones, judging the twelve tribes of Israel. And everyone who has left houses or brothers or sisters or father or mother or children or fields, for my name's sake, will receive a hundredfold, and will inherit eternal life. But many who are first will be last, and the last will be first."

- The trouble with possessions is that they can too easily possess us. Jesus calls for radical change in our lives, a change that can seem unattainable. However, he reminds us that, while something may seem impossible for mortals, for God, all things are possible.

- Do I believe that God will ask nothing of me that I am not, with his help, capable of doing?

Wednesday 19th August
Matthew 20:1–16

Jesus said to his disciples, "For the kingdom of heaven is like a landowner who went out early in the morning to hire laborers for his vineyard. After agreeing with the laborers for the usual daily wage, he sent them into his vineyard. When he went out about nine o'clock, he saw others standing idle in the marketplace; and he said to them, 'You also go into the vineyard, and I will pay you whatever is right.' So they went. When he went out again about noon and about three o'clock, he did the same. And about five o'clock he went out and found others standing around; and he said to them, 'Why are you standing here idle all day?' They said to him, 'Because no one has hired us.' He said to them, 'You also go into the vineyard.' When evening came, the owner of the vineyard said to his manager, 'Call the laborers and give them their pay, beginning with the last and then going to the first.' When those hired about five o'clock came, each of them received the usual daily wage. Now when the first came, they thought they would receive more; but each of them also received the usual daily wage. And when they received it, they grumbled against the landowner, saying, 'These last worked only one hour, and you have made them equal to us who have borne the burden of the day and the scorching heat.' But he replied to one of them, 'Friend, I am doing you no wrong; did you not agree with me for the usual daily wage? Take what belongs to you and go; I choose to give to this last the same as I give to you. Am I not allowed to do what I choose with what belongs to me? Or are you envious because I am generous?' So the last will be first, and the first will be last."

- In a well-balanced system, the fewer hours a person worked, the less pay he should have received. But the vineyard owner knew that what he offered the workers was minimal and that, to give a person less, he would leave families hungry. He went beyond justice, motivated by compassion.

- What is my gut reaction to this story? I bring my feelings to God in prayer.

Thursday 20th August
Saint Bernard, Abbot and Doctor of the Church
Matthew 22:1–14

Once more Jesus spoke to them in parables, saying: "The kingdom of heaven may be compared to a king who gave a wedding banquet for his son. He sent his slaves to call those who had been invited to the wedding banquet, but they would not come. Again he sent other slaves, saying, 'Tell those who have been invited: Look, I have prepared my dinner, my oxen and my fat calves have been slaughtered, and everything is ready; come to the wedding banquet.' But they made light of it and went away, one to his farm, another to his business, while the rest seized his slaves, maltreated them, and killed them. The king was enraged. He sent his troops, destroyed those murderers, and burned their city. Then he said to his slaves, 'The wedding is ready, but those invited were not worthy. Go therefore into the main streets, and invite everyone you find to the wedding banquet.' Those slaves went out into the streets and gathered all whom they found, both good and bad; so the wedding hall was filled with guests. But when the king came in to see the guests, he noticed a man there who was not wearing a wedding robe, and he said to him, 'Friend, how did you get in here without a wedding robe?' And he was speechless. Then the king said to the attendants, 'Bind him hand and foot, and throw him into the outer darkness, where there will be weeping and gnashing of teeth.' For many are called, but few are chosen."

- I ask God to help me to respond as best I can to this real invitation. Is a quiet voice whispering to me?

- O Lord, how we need your constant invitation to come to you and learn from you. Rid us of our garments of selfishness, our judgmental attitudes, our stubborn hearts, and clothe us instead with your garments of salvation.

Friday 21st August
Saint Pius X, Pope
Matthew 22:34–40

When the Pharisees heard that Jesus had silenced the Sadducees, they gathered together, and one of them, a lawyer, asked him a question to test him. "Teacher, which commandment in the law is the greatest?" He said to him, "'You shall love the Lord your God with all your heart, and with all your soul, and with all your mind.' This is the greatest and first commandment. And a second is like it: 'You shall love your neighbor as yourself.' On these two commandments hang all the law and the prophets."

- We cannot love God and then refuse to love our neighbor. Jesus extends the meaning of *neighbor* to include every single person and not just the people of one's own race, religion, or family.

- God's standard of love is the love of Jesus who died for us. "God proves his love for us in that while we still were sinners Christ died for us" (Romans 5:8). While Jesus praises the lawyer, the man must make the crucial step of committing himself to follow Jesus.

Saturday 22nd August
The Queenship of the Blessed Virgin Mary
Matthew 23:1–12

Then Jesus said to the crowds and to his disciples, "The scribes and the Pharisees sit on Moses' seat; therefore, do whatever they teach you and follow it; but do not do as they do, for they do not practice what they teach. They tie up heavy burdens, hard to bear, and lay them on the shoulders of others; but they themselves are unwilling to lift a finger to move them. They do all their deeds to be seen by others; for they make their phylacteries broad and their fringes long. They love to have the place of honor at banquets and the best seats in the synagogues, and to be greeted with respect in the marketplaces, and to have people call them rabbi. But you are not to be called rabbi, for you have one teacher, and you are all students. And call no one your father on earth, for you have one Father—the one in heaven. Nor are you to be called instructors, for you have one instructor, the Messiah. The greatest among you will be your servant. All who exalt themselves will be humbled, and all who humble themselves will be exalted."

- One of Jesus' gravest judgments of the religious leaders was that they made life burdensome for others. They weighed down the people with unnecessary regulations and petty rules. How do I see people in power today burdening those over whom they have power?

- I pray for clarity of vision, to look always to the Father and to learn from the Son how to treat others.

Twenty-First Week in Ordinary Time
August 23—August 29

Something to think and pray about each day this week:

Speed and activity conquer all. But cultivating a recollected heart that enters readily into prayer and contemplation of the deepest, most meaningful things is not something we can do quickly or busily. Recollection is not a process of efficiency or even a personal achievement; it is rooted more in emptiness, stillness. It is a hidden gift from God that requires patience, practice, repetition, and, ultimately, humility, the decision to make ourselves available, without an agenda, to the work of the Holy Spirit. To our distracted world, the practice of spiritual recollection might even look like a waste of time. Meekness and interiority are seen as weaknesses to be overcome, even medicated or educated out of us with assertiveness training.

—Elizabeth M. Kelly, *Jesus Approaches*

The Presence of God

Dear Jesus, I come to you today longing for your presence. I desire to love you as you love me. May nothing ever separate me from you.

Freedom

Lord, grant me the grace to have freedom of the Spirit. Cleanse my heart and soul so that I may live joyously in your love.

Consciousness

Where am I with God? With others?
Do I have something to be grateful for? Then I give thanks.
Is there something I am sorry for? Then I ask forgiveness.

The Word

The word of God comes down to us through the Scriptures. May the Holy Spirit enlighten my mind and my heart to respond to the Gospel teachings. (Please turn to the Scripture on the following pages. Inspiration points are there, should you need them. When you are ready, return here to continue.)

Conversation

How has God's word moved me? Has it left me cold?
Has it consoled me or moved me to act in a new way?
I imagine Jesus standing or sitting beside me;
I turn and share my feelings with him.

Conclusion

I thank God for these moments we have spent together and for any insights I have been given concerning the text.

Sunday 23rd August
Twenty-First Sunday in Ordinary Time
Matthew 16:13–20

Now when Jesus came into the district of Caesarea Philippi, he asked his disciples, "Who do people say that the Son of Man is?" And they said, "Some say John the Baptist, but others Elijah, and still others Jeremiah or one of the prophets." He said to them, "But who do you say that I am?" Simon Peter answered, "You are the Messiah, the Son of the living God." And Jesus answered him, "Blessed are you, Simon son of Jonah! For flesh and blood has not revealed this to you, but my Father in heaven. And I tell you, you are Peter, and on this rock I will build my church, and the gates of Hades will not prevail against it. I will give you the keys of the kingdom of heaven, and whatever you bind on earth will be bound in heaven, and whatever you loose on earth will be loosed in heaven." Then he sternly ordered the disciples not to tell anyone that he was the Messiah.

- Jesus could trust Peter to be honest—he would say what was on his mind and in his heart. As Jesus asks me the same question, I answer honestly, knowing that nothing I say will alienate Jesus.

- Am I open to Jesus' question, "Who do *you* say that I am?" This text has been used so often for apologetic purposes that it is hard to recapture the drama, the uncertain silence, that must have followed Jesus' question. He wondered what they would say and wonders what I say to the same question. Lord, I linger with this question: *What are you to me?*

Monday 24th August
Saint Bartholomew, Apostle
John 1:45–51

Philip found Nathanael and said to him, "We have found him about whom Moses in the law and also the prophets wrote, Jesus son of Joseph from Nazareth." Nathanael said to him, "Can anything good come out of Nazareth?" Philip said to him, "Come and see." When Jesus saw Nathanael coming toward him, he said of him, "Here is truly an Israelite in whom there is no deceit!" Nathanael asked him, "Where did you get to know me?" Jesus answered, "I saw you under the fig tree before Philip called you." Nathanael replied, "Rabbi, you are the Son of God! You are the King of Israel!" Jesus answered, "Do you believe because I told you that I saw you under the fig tree? You will see greater things than these." And he said to him, "Very truly, I tell you, you will see heaven opened and the angels of God ascending and descending upon the Son of Man."

- Saint Bartholomew, whose feast we celebrate today, is listed among the twelve apostles in the synoptic Gospels (Matthew, Mark, and Luke) but is not mentioned by the name Bartholomew in the Gospel of John. He also appears as one of the witnesses of the Ascension. There are many references to him in nonhistorical literature.

- Nathanael, whom some commentators identify with Bartholomew, is promised that as Israel (Jacob) of the Old Testament saw the glory of God in the vision of the ladder, so he (Nathanael), who is worthy of the name Israel, will see the glory of the Son of Man at the miracle at Cana. I pray today for the grace to see the glory of the Lord in all that is around me. "The World is charged with the grandeur of God" (Gerard Manley Hopkins).

Tuesday 25th August
Matthew 23:23–26

Jesus said, "Woe to you, scribes and Pharisees, hypocrites! For you tithe mint, dill, and cummin, and have neglected the weightier matters of the law: justice and mercy and faith. It is these you ought to have practiced without neglecting the others. You blind guides! You strain out a gnat but swallow a camel! Woe to you, scribes and Pharisees, hypocrites! For you clean the outside of the cup and of the plate, but inside they are full of greed and self-indulgence. You blind Pharisee! First clean the inside of the cup, so that the outside also may become clean."

- Attention to outward appearance is not a modern phenomenon: archaeologists find cosmetics and body art in almost every ancient culture. Jesus reminds us that the more attention we pay to the outside, the less likely we are to give care to where life really is. I consider how God sees me and how God wants me to resist any urge to present only my best side. God loves me as I am and invites me to see myself for who I am.

- Outsiders are often shocked at the hypocrisy of Christians who worship God on Sundays and then tear apart their neighbor's reputation during the rest of the week. Am I ever guilty? Cleaning "the inside of the cup" takes constant vigilance.

Wednesday 26th August
Matthew 23:27–32

"Woe to you, scribes and Pharisees, hypocrites! For you are like whitewashed tombs, which on the outside look beautiful, but inside they are full of the bones of the dead and of all kinds of filth. So you also on the outside look righteous to others, but inside you are full of hypocrisy and lawlessness. Woe to you, scribes and Pharisees, hypocrites! For you build the tombs of the prophets and decorate the graves of the righteous, and you say, 'If we had lived in the days of our ancestors, we would not have taken part with them in shedding the blood of the prophets.' Thus you testify against yourselves that you are descendants of those who murdered the prophets. Fill up, then, the measure of your ancestors."

- How do I regard those with whom I disagree strongly? Do I personalize social and political differences? Can I relate in any way to those Jesus is rebuking in this passage?

- Jesus challenges the scribes and Pharisees to look at what is going on in their inner selves, the part they hide from one another, and indeed, from themselves. Father, we, too, can live in an unrealistic way, doing our own thing and having no concern for how we treat those whose paths we cross.

Thursday 27th August
Saint Monica
Matthew 24:42–51

"Keep awake therefore, for you do not know on what day your Lord is coming. But understand this: if the owner of the house had known in what part of the night the thief was coming, he would have stayed awake and would not have let his house be broken into. Therefore you also must be ready, for the Son of Man is coming at an unexpected hour. Who then is the faithful and wise slave, whom his master has put in charge of his household, to give the other slaves their allowance of food at the proper time? Blessed is that slave whom his master will find at work when he arrives. Truly I tell you, he will put that one in charge of all his possessions.

But if that wicked slave says to himself, 'My master is delayed,' and he begins to beat his fellow slaves, and eats and drinks with drunkards, the master of that slave will come on a day when he does not expect him and at an hour that he does not know. He will cut him in pieces and put him with the hypocrites, where there will be weeping and gnashing of teeth."

- Throughout the gospels Jesus speaks about being "awake" and paying attention. Am I so preoccupied with the busyness of life and my own particular cares and concerns that I sometimes forget to watch and pray?

- The idea that God might come at any hour makes some people nervous and afraid. If I let Jesus lead me into a deeper love of God, I realize that I have nothing to fear but am able—at any time—to say to God, "Look, here I am."

Friday 28th August
Saint Augustine, Bishop and Doctor of the Church
Matthew 25:1–13

"Then the kingdom of heaven will be like this. Ten bridesmaids took their lamps and went to meet the bridegroom. Five of them were foolish, and five were wise. When the foolish took their lamps, they took no oil with them; but the wise took flasks of oil with their lamps. As the bridegroom was delayed, all of them became drowsy and slept. But at midnight there was a shout, 'Look! Here is the bridegroom! Come out to meet him.' Then all those bridesmaids got up and trimmed their lamps. The foolish said to the wise, 'Give us some of your oil, for our lamps are going out.' But the wise replied, 'No! there will not be enough for you and for us; you had better go to the dealers and buy some for yourselves.' And while they went to buy it, the bridegroom came, and those who were ready went with him into the wedding banquet; and the door was shut. Later the other bridesmaids came also, saying, 'Lord, lord, open to us.' But he replied, 'Truly I tell you, I do not know you.'" Keep awake therefore, for you know neither the day nor the hour."

- The foolish and the wise are often contrasted in the Bible. The foolish were those who thought they knew exactly when the groom would arrive, so, unlike the wise, they took just enough oil for the wait, and then discovered it was not enough. They were left out not because they were wicked but because they were caught unprepared by the groom's arrival. The challenge to be wise is always linked to a humility and flexibility.

- Father, you wait patiently for us to turn to you and accept all that you are offering us through the power of your Holy Spirit. Help us to keep our lamps lit with the oil of prayer. With that light to help us, we can do good works and share your love with others.

Saturday 29th August
The Passion of Saint John the Baptist
Mark 6:17–29

For Herod himself had sent men who arrested John, bound him, and put him in prison on account of Herodias, his brother Philip's wife, because Herod had married her. For John had been telling Herod, "It is not lawful for you to have your brother's wife." And Herodias had a grudge against him, and wanted to kill him. But she could not, for Herod feared John, knowing that he was a righteous and holy man, and he protected him. When he heard him, he was greatly perplexed; and yet he liked to listen to him. But an opportunity came when Herod on his birthday gave a banquet for his courtiers and officers and for the leaders of Galilee. When his daughter Herodias came in and danced, she pleased Herod and his guests; and the king said to the girl, "Ask me for whatever you wish, and I will give it." And he solemnly swore to her, "Whatever you ask me, I will give you, even half of my kingdom." She went out and said to her mother, "What should I ask for?" She replied, "The head of John the baptizer." Immediately she rushed back to the king and requested, "I want you to give me at once the head of John the Baptist on a platter." The king was deeply grieved; yet out of regard for his oaths and for the guests, he did not want to refuse her. Immediately the king sent a soldier of the guard with orders to bring John's head. He went and beheaded him in the prison, brought his head on a platter, and gave it to the girl. Then the girl gave it to her mother. When his disciples heard about it, they came and took his body, and laid it in a tomb."

- John the Baptist was beheaded because he spoke truth to power. The man who prepared the way for Jesus was executed at the whim of a corrupt ruler. Those who work for justice in the world or witness to their faith today often face difficult and even life-threatening situations. I pause to remember them in prayer.

- When it came to John the Baptist, Herod was what we would call conflicted. He would not repent and follow John, yet he tried to protect him and wanted to listen to him. In the end, Herod chose against John. Wavering between opposite loyalties or principles usually comes to a bad ending. Am I wavering today?

August 30—September 5

Something to think and pray about each day this week:

I urge you to ask God to purge from your heart the vestiges of fear that produce feelings of insignificance and unworthiness. You do God no favor by thinking stingily or meanly about the person who is the apple of God's eye—you. In *The Tempest of God*, the Carmelite Iain Matthew writes very movingly of the spirituality of St. John of the Cross, the sixteenth-century Spanish Carmelite mystic. At one point, Matthew notes John's insistence on faith rather than evidence for the development of the relationship with God. Matthew goes on: "The danger envisaged is not so much that we shall trust in the wrong thing, but that we shall stop trusting at all; that, while we may never say it in so many words, we shall cease to believe that we are a factor in God's life."

A factor in God's life! That is how much God values each one of us, according to one of the great mystics and saints of Christianity.

—William A. Barry, SJ, *A Friendship Like No Other*

The Presence of God
God is with me, but more,
God is within me, giving me existence.
Let me dwell for a moment on God's life-giving presence
in my body, my mind, my heart,
and in the whole of my life.

Freedom
Lord, you created me to live in freedom. May your Holy Spirit guide me
to follow you freely. Instill in my heart a desire to know and love you
more each day.

Consciousness
In God's loving presence I unwind the past day,
starting from now and looking back, moment by moment.
I gather in all the goodness and light, in gratitude.
I attend to the shadows and what they say to me,
seeking healing, courage, forgiveness.

The Word
God speaks to each of us individually. I listen attentively to hear what he
is saying to me. Read the text a few times, then listen. (Please turn to the
Scripture on the following pages. Inspiration points are there, should you
need them. When you are ready, return here to continue.)

Conversation
Jesus, you always welcomed little children when you walked on this earth.
Teach me to have a childlike trust in you. Teach me to live in the knowledge that you will never abandon me.

Conclusion
I thank God for these moments we have spent together and for any insights I have been given concerning the text.

Sunday 30th August
Twenty-Second Sunday in Ordinary Time
Matthew 16:21–27

From that time on, Jesus began to show his disciples that he must go to Jerusalem and undergo great suffering at the hands of the elders and chief priests and scribes, and be killed, and on the third day be raised. And Peter took him aside and began to rebuke him, saying, "God forbid it, Lord! This must never happen to you." But he turned and said to Peter, "Get behind me, Satan! You are a stumbling block to me; for you are setting your mind not on divine things but on human things." Then Jesus told his disciples, "If any want to become my followers, let them deny themselves and take up their cross and follow me. For those who want to save their life will lose it, and those who lose their life for my sake will find it. For what will it profit them if they gain the whole world but forfeit their life? Or what will they give in return for their life? For the Son of Man is to come with his angels in the glory of his Father, and then he will repay everyone for what has been done."

• Jesus knew very well what it would mean to make love the greatest commandment and to remain close to the poor. Yet he did not shy away from his mission; on the contrary, he fiercely scolded his closest friend, even calling him Satan. He then calls us to follow him on his way to the cross by carrying our own cross every day. I ask Jesus to defend me from the traps of Satan and to give me an ever-greater desire to be his true disciple.

• Our culture seems to claim that those who want to save their lives can do so, mostly by possessing more things and living in ever greater comfort. Jesus pulls no punches; he challenges us to be ready to lose our lives to be able to save them. I ask myself what this means to me, here and now. Do I feel called to let go of something precious to me so that I can live more fully?

Monday 31st August
Luke 4:16–30

When he came to Nazareth, where he had been brought up, he went to the synagogue on the sabbath day, as was his custom. He stood up to read, and the scroll of the prophet Isaiah was given to him. He unrolled the scroll and found the place where it was written: "The Spirit of the Lord is upon me, because he has anointed me to bring Good News to the poor. He has sent me to proclaim release to the captives and recovery of sight to the blind, to let the oppressed go free, to proclaim the year of the Lord's favor." And he rolled up the scroll, gave it back to the attendant, and sat down. The eyes of all in the synagogue were fixed on him. Then he began to say to them, "Today this scripture has been fulfilled in your hearing." All spoke well of him and were amazed at the gracious words that came from his mouth. They said, "Is not this Joseph's son?" He said to them, "Doubtless you will quote to me this proverb, 'Doctor, cure yourself!' And you will say, 'Do here also in your hometown the things that we have heard you did at Capernaum.'" And he said, "Truly I tell you, no prophet is accepted in the prophet's hometown. But the truth is, there were many widows in Israel in the time of Elijah, when the heaven was shut up three years and six months, and there was a severe famine over all the land; yet Elijah was sent to none of them except to a widow at Zarephath in Sidon. There were also many lepers in Israel in the time of the prophet Elisha, and none of them was cleansed except Naaman the Syrian." When they heard this, all in the synagogue were filled with rage. They got up, drove him out of the town, and led him to the brow of the hill on which their town was built, so that they might hurl him off the cliff. But he passed through the midst of them and went on his way.

- Like the people of Nazareth, I can easily consider that I know Jesus well enough that he should not surprise or shock me. I pray for being able to accept the mystery of my relationship to Jesus, for an open, listening heart.

- Familiarity with Jesus left his listeners unimpressed. The word of God made flesh was reading the word of God to them, and it fell upon deaf ears. Today, let me consciously look for the extraordinary amidst the ordinary.

Tuesday 1st September
Luke 4:31–37

He went down to Capernaum, a city in Galilee, and was teaching them on the sabbath. They were astounded at his teaching, because he spoke with authority. In the synagogue there was a man who had the spirit of an unclean demon, and he cried out with a loud voice, "Let us alone! What have you to do with us, Jesus of Nazareth? Have you come to destroy us? I know who you are, the Holy One of God." But Jesus rebuked him, saying, "Be silent, and come out of him!" When the demon had thrown him down before them, he came out of him without having done him any harm. They were all amazed and kept saying to one another, "What kind of utterance is this? For with authority and power he commands the unclean spirits, and out they come!" And a report about him began to reach every place in the region.

- The people are impressed because Jesus speaks with authority, the authority of his personal integrity and charisma. Often we run the risk of separating the message from his person, reducing it to a mere moral code. I ask to be given the grace to listen to Jesus and to let myself be touched by his authority.

- The Gospels do not shy away from presenting the opposition Jesus had to face whenever he expelled demons. It is no wonder that we, too, find our struggles with evil so difficult. I pray for trust in the power of Jesus even in the face of the strongest opposition. I recall that he is sharing this power with me.

Wednesday 2nd September
Luke 4:38–44

After leaving the synagogue Jesus entered Simon's house. Now Simon's mother-in-law was suffering from a high fever, and they asked him about her. Then he stood over her and rebuked the fever, and it left her. Immediately she got up and began to serve them. As the sun was setting, all those who had any who were sick with various kinds of diseases brought them to him; and he laid his hands on each of them and cured them. Demons also came out of many, shouting, "You are the Son of God!" But he rebuked them and would not allow them to speak, because they knew that he was the Messiah. At daybreak he departed and went into a deserted place. And the crowds were looking for him; and when they reached him, they wanted to prevent him from leaving them. But he said to them, "I must proclaim the Good News of the kingdom of God to the other cities also; for I was sent for this purpose." So he continued proclaiming the message in the synagogues of Judea.

- Jesus is supremely free; his decisions are not taken according to his ratings but by his sense of mission. I ask for greater freedom in my decisions, big or small.

- It may seem surprising that Jesus turned away the crowds who went looking for him. His point of view was different from what might be expected. He spoke from the still point of his life, from his core relationship with his Father. I need my moments of stillness and reflection to anchor myself and rediscover my true identity and direction.

Thursday 3rd September
Saint Gregory the Great, Pope and Doctor of the Church
Luke 5:1–11

Once while Jesus was standing beside the lake of Gennesaret, and the crowd was pressing in on him to hear the word of God, he saw two boats there at the shore of the lake; the fishermen had gone out of them and were washing their nets. He got into one of the boats, the one belonging to Simon, and asked him to put out a little way from the shore. Then he sat down and taught the crowds from the boat. When he had finished speaking, he said to Simon, "Put out into the deep water and let down your nets for a catch." Simon answered, "Master, we have worked all night long but have caught nothing. Yet if you say so, I will let down the nets." When they had done this, they caught so many fish that their nets were beginning to break. So they signaled to their partners in the other boat to come and help them. And they came and filled both boats, so that they began to sink. But when Simon Peter saw it, he fell down at Jesus' knees, saying, "Go away from me, Lord, for I am a sinful man!" For he and all who were with him were amazed at the catch of fish that they had taken; and so also were James and John, sons of Zebedee, who were partners with Simon. Then Jesus said to Simon, "Do not be afraid; from now on you will be catching people." When they had brought their boats to shore, they left everything and followed him.

- "Put out into the deep water and let your nets down for a catch." This was the motto Saint John Paul II chose for the church in the third millennium. I pray for the trust Peter had when faced with this stark command, which seemingly did not make much sense. I ask this grace for the whole church, that the community of believers may be full of courage as it carries out its mission to take the gospel to the whole world.

- I ponder Jesus' response to Peter's confession of himself as a sinner. "Do not be afraid: from now on you will be catching people." Peter is given his mission when he realizes his sinfulness. This insight makes him a better apostle, for he can understand better those he is sent to; he knows he shares their need for mercy and salvation.

Friday 4th September
Luke 5:33–39

[Then the Pharisees and the scribes said to Jesus,] "John's disciples, like the disciples of the Pharisees, frequently fast and pray, but your disciples eat and drink." Jesus said to them, "You cannot make wedding guests fast while the bridegroom is with them, can you? The days will come when the bridegroom will be taken away from them, and then they will fast in those days." He also told them a parable: "No one tears a piece from a new garment and sews it on an old garment; otherwise the new will be torn, and the piece from the new will not match the old. And no one puts new wine into old wineskins; otherwise the new wine will burst the skins and will be spilled, and the skins will be destroyed. But new wine must be put into fresh wineskins. And no one after drinking old wine desires new wine, but says, 'The old is good.'"

- The disciples did what people often do: they made comparisons. Jesus invites them not to look out but to look in and to notice their own attitudes. He does not want them—or us—to be a patchwork of mismatched patterns and practices. He invites us to be made anew, to let go of anything that might hold us back or impair our ability to receive the Good News.

- The Pharisees saw different ways of living and made comparisons; Jesus simply sought life. Jesus saw the ordinary things of the world—torn clothes, spilled wine—and recognized how God is at work in us. How might I look more closely at the bits and pieces of my every day?

Saturday 5th September
Luke 6:1–5

One sabbath while Jesus was going through the grainfields, his disciples plucked some heads of grain, rubbed them in their hands, and ate them. But some of the Pharisees said, "Why are you doing what is not lawful on the sabbath?" Jesus answered, "Have you not read what David did when he and his companions were hungry? He entered the house of God and took and ate the bread of the Presence, which it is not lawful for any but the priests to eat, and gave some to his companions?" Then he said to them, "The Son of Man is lord of the sabbath."

- The Son of Man is lord of the sabbath! No wonder the Jews found Jesus difficult; they rightly understood he was claiming to be God himself. We sometimes reduce Jesus to his message of universal love and forgiveness and are not ready to accept his claim that he is also our Lord and God.

- Any time is a good time to do good, and laws are good only when they are in the service of love. God's central concern is the well-being and happiness of humankind. Let these be my central concern likewise. Pope Francis urges us not to be afraid of making mistakes in our efforts to do good.

September 6—September 12

Something to think and pray about each day this week:

Christ reveals himself in the deeply messy, profoundly awkward world of face-to-face human interaction with people in trouble, conflict, doubt, hunger, thirst, and pain. The real encounter with Christ takes place not when we are all dressed up and polished and nicely groomed and brandishing our résumés but in our broken humanity. Encounter with Christ happens in our longing for a kingdom that is not of this world and that we must search for and work for with all our might in this world.

We're called to offer up our energy, time, and hearts—our very bodies—to "the poor": which is to say, people who, for all our intelligence backed by willpower, we are never going to be able to rescue, shape up, or "fix."

—Heather King, *Holy Desperation*

The Presence of God

"Come to me, all you who are weary and are carrying heavy burdens, and I will give you rest." Here I am, Lord. I come to seek your presence. I long for your healing power.

Freedom

By God's grace I was born to live in freedom. Free to enjoy the pleasures he created for me. Dear Lord, grant that I may live as you intended, with complete confidence in your loving care.

Consciousness

Knowing that God loves me unconditionally, I look honestly over the past day, its events, and my feelings. Do I have something to be grateful for? Then I give thanks. Is there something I am sorry for? Then I ask forgiveness.

The Word

God speaks to each of us individually. I listen attentively to hear what he is saying to me. Read the text a few times, then listen. (Please turn to the Scripture on the following pages. Inspiration points are there, should you need them. When you are ready, return here to continue.)

Conversation

I know with certainty that there were times when you carried me, Lord. There were times when it was through your strength that I got through the dark times in my life.

Conclusion

Glory be to the Father, and to the Son, and to the Holy Spirit,
As it was in the beginning, is now and ever shall be,
World without end. Amen.

Sunday 6th September
Twenty-Third Sunday in Ordinary Time
Matthew 18:15–20

"If another member of the church sins against you, go and point out the fault when the two of you are alone. If the member listens to you, you have regained that one. But if you are not listened to, take one or two others along with you, so that every word may be confirmed by the evidence of two or three witnesses. If the member refuses to listen to them, tell it to the church; and if the offender refuses to listen even to the church, let such a one be to you as a Gentile and a tax collector. Truly I tell you, whatever you bind on earth will be bound in heaven, and whatever you loose on earth will be loosed in heaven. Again, truly I tell you, if two of you agree on earth about anything you ask, it will be done for you by my Father in heaven. For where two or three are gathered in my name, I am there among them."

- The fourth discourse of Matthew's Gospel is addressed to the leading disciples. It gives the rules for the Christian community. It emphasizes the role of dialogue, which is another way of saying that we should at all times seek consensus. It accepts that this is not always possible, and the consequences are clear.

- To what extent do I seek consensus? And to what extent do I try to prevail with my own will, plan, or opinion?

Monday 7th September
Luke 6:6–11

On another sabbath Jesus entered the synagogue and taught, and there was a man there whose right hand was withered. The scribes and the Pharisees watched him to see whether he would cure on the sabbath, so that they might find an accusation against him. Even though he knew what they were thinking, he said to the man who had the withered hand, "Come and stand here." He got up and stood there. Then Jesus said to them, "I ask you, is it lawful to do good or to do harm on the sabbath, to save life or to destroy it?" After looking around at all of them, he said to him, "Stretch out your hand." He did so, and his hand was restored. But they were filled with fury and discussed with one another what they might do to Jesus.

- As I watch the scribes and Pharisees react to Jesus curing a man, I am reminded of my own tendency to close my heart to the suffering of others and even to the presence of God. I look at Jesus and ask to have his compassionate heart, so sensitive and free when faced by human suffering.

- Lord, our church suffers today from those who use their position and power to dominate others. Reveal to me the ways you call me to stretch out my hand to empower those around me.

Tuesday 8th September
The Nativity of the Blessed Virgin Mary
Matthew 1:1–16, 18–23

An account of the genealogy of Jesus the Messiah, the son of David, the son of Abraham. Abraham was the father of Isaac, and Isaac the father of Jacob, and Jacob the father of Judah and his brothers, and Judah the father of Perez and Zerah by Tamar, and Perez the father of Hezron, and Hezron the father of Aram, and Aram the father of Aminadab, and Aminadab the father of Nahshon, and Nahshon the father of Salmon, and Salmon the father of Boaz by Rahab, and Boaz the father of Obed by Ruth, and Obed the father of Jesse, and Jesse the father of King David. And David was the father of Solomon by the wife of Uriah, and Solomon the father of Rehoboam, and Rehoboam the father of Abijah, and Abijah the father of Asaph, and Asaph the father of Jehoshaphat, and Jehoshaphat the father of Joram, and Joram the father of Uzziah, and Uzziah the father of Jotham, and Jotham the father of Ahaz, and Ahaz the father of Hezekiah, and Hezekiah the father of Manasseh, and Manasseh the father of Amos, and Amos the father of Josiah, and Josiah the father of Jechoniah and his brothers, at the time of the deportation to Babylon. And after the deportation to Babylon: Jechoniah was the father of Salathiel, and Salathiel the father of Zerubbabel, and Zerubbabel the father of Abiud, and Abiud the father of Eliakim, and Eliakim the father of Azor, and Azor the father of Zadok, and Zadok the father of Achim, and Achim the father of Eliud, and Eliud the father of Eleazar, and Eleazar the father of Matthan, and Matthan the father of Jacob, and Jacob the father of Joseph the husband of Mary, of whom Jesus was born, who is called the Messiah. . . .

Now the birth of Jesus the Messiah took place in this way. When his mother Mary had been engaged to Joseph, but before they lived together, she was found to be with child from the Holy Spirit. Her husband Joseph, being a righteous man and unwilling to expose her to public disgrace, planned to dismiss her quietly. But just when he had resolved to do this, an angel of the Lord appeared to him in a dream and said, "Joseph, son of David, do not be afraid to take Mary as your wife, for the child conceived in her is from the Holy Spirit. She will bear a son, and you are to name him Jesus, for he will save his people from their sins." All this took place to fulfill what had been spoken by the Lord through the prophet: "Look, the virgin shall conceive and bear a son, and they shall name him Emmanuel,' which means, 'God is with us.'"

- *Emmanuel* means "God is with us." This is the most consoling of statements. Often I can be lonely and wish for company; I can feel that there is no one around for me. Especially as I get older, I sense that I am on a lonely journey. But here is Good News: God is with me! This is my salvation, that God is never far away.

- This message is repeated over and over in Scripture, so I want to take it seriously, as Mary and the others did. Instead of running away from solitude when it comes, I can use it as an opportunity to be with my God. God is with me, so let me be with God! I thank God for the constant opportunity for prayer.

Wednesday 9th September
Saint Peter Claver, Priest
Luke 6:20–26

Then he looked up at his disciples and said: "Blessed are you who are poor, for yours is the kingdom of God. Blessed are you who are hungry now, for you will be filled. Blessed are you who weep now, for you will laugh. Blessed are you when people hate you, and when they exclude you, revile you, and defame you on account of the Son of Man. Rejoice on that day and leap for joy, for surely your reward is great in heaven; for that is what their ancestors did to the prophets. But woe to you who are rich, for you have received your consolation. Woe to you who are full now, for you will be hungry. Woe to you who are laughing now, for you will mourn and weep. Woe to you when all speak well of you, for that is what their ancestors did to the false prophets."

- I try to see which beatitude touches me today, whether because it helps me rejoice in God's gifts to me or because I feel a resistance in my heart. I pray for a listening heart.

- I ask myself to what extent I understand and live the Christian life in the perspective of the beatitudes, as the seeking of blessedness and happiness, and beyond merely living by the rules.

Thursday 10th September
Luke 6:27–38

"But I say to you that listen, Love your enemies, do good to those who hate you, bless those who curse you, pray for those who abuse you. If anyone strikes you on the cheek, offer the other also; and from anyone who takes away your coat do not withhold even your shirt. Give to everyone who begs from you; and if anyone takes away your goods, do not ask for them again. Do to others as you would have them do to you. If you love those who love you, what credit is that to you? For even sinners love those who love them. If you do good to those who do good to you, what credit is that to you? For even sinners do the same. If you lend to those from whom you hope to receive, what credit is that to you? Even sinners lend to sinners, to receive as much again. But love your enemies, do good, and lend, expecting nothing in return. Your reward will be great, and you will be children of the Most High; for he is kind to the ungrateful and the wicked. Be merciful, just as your Father is merciful. Do not judge, and you will not be judged; do not condemn, and you will not be condemned. Forgive, and you will be forgiven; give, and it will be given to you. A good measure, pressed down, shaken together, running over, will be put into your lap; for the measure you give will be the measure you get back."

- Jesus, again you turn our thinking upside down! Love of enemies is so contrary to human nature, but that is what you demand of us. But, Lord, I am what you call a sinner, because when others offend me I close my heart to them and punish them as best I can.

- You ask me now to bring my enemies into my heart and show mercy to them. Lord, change my heart or I will never become "a child of the Most High." Let me spend time pondering how merciful you are to me, even when I am "ungrateful and wicked." That will make me pause before judging and condemning my enemies.

Friday 11th September
Luke 6:39–42

He also told them a parable: "Can a blind person guide a blind person? Will not both fall into a pit? A disciple is not above the teacher, but everyone who is fully qualified will be like the teacher. Why do you see the speck in your neighbor's eye, but do not notice the log in your own eye? Or how can you say to your neighbor, 'Friend, let me take out the speck in your eye,' when you yourself do not see the log in your own eye? You hypocrite, first take the log out of your own eye, and then you will see clearly to take the speck out of your neighbor's eye."

- Instead of seeking healing, the person with the plank in their eye can become adept at spotting the splinters of others. If I cannot look out at the world and find what is to be praised and blessed, I need to look in to see what is hampering me, to recognize how I may be blinded to the work of God in others. As I pray for my daily bread, I pray also that I may recognize and accept it.

- God sees each of us from the inside. God sees us with a generous and compassionate gaze. God does not despise or condemn us for our shortcomings and failings. Lord, today make me gaze at annoying people as kindly as you do.

Saturday 12th September
Luke 6:43–49

[Jesus said to the people,] "No good tree bears bad fruit, nor again does a bad tree bear good fruit; for each tree is known by its own fruit. Figs are not gathered from thorns, nor are grapes picked from a bramble bush. The good person out of the good treasure of the heart produces good, and the evil person out of evil treasure produces evil; for it is out of the abundance of the heart that the mouth speaks. Why do you call me 'Lord, Lord', and do not do what I tell you? I will show you what someone is like who comes to me, hears my words, and acts on them. That one is like a man building a house, who dug deeply and laid the foundation on rock; when a flood arose, the river burst against that house but could not shake it, because it had been well built. But the one who hears and does not act is like a man who built a house on the ground without a foundation. When the river burst against it, immediately it fell, and great was the ruin of that house."

- Pope Francis encourages us to be people of discernment, who know how to identify and choose what is best, beyond a black-and-white attitude. Today's reading provides a basic discernment criterion: What fruit does each choice produce? I look at my options and try to assess the fruit of each.

- In our deeply relativistic times, Jesus' teaching about building our lives on his words sounds like a real challenge. I ask to understand what it means in my own life, to see where my life is built on sand and where it is built on solid rock.

September 13—September 19

Something to think and pray about each day this week:

Telling God about our joys and successes is rather easy. It's another matter to tell the truth about our sad moments. All of us get down at times. Think of some time when you have felt down in the dumps, ill at ease, sad, even depressed. Did you try to tell a friend how you were feeling? If so, what happened?

If your friend listened with sympathy and compassion, you were fortunate indeed. Often when we try to tell others, even friends, how sad we are, they want to give advice, remind us that others are worse off, or tell us their own troubles. Many people, I believe, are poor listeners, like a bishop who, in a homily to his priests, admitted that as soon as someone began to tell him some problem, he started to think of solutions. It's not easy to find someone who really listens. Sometimes we have to tell our friends that we just want them to listen, not to offer advice right away. And sometimes our friends need to remind us to do the same.

—William A. Barry, SJ, *Praying the Truth*

The Presence of God

As I sit here, the beating of my heart,
the ebb and flow of my breathing, the movements of my mind
are all signs of God's ongoing creation of me.
I pause for a moment and become aware
of this presence of God within me.

Freedom

I will ask God's help
to be free from my own preoccupations,
to be open to God in this time of prayer,
to come to know, love, and serve God more.

Consciousness

At this moment, Lord, I turn my thoughts to you.
I will leave aside my chores and preoccupations.
I will take rest and refreshment in your presence.

The Word

Now I turn to the Scripture set out for me this day. I read slowly over the
words and see if any sentence or sentiment appeals to me. (Please turn to
the Scripture on the following pages. Inspiration points are there, should
you need them. When you are ready, return here to continue.)

Conversation

Begin to talk to Jesus about the Scripture you have just read. What part
of it strikes a chord in you? Perhaps the words of a friend—or some story
you have heard recently—will slowly rise to the surface of your consciousness. If so, does the story throw light on what the Scripture passage may
be saying to you?

Conclusion

Glory be to the Father, and to the Son, and to the Holy Spirit,
As it was in the beginning, is now and ever shall be,
World without end. Amen.

Sunday 13th September
Twenty-Fourth Sunday in Ordinary Time
Matthew 18:21–35

Then Peter came and said to him, "Lord, if another member of the church sins against me, how often should I forgive? As many as seven times?" Jesus said to him, "Not seven times, but, I tell you, seventy-seven times. For this reason the kingdom of heaven may be compared to a king who wished to settle accounts with his slaves. When he began the reckoning, one who owed him ten thousand talents was brought to him; and, as he could not pay, his lord ordered him to be sold, together with his wife and children and all his possessions, and payment to be made. So the slave fell on his knees before him, saying, 'Have patience with me, and I will pay you everything.' And out of pity for him, the lord of that slave released him and forgave him the debt. But that same slave, as he went out, came upon one of his fellow slaves who owed him a hundred denarii; and seizing him by the throat, he said, 'Pay what you owe.' Then his fellow-slave fell down and pleaded with him, 'Have patience with me, and I will pay you.' But he refused; then he went and threw him into prison until he should pay the debt. When his fellow slaves saw what had happened, they were greatly distressed, and they went and reported to their lord all that had taken place. Then his lord summoned him and said to him, 'You wicked slave! I forgave you all that debt because you pleaded with me. Should you not have had mercy on your fellow slave, as I had mercy on you?' And in anger his lord handed him over to be tortured until he should pay his entire debt. So my heavenly Father will also do to every one of you, if you do not forgive your brother or sister from your heart."

- Peter, like most of us, believed that forgiveness must have a limit—it only made sense. But the forgiveness Jesus embodies goes beyond sense or even a logical balance sheet. Such forgiveness is countercultural in a world that must always find a place for blame. How countercultural is forgiveness for me personally? God's love is limitless, endless, ongoing. This is how the Lord loves you. "I forgave you all that debt" (Matthew 18:32).

- Thank you, Lord, for forgiving me seventy-seven times and more. Give me the grace to forgive someone today.

Monday 14th September
The Exaltation of the Holy Cross
John 3:13–17

"No one has ascended into heaven except the one who descended from heaven, the Son of Man. And just as Moses lifted up the serpent in the wilderness, so must the Son of Man be lifted up, that whoever believes in him may have eternal life. For God so loved the world that he gave his only Son, so that everyone who believes in him may not perish but may have eternal life. Indeed, God did not send the Son into the world to condemn the world, but in order that the world might be saved through him."

- In our exaltation of the cross lies a fundamental tenet of our faith in Jesus Christ. We believe that the suffering of Jesus brought us salvation and that we are called to express this faith by joining our own suffering with his. I believe that doing this saves my suffering from meaninglessness and furthers the salvation of the world.

- I gaze in wonder at the depth of God's wisdom and mercy. I adore the crucified Jesus and ask for a deep sense of gratitude in front of this mystery.

Tuesday 15th September
Our Lady of Sorrows
John 19:25–27

Meanwhile, standing near the cross of Jesus were his mother, and his mother's sister, Mary the wife of Clopas, and Mary Magdalene. When Jesus saw his mother and the disciple whom he loved standing beside her, he said to his mother, "Woman, here is your son." Then he said to the disciple, "Here is your mother." And from that hour the disciple took her into his own home.

- Today's Gospel reading focuses on the gift that Jesus gives from the cross: giving his mother to John, and John to his mother. This has been interpreted as John representing us, the church, as the Body of Christ. This means that Mary is following the same role of looking after us as she had when she looked after Jesus. It means that Jesus who gave us the beautiful sacrament of the Eucharist is seeing us as other Christs under the care of his mother.

- Mary is indeed Our Lady of Sorrows, having watched her son suffer and die. She has become the mother of all and thus sorrows with each of us when we suffer. I meditate on the motherly compassion that fills the universe.

Wednesday 16th September
Saints Cornelius, Pope, and Cyprian, Bishop, Martyrs
Luke 7:31–35

"To what then will I compare the people of this generation, and what are they like? They are like children sitting in the marketplace and calling to one another, 'We played the flute for you, and you did not dance; we wailed, and you did not weep.' For John the Baptist has come eating no bread and drinking no wine, and you say, 'He has a demon'; the Son of Man has come eating and drinking, and you say, 'Look, a glutton and a drunkard, a friend of tax collectors and sinners!' Nevertheless, wisdom is vindicated by all her children."

- Children can complain and change their minds quickly, but Jesus points out how adults can be hardheaded and impossible to please. Am I fickle, difficult to please, shifting in my beliefs and attitudes? I pray today for stability, grounded in gratitude and a teachable spirit.

- Lord, I, too, can be contrary of heart, blind and deaf to your truth. I go through periods of negativity and complaint, when nothing seems to please me. Come to me in my poverty of spirit. Reveal love's wisdom to me, and let me be counted among your children.

Thursday 17th September
Luke 7:36–50

One of the Pharisees asked Jesus to eat with him, and he went into the Pharisee's house and took his place at the table. And a woman in the city, who was a sinner, having learned that he was eating in the Pharisee's house, brought an alabaster jar of ointment. She stood behind him at his feet, weeping, and began to bathe his feet with her tears and to dry them with her hair. Then she continued kissing his feet and anointing them with the ointment. Now when the Pharisee who had invited him saw it, he said to himself, "If this man were a prophet, he would have known who and what kind of woman this is who is touching him—that she is a sinner." Jesus spoke up and said to him, "Simon, I have something to say to you." "Teacher," he replied, "speak." "A certain creditor had two debtors; one owed five hundred denarii, and the other fifty. When they could not pay, he canceled the debts for both of them. Now which of them will love him more?" Simon answered, "I suppose the one for whom he canceled the greater debt." And Jesus said to him, "You have judged rightly." Then turning toward the woman, he said to Simon, "Do you see this woman? I entered your house; you gave me no water for my feet, but she has bathed my feet with her tears and dried them with her hair. You gave me no kiss, but from the time I came in she has not stopped kissing my feet. You did not anoint my head with oil, but she has anointed my feet with ointment. Therefore, I tell you, her sins, which were many, have been forgiven; hence she has shown great love. But the one to whom little is forgiven, loves little." Then he said to her, "Your sins are forgiven." But those who were at the table with him began to say among themselves, "Who is this who even forgives sins?" And he said to the woman, "Your faith has saved you; go in peace."

- Simon had life mapped out: he had decided who deserved his attention and how they might be honored. He invited Jesus as a guest but withheld courtesy; he was prepared to listen to the words of Jesus but not ready to receive them in his heart. I ask God to help me, as I review my life, to recognize and remove any ways in which I resist God's Word.

- The Pharisee is surprised and shocked when Jesus allows a sinner to touch him. He has yet to understand that Jesus welcomes and heals sinners. But he does not think of himself as in need of healing. Did he perhaps reflect later over this incident and learn something? All sinners have a future—Lord, let me never despair of myself, since you do not do so. Forgiveness is for all, and the greater the need the more generous is God's response.

Friday 18th September
Luke 8:1–3

Soon afterwards he went on through cities and villages, proclaiming and bringing the Good News of the kingdom of God. The twelve were with him, as well as some women who had been cured of evil spirits and infirmities: Mary, called Magdalene, from whom seven demons had gone out, and Joanna, the wife of Herod's steward Chuza, and Susanna, and many others, who provided for them out of their resources.

- Jesus always understood his mission as something to be carried out with others, never on his own. I look at the ones he chose—quite an unlikely group—and I ask myself what he wants to tell us through this choice.

- Saint Luke always speaks favorably of women and highlights their positive response to Jesus. He is the only Gospel writer who gives us this detail of the women who traveled with Jesus. The scene gives an image of the infant church. It is on the move and is made up of ordinary women and men who are centered on Jesus.

Saturday 19th September
Luke 8:4–15

When a great crowd gathered and people from town after town came to Jesus, he said in a parable: "A sower went out to sow his seed; and as he sowed, some fell on the path and was trampled on, and the birds of the air ate it up. Some fell on the rock; and as it grew up, it withered for lack of moisture. Some fell among thorns, and the thorns grew with it and choked it. Some fell into good soil, and when it grew, it produced a hundredfold." As he said this, he called out, "Let anyone with ears to hear listen!" Then his disciples asked him what this parable meant. He said, "To you it has been given to know the secrets of the kingdom of God; but to others I speak in parables, so that 'looking they may not perceive, and listening they may not understand.' Now the parable is this: The seed is the word of God. The ones on the path are those who have heard; then the devil comes and takes away the word from their hearts, so that they may not believe and be saved. The ones on the rock are those who, when they hear the word, receive it with joy. But these have no root; they believe only for a while and in a time of testing fall away. As for what fell among the thorns, these are the ones who hear; but as they go on their way, they are choked by the cares and riches and pleasures of life, and their fruit does not mature. But as for that in the good soil, these are the ones who, when they hear the word, hold it fast in an honest and good heart, and bear fruit with patient endurance."

- Some commentators see in this parable the kernel of the whole gospel. The seed is sown, its fruitfulness neither automatic nor assured for every heart. But when it lands on good ground, it bears fruit of surprising abundance, which more than makes up for the seed that falls on poor soil. Do I share the optimism of the parable, or am I rather a prophet of doom?

- I look at what goes on in my own heart when I hear the word, and I ask for an honest and good heart that welcomes the seed so that it bears abundant fruit with patient endurance.

September 20—September 26

Something to think and pray about each day this week:

Forgiveness is possible, even in the dire circumstances of brutal evil that one party perpetrates on another, because we are made in the image and likeness of God. God forgives us for crucifying Jesus. And, as Archbishop Tutu reminds us, our future and the future of our world, and of God's loving enterprise in the world, depend on our being able to ask for and to give forgiveness. In an article by Alex Perry about the musical *Truth in Translation*, the director, Michael Lessac, says that he aimed to tell the story of an "evolutionary step for humanity" when South Africa did "something that no other country in the world has ever done: forgive the past to survive the future." In the same article, Nelson Mandela talks about the African term *ubuntu*, referring to the fact that everyone, no matter their color, religion, or even their status as friend or enemy, is tied to everyone else. "The question is," says Mandela, "are you going to . . . enable the community around you to be able to improve?" Forgiveness is about enabling our communities to improve.

—William A. Barry, SJ, *Changed Heart, Changed World*

The Presence of God

"Be still, and know that I am God!" Lord, your words lead us to the calmness and greatness of your presence.

Freedom

Leave me here freely all alone. / In cell where never sunlight shone. / Should no one ever speak to me. / This golden silence makes me free!

—Part of a poem by Bl. Titus Brandsma, written while he was a prisoner at Dachau concentration camp

Consciousness

Knowing that God loves me unconditionally, I can afford to be honest about how I am.

How has the day been, and how do I feel now? I share my feelings openly with the Lord.

The Word

I take my time to read the word of God slowly, a few times, allowing myself to dwell on anything that strikes me. (Please turn to the Scripture on the following pages. Inspiration points are there, should you need them. When you are ready, return here to continue.)

Conversation

Sometimes I wonder what I might say if I were to meet you in person, Lord.

I think I might say, "Thank you" because you are always there for me.

Conclusion

I thank God for these moments we have spent together and for any insights I have been given concerning the text.

Sunday 20th September
Twenty-Fifth Sunday in Ordinary Time
Matthew 20:1–16

Jesus said to his disciples, "For the kingdom of heaven is like a land-owner who went out early in the morning to hire laborers for his vineyard. After agreeing with the laborers for the usual daily wage, he sent them into his vineyard. When he went out about nine o'clock, he saw others standing idle in the marketplace; and he said to them, 'You also go into the vineyard, and I will pay you whatever is right.' So they went. When he went out again about noon and about three o'clock, he did the same. And about five o'clock he went out and found others standing around; and he said to them, 'Why are you standing here idle all day?' They said to him, 'Because no one has hired us.' He said to them, 'You also go into the vineyard.' When evening came, the owner of the vineyard said to his manager, 'Call the laborers and give them their pay, beginning with the last and then going to the first.' When those hired about five o'clock came, each of them received the usual daily wage. Now when the first came, they thought they would receive more; but each of them also received the usual daily wage. And when they received it, they grumbled against the landowner, saying, 'These last worked only one hour, and you have made them equal to us who have borne the burden of the day and the scorching heat.' But he replied to one of them, 'Friend, I am doing you no wrong; did you not agree with me for the usual daily wage? Take what belongs to you and go; I choose to give to this last the same as I give to you. Am I not allowed to do what I choose with what belongs to me? Or are you envious because I am generous?' So the last will be first, and the first will be last."

- Envy is arguably the most poisonous of the deadly sins. Not only do the envious loathe others for what they have, but they also loathe themselves for not having it. We are all coworkers in God's vineyard. We can each be confident that he will deal not only justly but generously with us.

- The vineyard owner, in his mercy, rewarded all equally. When am I tempted to consider my work and time more valuable than others'?

Monday 21st September
Saint Matthew, Apostle and Evangelist
Matthew 9:9–13

As Jesus was walking along, he saw a man called Matthew sitting at the tax booth; and he said to him, "Follow me." And he got up and followed him. And as he sat at dinner in the house, many tax collectors and sinners came and were sitting with him and his disciples. When the Pharisees saw this, they said to his disciples, "Why does your teacher eat with tax collectors and sinners?" But when he heard this, he said, "Those who are well have no need of a physician, but those who are sick. Go and learn what this means, 'I desire mercy, not sacrifice.' For I have come to call not the righteous but sinners."

- Jesus must have been an extraordinary leader, to be able to call Matthew to leave his work, his world of contacts and relationships, and follow him: "He got up and followed him." It was a choice that brought joy, a joy that Matthew wanted to share with his colleagues. How open am I to follow what God calls me to? Is it a joy or a sacrifice for me? Do I share this with my companions?

- "I desire mercy, not sacrifice." Here are two visions of religion put into stark contrast: Is religion primarily observation of rules and laws, or is it a loving and merciful relationship to God and to others? This discussion was as lively in Jesus' time as it is nowadays, as Pope Francis challenges us to put mercy at the center of our Christian life and draw the practical consequences. I ask for the grace to grasp the meaning of all this, to make the right choices.

Tuesday 22nd September
Luke 8:19–21

Then Jesus' mother and his brothers came to him, but they could not reach him because of the crowd. And he was told, "Your mother and your brothers are standing outside, wanting to see you." But he said to them, "My mother and my brothers are those who hear the word of God and do it."

- *Hearing* the word and *doing* it: for Jesus, these two verbs go together. Once he said that those who do so are building their life on rock rather than on sand so that they can be strong in the midst of difficulties.

- Jesus identifies those who hear the word of God and do it with his innermost circle, with his own mother and brothers. I thank Jesus for this great compliment, and I ask for the grace to be able to put into practice the word of God in my life, not as an obligation but as a privilege.

Wednesday 23rd September
Saint Pius of Pietrelcina, Priest
Luke 9:1–6

Then Jesus called the twelve together and gave them power and authority over all demons and to cure diseases, and he sent them out to proclaim the kingdom of God and to heal. He said to them, "Take nothing for your journey, no staff, nor bag, nor bread, nor money—not even an extra tunic. Whatever house you enter, stay there, and leave from there. Wherever they do not welcome you, as you are leaving that town shake the dust off your feet as a testimony against them." They departed and went through the villages, bringing the Good News and curing diseases everywhere.

- Jesus suggests that we live in a simple way and not be encumbered by niggling concerns. It will be difficult for us to bring Good News if we are concerned with our own details. We will be able to travel more lightly if we can make what matters to Jesus matter to us.

- The disciples of Jesus are to move on if they are not welcomed. Hostility can cling like dust to the feet and hinder further growth. It is the same with our personal life. Prayer invites us to let go of hostility, antipathy, and hurt, both from us to another and from another to ourselves.

Thursday 24th September
Luke 9:7–9

Now Herod the ruler heard about all that had taken place, and he was perplexed, because it was said by some that John had been raised from the dead, by some that Elijah had appeared, and by others that one of the ancient prophets had arisen. Herod said, "John I beheaded; but who is this about whom I hear such things?" And he tried to see [Jesus].

- Herod has beheaded John the Baptist, but now Jesus is on the scene and is making headlines. Herod is perplexed and anxious. He tries to see Jesus, but more from fear and bad conscience than from genuine desire. A true disciple has a faith-filled desire to know Jesus and to grow in an ever-deepening relationship with him.

- Lord, faith is a prerequisite for sight. Only by truly accepting you and embracing your way can I hope to see you. Strengthen my faith, Lord.

Friday 25th September
Luke 9:18–22

Once when Jesus was praying alone, with only the disciples near him, he asked them, "Who do the crowds say that I am?" They answered, "John the Baptist; but others, Elijah; and still others, that one of the ancient prophets has arisen." He said to them, "But who do you say that I am?" Peter answered, "The Messiah of God." He sternly ordered and commanded them not to tell anyone, saying, "The Son of Man must undergo great suffering, and be rejected by the elders, chief priests, and scribes, and be killed, and on the third day be raised."

- The crowds referred to their history, recognizing how God had worked in the past. The disciples realized how God was working among them in their present. I give thanks for my history, for my story. As I see where God has worked, I pray for confidence that God is working now, for hope in God's continuing goodness, and for the strength I need to follow God's Word.

- This is a crucial moment in Jesus' life. He asks the question that lies at the heart of Christian faith and theology: "Who do you say that I am?" Peter becomes the spokesperson for this little contingent of believers. Only later will they grasp how the term *Messiah* is understood by Jesus. Suffering, rejection, and death await him, but they are followed by glory. Lord, to follow you I, too, must embark on a personal discovery of who you are. Give me the grace to walk this faith journey. May I not keep you at arm's length by putting a protective shield around myself, but help me rather to daily embrace you on the path of discipleship, with its pains and joys.

Saturday 26th September
Luke 9:43b–45

While everyone was amazed at all that [Jesus] was doing, he said to his disciples, "Let these words sink into your ears: The Son of Man is going to be betrayed into human hands." But they did not understand this saying; its meaning was concealed from them, so that they could not perceive it. And they were afraid to ask him about this saying.

- We cannot but admire the skill of Luke in painting the starkest of contrasts between the amazement of everyone at all that Jesus was doing, and their lack of understanding of his future suffering. Jesus is the Savior who shows us the greatness of God through his suffering for us.

- Like the disciples, we are frightened by suffering and its apparent meaninglessness. I bring some suffering I know to my prayer, and I try to ask Jesus what it means.

September 27—October 3

Something to think and pray about each day this week:

We find it extremely hard to accept undeserved service and forgiveness and love from anyone, and especially from Jesus. For we cannot do anything to earn his love; worse yet, we know how often we betray him and what he stands for. And he tells us what he is about: "Do you know what I have done to you? You call me Teacher and Lord—and you are right, for that is what I am. So if I, your Lord and Teacher, have washed your feet, you also ought to wash one another's feet. For I have set you an example, that you also should do as I have done to you" (John 13:12–15).

Perhaps part of our reluctance to accept his forgiveness derives from the realization that we will then be called to give up our own grudges. But the deepest level of reluctance comes, it seems, from the difficulty of accepting an absolutely free gift. But when we do accept it, we can experience the effusion of Peter: "Lord, not my feet only but also my hands and my head!" (John 13:9).

—William A. Barry, SJ, *Seek My Face*

The Presence of God

Dear Jesus, as I call on you today, I realize that often I come asking for favors. Today I'd like just to be in your presence. Draw my heart in response to your love.

Freedom

God my creator, you gave me life and the gift of freedom. Through your love I exist in this world. May I never take the gift of life for granted. May I always respect others' right to life.

Consciousness

Dear Lord, help me to remember that you gave me life. Teach me to slow down, to be still and enjoy the pleasures created for me. To be aware of the beauty that surrounds me: the marvel of mountains, the calmness of lakes, the fragility of a flower petal. I need to remember that all these things come from you.

The Word

The word of God comes down to us through the Scriptures. May the Holy Spirit enlighten my mind and my heart to respond to the Gospel teachings. (Please turn to the Scripture on the following pages. Inspiration points are there, should you need them. When you are ready, return here to continue.)

Conversation

What feelings are rising in me as I pray and reflect on God's word? I imagine Jesus himself sitting or standing near me, and I open my heart to him.

Conclusion

I thank God for these moments we have spent together and for any insights I have been given concerning the text.

Sunday 27th September
Twenty-Sixth Sunday in Ordinary Time
Matthew 21:28–32

"What do you think? A man had two sons; he went to the first and said, 'Son, go and work in the vineyard today.' He answered, 'I will not'; but later he changed his mind and went. The father went to the second and said the same; and he answered, 'I go, sir'; but he did not go. Which of the two did the will of his father?" They said, "The first." Jesus said to them, "Truly I tell you, the tax collectors and the prostitutes are going into the kingdom of God ahead of you. For John came to you in the way of righteousness and you did not believe him, but the tax collectors and the prostitutes believed him; and even after you saw it, you did not change your minds and believe him."

- The Lord has always prepared great things for the people he chose as his own. But when the offer of these gifts came to be made through God's envoys, the prophets, the people turned it all down. The preaching of John the Baptist is only the latest example: his appeal for belief was rejected by his own people but accepted by the prostitutes and the collectors of the Roman taxes.

- Lord, help us remember the prophets' warnings against pride. May I never presume upon your faithfulness to me by disregarding your will and forgetting all you have given me and taught me thus far.

Monday 28th September
Luke 9:46–50

An argument arose among them as to which one of them was the greatest. But Jesus, aware of their inner thoughts, took a little child and put it by his side, and said to them, "Whoever welcomes this child in my name welcomes me, and whoever welcomes me welcomes the one who sent me; for the least among all of you is the greatest." John answered, "Master, we saw someone casting out demons in your name, and we tried to stop him, because he does not follow with us." But Jesus said to him, "Do not stop him; for whoever is not against you is for you."

- Jesus' own disciples, even in his presence, show unpleasant signs of ambition, as they jockey for key positions of influence. The only antidote to this kind of arrogance is humility. Jesus points to the dependence of the child as our model. It is moving to see Jesus taking pains to teach the disciples these basic lessons, repeating the same lesson again and again.

- Am I free of the attachment to position and influence in the community? Do I have the generosity to appreciate God's work in others? Can I show patience to my fellow Christians, which Jesus shows to the disciples, as he constantly tries to show them a better way?

Tuesday 29th September
Saints Michael, Gabriel and Raphael, Archangels
John 1:47–51

When Jesus saw Nathanael coming toward him, he said of him, "Here is truly an Israelite in whom there is no deceit!" Nathanael asked him, "Where did you get to know me?" Jesus answered, "I saw you under the fig tree before Philip called you." Nathanael replied, "Rabbi, you are the Son of God! You are the King of Israel!" Jesus answered, "Do you believe because I told you that I saw you under the fig tree? You will see greater things than these." And he said to him, "Very truly, I tell you, you will see heaven opened and the angels of God ascending and descending upon the Son of Man."

- Jesus, when you see me coming toward you, what do you say? Help me to be like Nathanael, whose heart was without deceit. He was genuine: he asked Jesus a straight question and followed up with a dramatic statement of his belief, which must have pleased Jesus.

- Jesus, you rewarded Nathanael by hinting at a new level of disclosure and intimacy between yourself and him. Please be patient with me and grant that I may "see you more clearly, love you more dearly, and follow you more nearly," as the old prayer puts it.

Wednesday 30th September
Saint Jerome, Priest and Doctor of the Church
Luke 9:57–62

As they were going along the road, someone said to him, "I will follow you wherever you go." And Jesus said to him, "Foxes have holes, and birds of the air have nests; but the Son of Man has nowhere to lay his head." To another he said, "Follow me." But he said, "Lord, first let me go and bury my father." But Jesus said to him, "Let the dead bury their own dead; but as for you, go and proclaim the kingdom of God." Another said, "I will follow you, Lord; but let me first say farewell to those at my home." Jesus said to him, "No one who puts a hand to the plough and looks back is fit for the kingdom of God."

- In this passage from Luke, people admire Jesus and are inspired by him and thus say, "I will follow you." But they have their own concerns to deal with first. Jesus asks if they really know what it means to follow him. He has nowhere to lay his head. His life follows a path that cannot be predicted and planned with certainty of security, wealth, or ease.

- We are inspired by how Saint Jerome totally handed himself over to the call of Jesus? When we die, we will have no choice but to do the same. But to what degree can we hand ourselves over to Jesus now? Can those practical concerns of family ties and work become a path rather than a block to following the Lord? Can we inspire others by the way we relate to them and the way we go about our daily tasks? How close can we get now to being like the many saints who have followed Jesus?

Thursday 1st October
Saint Thérèse of the Child Jesus, Virgin and Doctor of the Church
Luke 10:1–12

After this the Lord appointed seventy others and sent them on ahead of him in pairs to every town and place where he himself intended to go. He said to them, "The harvest is plentiful, but the laborers are few; therefore ask the Lord of the harvest to send out laborers into his harvest. Go on your way. See, I am sending you out like lambs into the midst of wolves. Carry no purse, no bag, no sandals; and greet no one on the road. Whatever house you enter, first say, 'Peace to this house!' And if anyone is there who shares in peace, your peace will rest on that person; but if not, it will return to you. Remain in the same house, eating and drinking whatever they provide, for the laborer deserves to be paid. Do not move about from house to house. Whenever you enter a town and its people welcome you, eat what is set before you; cure the sick who are there, and say to them, 'The kingdom of God has come near to you.' But whenever you enter a town and they do not welcome you, go out into its streets and say, 'Even the dust of your town that clings to our feet, we wipe off in protest against you. Yet know this: the kingdom of God has come near.' I tell you, on that day it will be more tolerable for Sodom than for that town."

• Jesus sends out a large group of his followers on mission ahead of him, leaving them in no doubt about the challenges awaiting them, how many people will not welcome them. We get a picture of the unredeemed world in which peace is patchy and love is often lacking. Do what you can, he tells them, to offer healing, comfort, peace, and harmony.

• To spread God's kingdom, Jesus chooses to depend on the various gifts of his chosen ones. He sends us out just as we are. We carry little except our limited strengths and our frailties. The gift of peace that we can bring, to those who accept us, is more precious than any casual roadside conversation. Lord, give me this peace, this tranquility of spirit.

Friday 2nd October
The Holy Guardian Angels
Matthew 18:1–5, 10

At that time the disciples came to Jesus and asked, "Who is the greatest in the kingdom of heaven?" He called a child, whom he put among them, and said, "Truly I tell you, unless you change and become like children, you will never enter the kingdom of heaven. Whoever becomes humble like this child is the greatest in the kingdom of heaven. Whoever welcomes one such child in my name welcomes me. . . . Take care that you do not despise one of these little ones; for, I tell you, in heaven their angels continually see the face of my Father in heaven."

• In today's Gospel story, Jesus confuses his disciples. He points at the gifts of children—their innocence, humility, and honesty—as marks of true greatness. Political, economic, or intellectual power is not a sign of greatness. Jesus puzzled the disciples by telling them to become like little children. Am I free to challenge my friends, my family, or my work colleagues with childlike fearlessness when my heart tells me that something is not right?

- The clear heart and the simple honesty of a child make us sit up and pay attention and smile in admiration. I pause in silence to reflect on the true greatness to be found in a child, and I pray for those who have children in their care.

Saturday 3rd October
Luke 10:17–24

The seventy returned with joy, saying, "Lord, in your name even the demons submit to us!" He said to them, "I watched Satan fall from heaven like a flash of lightning. See, I have given you authority to tread on snakes and scorpions, and over all the power of the enemy; and nothing will hurt you. Nevertheless, do not rejoice at this, that the spirits submit to you, but rejoice that your names are written in heaven." At that same hour Jesus rejoiced in the Holy Spirit and said, "I thank you, Father, Lord of heaven and earth, because you have hidden these things from the wise and the intelligent and have revealed them to infants; yes, Father, for such was your gracious will. All things have been handed over to me by my Father; and no one knows who the Son is except the Father, or who the Father is except the Son and anyone to whom the Son chooses to reveal him." Then turning to the disciples, Jesus said to them privately, "Blessed are the eyes that see what you see! For I tell you that many prophets and kings desired to see what you see, but did not see it, and to hear what you hear, but did not hear it."

- The seventy disciples return to Jesus, delighted with themselves. Their mission to bring peace and reconciliation has overcome hatred and evil. But Jesus reminds the disciples that the power working in them comes from the love God has for them. Then he draws them into the circle of his divine origin: "Blessed are the eyes that see what you see."

- It is in the sharing of our personalities and gifts that others are healed. And in our very acts of generosity we enter, often unaware, the divinity of our human nature. I dwell for a short time on some experience of being with a person or a group when I was a positive and helpful presence. How did I feel after the experience? Do I have a sense of my gifts having a source beyond me? Naming God as the source of all that I am may not come easily. I ask for a deeper awareness of the mystery to whom I belong.

Twenty-Seventh Week in Ordinary Time
October 4—October 10

Something to think and pray about each day this week:

Do you remember how you reacted when you first heard that heaven would consist of the beatific vision? "What's that?" you might have said in your head, if not out loud. When it was explained that the beatific vision meant looking at and enjoying God for all eternity, did you wonder if you'd be bored, if there would be something else to do? Being polite before God, if you did have such thoughts, you were probably like me and kept them to yourself. After all, heaven is a long way off, and there are still a lot of interesting things to do and see here on earth. The beatific vision could take care of itself, whatever it might mean.

—William A. Barry, SJ, *God's Passionate Desire*

The Presence of God

"I am standing at the door, knocking" says the Lord. What a wonderful privilege that the Lord of all creation desires to come to me. I welcome his presence.

Freedom

Everything has the potential to draw forth from me a fuller love and life. Yet my desires are often fixed, caught, on illusions of fulfillment. I ask that God, through my freedom, may orchestrate my desires in a vibrant loving melody rich in harmony.

Consciousness

To be conscious about something is to be aware of it.

Dear Lord, help me to remember that you gave me life.

Thank you for the gift of life.

Teach me to slow down, to be still and enjoy the pleasures created for me. To be aware of the beauty that surrounds me: the marvel of mountains, the calmness of lakes, the fragility of a flower petal. I need to remember that all these things come from you.

The Word

I read the word of God slowly, a few times over, and I listen to what God is saying to me. (Please turn to the Scripture on the following pages. Inspiration points are there, should you need them. When you are ready, return here to continue.)

Conversation

What feelings are rising in me as I pray and reflect on God's word? I imagine Jesus himself sitting or standing near me, and I open my heart to him.

Conclusion

I thank God for these moments we have spent together and for any insights I have been given concerning the text.

Sunday 4th October
Twenty-Seventh Sunday in Ordinary Time
Matthew 21:33–43

"Listen to another parable. There was a landowner who planted a vineyard, put a fence around it, dug a wine press in it, and built a watchtower. Then he leased it to tenants and went to another country. When the harvest time had come, he sent his slaves to the tenants to collect his produce. But the tenants seized his slaves and beat one, killed another, and stoned another. Again he sent other slaves, more than the first; and they treated them in the same way. Finally he sent his son to them, saying, 'They will respect my son.' But when the tenants saw the son, they said to themselves, 'This is the heir; come, let us kill him and get his inheritance.' So they seized him, threw him out of the vineyard, and killed him. Now when the owner of the vineyard comes, what will he do to those tenants?" They said to him, "He will put those wretches to a miserable death, and lease the vineyard to other tenants who will give him the produce at the harvest time." Jesus said to them, "Have you never read in the scriptures: 'The stone that the builders rejected / has become the cornerstone; / this was the Lord's doing, / and it is amazing in our eyes'? Therefore I tell you, the kingdom of God will be taken away from you and given to a people that produces the fruits of the kingdom."

- The parable is clear. The tenants refuse to pay the rent. The rent collectors get beaten up. The landlord's son is killed. The listeners understand that the story doesn't end well for the tenants. Jesus develops the further point. The builders reject the very stone that will become the cornerstone.

- The account of Jesus' suffering, death, and resurrection was the original focus for the Gospels of Matthew, Mark, and Luke. This parable gives it to us in a nutshell. "This was the Lord's doing, and it is amazing in our eyes." I may not have a landlord. But who is the lord of my life?

Monday 5th October
Luke 10:25–37

A lawyer stood up to test Jesus. "Teacher," he said, "what must I do to inherit eternal life?" He said to him, "What is written in the law? What do you read there?" He answered, "You shall love the Lord your God with all your heart, and with all your soul, and with all your strength, and with all your mind; and your neighbor as yourself." And he said to him, "You have given the right answer; do this, and you will live." But wanting to justify himself, he asked Jesus, "And who is my neighbor?" Jesus replied, "A man was going down from Jerusalem to Jericho, and fell into the hands of robbers, who stripped him, beat him, and went away, leaving him half dead. Now by chance a priest was going down that road; and when he saw him, he passed by on the other side. So likewise a Levite, when he came to the place and saw him, passed by on the other side. But a Samaritan while traveling came near him; and when he saw him, he was moved with pity. He went to him and bandaged his wounds, having poured oil and wine on them. Then he put him on his own animal, brought him to an inn, and took care of him. The next day he took out two denarii, gave them to the innkeeper, and said, 'Take care of him; and when I come back, I will repay you whatever more you spend.' Which of these three, do you think, was a neighbor to the man who fell into the hands of the robbers?" He said, "The one who showed him mercy." Jesus said to him, "Go and do likewise."

- Perhaps this is the most moving parable in Scripture. Why? Because it cuts to the roots of the world's prejudices. Remember, in Jesus' time, the Jews and the Samaritans despised one another. No matter what religion or nonreligion one follows, one can readily find the truth in this drama.

- When Jesus is asked the question, "Who is my neighbor?" he does not answer with a definition but by telling a story. This beautiful passage from the Gospel shows how the answer must come from the heart, not the head. In my prayer I can ask the Lord to help me, through my heart, to realize where today's path goes.

Tuesday 6th October
Luke 10:38–42

Now as they went on their way, Jesus entered a certain village, where a woman named Martha welcomed him into her home. She had a sister named Mary, who sat at the Lord's feet and listened to what he was saying. But Martha was distracted by her many tasks; so she came to him and asked, "Lord, do you not care that my sister has left me to do all the work by myself? Tell her then to help me." But the Lord answered her, "Martha, Martha, you are worried and distracted by many things; there is need of only one thing. Mary has chosen the better part, which will not be taken away from her."

- Jesus may seem to be preferring contemplation to action, praising Mary and criticizing Martha. Yet, he cannot be telling us to be content with sitting down to listen to his word, for he always insists that true listening to his word means putting it into practice. His objection to Martha is that she is too worried and distracted by many things to be able to really listen to him. Do I merit the same reproach? I ask for a pure heart, focused on what will not be taken away.

- Jesus was concerned about Martha burdening herself unnecessarily. He does not want her to worry so much. Imagine Jesus calling you by name—twice, gently. What would he say to you?

Wednesday 7th October
Our Lady of the Rosary
Luke 11:1–4

[Jesus] was praying in a certain place, and after he had finished, one of his disciples said to him, "Lord, teach us to pray, as John taught his disciples." He said to them, "When you pray, say: Father, hallowed be your name. Your kingdom come. Give us each day our daily bread. And forgive us our sins, for we ourselves forgive everyone indebted to us. And do not bring us to the time of trial."

- When the incarnate Son of God, the one closest to the Father, is asked to put into words the elements of true prayer, he responds with what we now call the Lord's Prayer or the Our Father. Identify one phrase of this prayer and meditate on it today.

- It is difficult to forgive even small hurts. What about the hurts of injustice, abuse, neglect? Jesus encourages us to think of these in prayer. One step toward forgiveness is to pray for someone—even when we can't talk to that person or think kindly of him or her.

Thursday 8th October
Luke 11:5–13

[Jesus] said to them, "Suppose one of you has a friend, and you go to him at midnight and say to him, 'Friend, lend me three loaves of bread; for a friend of mine has arrived, and I have nothing to set before him.' And he answers from within, 'Do not bother me; the door has already been locked, and my children are with me in bed; I cannot get up and give you anything.' I tell you, even though he will not get up and give him anything because he is his friend, at least because of his persistence he will get up and give him whatever he needs. So I say to you, Ask, and it will be given to you; search, and you will find; knock, and the door will be opened for you. For everyone who asks receives, and everyone who searches finds, and for everyone who knocks, the door will be opened. Is there anyone among you who, if your child asks for a fish, will give a snake instead of a fish? Or if the child asks for an egg, will give a scorpion? If you then, who are evil, know how to give good gifts to your children, how much more will the heavenly Father give the Holy Spirit to those who ask him!"

- Jesus wants me to persevere in my requests and says that he will give me what I need but not always what I want. I ask Jesus to guide me in knowing the difference.

- We may have been praying for ourselves or others for many years, and now we're tired of asking. Prayer is always heard by God but not always answered as we might wish. God, what do I receive from you when I pray and pray? Your presence? Understanding? Compassion?

Friday 9th October
Luke 11:15–26

Some of [the crowd] said of [Jesus], "He casts out demons by Beelzebul, the ruler of the demons." Others, to test him, kept demanding from him a sign from heaven. But he knew what they were thinking and said to them, "Every kingdom divided against itself becomes a desert, and house falls on house. If Satan also is divided against himself, how will his kingdom stand?—for you say that I cast out the demons by Beelzebul. Now if I cast out the demons by Beelzebul, by whom do your exorcists cast them out? Therefore they will be your judges. But if it is by the finger of God that I cast out the demons, then the kingdom of God has come to you. When a strong man, fully armed, guards his castle, his property is safe. But when one stronger than he attacks him and overpowers him, he takes away his armor in which he trusted and divides his plunder. Whoever is not with me is against me, and whoever does not gather with me scatters. When the unclean spirit has gone out of a person, it wanders through waterless regions looking for a resting place, but not finding any, it says, 'I will return to my house from which I came.' When it comes, it finds it swept and put in order. Then it goes and brings seven other spirits more evil than itself, and they enter and live there; and the last state of that person is worse than the first."

- Disbelief and denial swell and burst to the surface in today's Gospel. The people of Jesus' time deny that the good he does comes through the power of God. Jesus' self-defense is simple: evil cannot be overthrown by evil. Good overpowers evil. Evil paralyzes good.

- Trusting in the power of God means that we believe there is someone powerful and loving at the source of all the events of our lives, all the events in the world, and all the extraordinary events in the universe. I pause for a few moments of prayer for the world, in praise of the good that emanates from God.

Saturday 10th October
Luke 11:27–28

While Jesus was speaking, a woman in the crowd raised her voice and said to him, "Blessed is the womb that bore you and the breasts that nursed you!" But he said, "Blessed rather are those who hear the word of God and obey it!"

- The woman in the crowd appreciates what Jesus has said, praising and blessing his mother. Jesus, in reply, asks her to imagine instead those who listen and are obedient to the word of God. Do what they do, rather than applaud what they say. In today's culture we often encounter the terms *Follow* and *Like*. How am I tempted to offer my opinion more than act on what I believe?

- How much of my time goes to what is insignificant, and how much of it is spent on what is significant? How do I tell the difference?

Something to think and pray about each day this week:

What about the person who is trying to live a decent Christian life, even if not perfectly, say, a working mother and wife who tries her best to do an honest day's work and to take care of her family obligations? One such person felt great joy and peace in God's presence and looked forward to prayer. Soon, however, she experienced anxiety, feeling that she was being too proud to expect God to speak to her and that taking time for prayer like this was a luxury she could ill afford. She said to herself, "This is too highfalutin for the likes of me." God now seemed distant. Ignatius would say that the positive experiences come from God or the good spirit who wants to draw her into friendship, whereas the troubling thoughts come from the bad spirit or from her fears of closeness to God.

—William A. Barry, SJ, *Here's My Heart, Here's My Hand*

The Presence of God
Dear Jesus, I come to you today longing for your presence. I desire to love you as you love me. May nothing ever separate me from you.

Freedom
Lord grant me the grace to have freedom of the spirit. Cleanse my heart and soul so that I may live joyously in your love.

Consciousness
Where am I with God? With others?
Do I have something to be grateful for? Then I give thanks.
Is there something I am sorry for? Then I ask forgiveness.

The Word
The word of God comes down to us through the Scriptures. May the Holy Spirit enlighten my mind and my heart to respond to the Gospel teachings. (Please turn to the Scripture on the following pages. Inspiration points are there, should you need them. When you are ready, return here to continue.)

Conversation
How has God's word moved me? Has it left me cold?
Has it consoled me or moved me to act in a new way?
I imagine Jesus standing or sitting beside me;
I turn and share my feelings with him

Conclusion
I thank God for these moments we have spent together and for any insights I have been given concerning the text.

Sunday 11th October
Twenty-Eighth Sunday in Ordinary Time
Matthew 22:1–14

Once more Jesus spoke to them in parables, saying: "The kingdom of heaven may be compared to a king who gave a wedding banquet for his son. He sent his slaves to call those who had been invited to the wedding banquet, but they would not come. Again he sent other slaves, saying, 'Tell those who have been invited: Look, I have prepared my dinner, my oxen and my fat calves have been slaughtered, and everything is ready; come to the wedding banquet.' But they made light of it and went away, one to his farm, another to his business, while the rest seized his slaves, maltreated them, and killed them. The king was enraged. He sent his troops, destroyed those murderers, and burned their city. Then he said to his slaves, 'The wedding is ready, but those invited were not worthy. Go therefore into the main streets, and invite everyone you find to the wedding banquet.' Those slaves went out into the streets and gathered all whom they found, both good and bad; so the wedding hall was filled with guests. But when the king came in to see the guests, he noticed a man there who was not wearing a wedding robe, and he said to him, 'Friend, how did you get in here without a wedding robe?' And he was speechless. Then the king said to the attendants, 'Bind him hand and foot, and throw him into the outer darkness, where there will be weeping and gnashing of teeth.' For many are called, but few are chosen."

- God invites us to draw close, not because of our worthiness or in thanks for our efforts but in a generous sharing of life. This time of prayer is part of my response: I give it wholeheartedly to God.

- The "wedding robe" I wear is my awareness of my place before God. I pray that I may remain humble, be conscious of how I am blessed, and grow in trust as I respond to God's Spirit in my life.

Monday 12th October
Luke 11:29–32

When the crowds were increasing, he began to say, "This generation is an evil generation; it asks for a sign, but no sign will be given to it except the sign of Jonah. For just as Jonah became a sign to the people of Nineveh, so the Son of Man will be to this generation. The queen of the South will rise at the judgment with the people of this generation and condemn them, because she came from the ends of the earth to listen to the wisdom of Solomon, and see, something greater than Solomon is here! The people of Nineveh will rise up at the judgment with this generation and condemn it, because they repented at the proclamation of Jonah, and see, something greater than Jonah is here!"

- The Ninevites were moved to repentance by the prophetic sign of Jonah, which they recognized as the authentic word of God. Later God sends his Son into our world as the ultimate sign of his love for us.

- You, Lord Jesus, are the sign of signs. Those who go seeking further wonders have not truly seen you. In you I find all that I need to be fully human and to find my destiny with God.

Tuesday 13th October
Luke 11:37–41

While Jesus was speaking, a Pharisee invited him to dine with him; so he went in and took his place at the table. The Pharisee was amazed to see that he did not first wash before dinner. Then the Lord said to him, "Now you Pharisees clean the outside of the cup and of the dish, but inside you are full of greed and wickedness. You fools! Did not the one who made the outside make the inside also? So give for alms those things that are within; and see, everything will be clean for you."

- It can be too easy to conform to others' expectations. We miss out by not developing our own inner life. I ask Jesus for the gift of inner freedom from which good judgment comes.

- Jesus tells us that holiness lies in wholeness and integrity; we are invited to be of one piece, without deep contradictions. I bring my life before God fully and openly, asking that any divisions in me be healed—that I be made whole.

Wednesday 14th October
Luke 11:42–46

"But woe to you Pharisees! For you tithe mint and rue and herbs of all kinds, and neglect justice and the love of God; it is these you ought to have practiced, without neglecting the others. Woe to you Pharisees! For you love to have the seat of honor in the synagogues and to be greeted with respect in the marketplaces. Woe to you! For you are like unmarked graves, and people walk over them without realizing it." One of the lawyers answered him, "Teacher, when you say these things, you insult us too." And he said, "Woe also to you lawyers! For you load people with burdens hard to bear, and you yourselves do not lift a finger to ease them."

• Some people in authority use their position to demand that others recognize their position and conform to their plans in great detail. What can be lost are the core actions of true leadership: recognizing the needs of those in our care and serving them because we have the power to do so. In prayer today, I consider how I use whatever power I have to serve others.

• Jesus saw that the Pharisees and lawyers were self-satisfied and realized they were starving themselves. They paid attention to what was outside while neglecting the life of the spirit. Life is not about cosmetics and advertising, nor is it measured by conformity and approval.

Thursday 15th October
Saint Teresa of Jesus, Virgin and Doctor of the Church
Luke 11:47–54

Jesus said to the lawyers, "Woe to you! For you build the tombs of the prophets whom your ancestors killed. So you are witnesses and approve of the deeds of your ancestors; for they killed them, and you build their tombs. Therefore also the Wisdom of God said, 'I will send them prophets and apostles, some of whom they will kill and persecute,' so that this generation may be charged with the blood of all the prophets shed since the foundation of the world, from the blood of Abel to the blood of Zechariah, who perished between the altar and the sanctuary. Yes, I tell you, it will be charged against this generation. Woe to you lawyers! For you have taken away the key of knowledge; you did not enter yourselves, and you hindered those who were entering." When he went outside, the scribes and the Pharisees began to be very hostile toward him and to cross-examine him about many things, lying in wait for him, to catch him in something he might say.

• Contemporary society, especially in the West, has, for the most part, seemed resistant to formal religion and the proclamation of the gospel.

If, in many places, faith in religious beliefs has gone, have love and care of our neighbor gone with it? Are we in danger of entering the loveless but politically correct world of the scribes and Pharisees?

- Many prophets before Jesus suffered death for telling the truth; this would be Jesus' fate as well. It is a great freedom to be open to the truth and not embedded in our prejudices. I ask the Lord for the kind of security in my relationship with him that enables me to be more open-minded.

Friday 16th October
Luke 12:1–7

Meanwhile, when the crowd gathered by the thousands, so that they trampled on one another, Jesus began to speak first to his disciples, "Beware of the yeast of the Pharisees, that is, their hypocrisy. Nothing is covered up that will not be uncovered, and nothing secret that will not become known. Therefore whatever you have said in the dark will be heard in the light, and what you have whispered behind closed doors will be proclaimed from the housetops. I tell you, my friends, do not fear those who kill the body, and after that can do nothing more. But I will warn you whom to fear: fear him who, after he has killed, has authority to cast into hell. Yes, I tell you, fear him! Are not five sparrows sold for two pennies? Yet not one of them is forgotten in God's sight. But even the hairs of your head are all counted. Do not be afraid; you are of more value than many sparrows."

- Luke's Gospel continues to indicate that the tension is building up and the opposition to Jesus is becoming stronger as he heads toward Jerusalem. Anyone who follows him needs to be focused and ready for anything.
- People who are suffering or are on the fringes of society may not know that they are "of more value than many sparrows." Trusting that the millions of people who suffer terrible trials of injustice here on earth will find consolation in the life after death is a huge leap of faith. Do I believe this? Do I care even for the sparrows and the smallest details in the lives of people I know? How can I demonstrate this care?

Saturday 17th October
Saint Ignatius of Antioch, Bishop and Martyr
Luke 12:8–12

[Jesus said to the disciples,] "And I tell you, everyone who acknowledges me before others, the Son of Man also will acknowledge before the angels of God; but whoever denies me before others will be denied before the angels of God. And everyone who speaks a word against the Son of Man will be forgiven; but whoever blasphemes against the Holy Spirit will not be forgiven. When they bring you before the synagogues, the rulers, and the authorities, do not worry about how you are to defend yourselves or what you are to say; for the Holy Spirit will teach you at that very hour what you ought to say."

- There surely is something odd about a person who wanders through the flowers, the green fields, and looks up at the high mountains and then curses them—blasphemes against all of nature. The beauty of the world is only one tiny sparkle of the diamond light coming from the Holy Spirit. Look at the stars. Browse the amazing images of the galaxies. Think of the brilliant insights and the incredible talents of human beings. Inspirations in dark moments flow in to renew us. All of them are facets of the Holy Spirit.

- Not only does Jesus promise his constant presence in the lives of his faithful ones, but he also promises the help and inspiration of the Holy Spirit, especially in times of need. How do I feel when I consider that I may always call upon the help of the Holy Spirit?

October 18—October 24

Something to think and pray about each day this week:

So how do I let go of my anger? Generally, I bring it to prayer. The complaints come unbidden, so I might as well integrate it into prayer. What I've found helpful is to balance anger with gratitude. Near the end of my daily give-away year, I decided to intentionally note one thing each day that I was grateful for and to do this during morning prayer. I call this my "gratitude offensive."

It's been a good experience for me. As soon as I start fretting about the ills of our society, I call to mind that at least I have electricity and running water, or that we finally decided on which car to buy and had the money to buy it, or that my back pain and cold left in time for me to enjoy a dance weekend, or that there's a gentle breeze today, or . . . If it's a person I feel angry toward, I've taken it to confession and forced myself to think of a positive quality that person possesses and then hold him or her in prayer. This may take a lot of repetition. I keep reminding myself: Don't quibble over small stuff; let it go, and substitute gratitude. Remember Rule of Thumb #10, Part 1: Forgive others. It will lift your spirit.

—Susan V. Vogt, *Blessed by Less*

The Presence of God
God is with me, but even more astounding, God is within me.
Let me dwell for a moment on God's life-giving presence
in my body, in my mind, in my heart,
as I sit here, right now.

Freedom
Lord, may I never take the gift of freedom for granted. You gave me the
great blessing of freedom of spirit. Fill my spirit with your peace and joy.

Consciousness
I remind myself that I am in the presence of God, who is my strength in
times of weakness and my comforter in times of sorrow.

The Word
I take my time to read the word of God slowly, a few times, allowing myself to dwell on anything that strikes me. (Please turn to the Scripture on
the following pages. Inspiration points are there, should you need them.
When you are ready, return here to continue.)

Conversation
Jesus, you always welcomed little children when you walked on this earth.
Teach me to have a childlike trust in you. Teach me to live in the knowl-
edge that you will never abandon me.

Conclusion
Glory be to the Father, and to the Son, and to the Holy Spirit,
As it was in the beginning, is now and ever shall be,
World without end. Amen.

Sunday 18th October
Twenty-Ninth Sunday in Ordinary Time
Matthew 22:15–21

Then the Pharisees went and plotted to entrap him in what he said. So they sent their disciples to him, along with the Herodians, saying, "Teacher, we know that you are sincere, and teach the way of God in accordance with truth, and show deference to no one; for you do not regard people with partiality. Tell us, then, what you think. Is it lawful to pay taxes to the emperor, or not?" But Jesus, aware of their malice, said, "Why are you putting me to the test, you hypocrites? Show me the coin used for the tax." And they brought him a denarius. Then he said to them, "Whose head is this, and whose title?" They answered, "The emperor's." Then he said to them, "Give therefore to the emperor the things that are the emperor's, and to God the things that are God's."

- Jesus remains free and firm in the face of plots against him by the Pharisees, who try to catch him out and find a way to silence him with a barbed question. Is it right to pay taxes to a foreign power? If he says yes, he is against them, his own people. If he says no, they will report him to the Romans and have him arrested. You can see in the text the wisdom of his answer.

- To be a good citizen and to serve God are not in contradiction, because God works through all human systems and institutions to build the final community of love. God needs me to help build good relationships wherever I find myself.

Monday 19th October
Saints John de Brébeuf and Isaac Jogues, Priests, and Companions, Martyrs
Luke 12:13–21

Someone in the crowd said to Jesus, "Teacher, tell my brother to divide the family inheritance with me." But he said to him, "Friend, who set me to be a judge or arbitrator over you?" And he said to them, "Take care! Be on your guard against all kinds of greed; for one's life does not consist in the abundance of possessions." Then he told them a parable: "The land of a rich man produced abundantly. And he thought to himself, 'What should I do, for I have no place to store my crops?' Then he said, 'I will do this: I will pull down my barns and build larger ones, and there I will store all my grain and my goods. And I will say to my soul, Soul, you have ample goods laid up for many years; relax, eat, drink, be merry.' But God said to him, 'You fool! This very night your life is being demanded of you. And the things you have prepared, whose will they be?' So it is with those who store up treasures for themselves but are not rich toward God."

- What are we, in fact, living for? The demands of our way of life can make it difficult to put first things first. It is only in our relationship to Jesus that we can discover who we truly are, as Jesus sees us.

- In this parable, Jesus attacks greed and egotism. This rich man is living for this world and this life only, thinking only of himself, with no awareness of others' needs. All the rich man's ambitious planning is in vain because that same night he is to die. Who will inherit his substantial fortune, since he cannot take it with him, though he has lived as if he could? I ask Jesus to show me the real values and riches in my own life.

Tuesday 20th October
Luke 12:35–38

"Be dressed for action and have your lamps lit; be like those who are waiting for their master to return from the wedding banquet, so that they may open the door for him as soon as he comes and knocks. Blessed are those slaves whom the master finds alert when he comes; truly I tell you, he will fasten his belt and have them sit down to eat, and he will come and serve them. If he comes during the middle of the night, or near dawn, and finds them so, blessed are those slaves."

- It's a great gift to be alert to the fact that we have come from God and we are going back to God. This helps put our whole life into a proper perspective. Closeness to Jesus is what keeps this awareness alive.

- Are these words only about the end time, or is Jesus knocking at my door on a daily basis? Am I being challenged to recognize him in the guise of a stranger, a person who is ill or who needs an encouraging word or a gentle touch? Do I treasure these opportunities as an encounter with Christ? Lord, make me vigilant so that I may recognize your face in my encounters today.

Wednesday 21st October
Luke 12:39–48

Jesus said to the people, "But know this: if the owner of the house had known at what hour the thief was coming, he would not have let his house be broken into. You also must be ready, for the Son of Man is coming at an unexpected hour." Peter said, "Lord, are you telling this parable for us or for everyone?" And the Lord said, "Who then is the faithful and prudent manager whom his master will put in charge of his slaves, to give them their allowance of food at the proper time? Blessed is that slave whom his master will find at work when he arrives. Truly I tell you, he will put that one in charge of all his possessions. But if that slave says to himself, 'My master is delayed in coming,' and if he begins to beat the other slaves, men and women, and to eat and drink and get drunk, the master of that slave will come on a day when he does not expect him and at an hour that he does not know, and will cut him in pieces, and put him with the unfaithful. That slave who knew what his master wanted, but did not prepare himself or do what was wanted, will receive a severe beating. But one who did not know and did what deserved a beating will receive a light beating. From everyone to whom much has been given, much will be required; and from one to whom much has been entrusted, even more will be demanded."

- Today's Gospel reading continues the message of being awake, alert, and ready. Each day is a microcosm of life, and we are called to live it as fully and as meaningfully as possible. "The glory of God is the human person fully alive!" So says Saint Irenaeus.

- Prayer times are our moments of being ready: in common worship, personal prayer time, and casual moments. The Lord can touch our lives at any time with a mood of peace, a challenge, or a word of Scripture. Prayer is God's gift to us and God's work within us.

Thursday 22nd October
Luke 12:49–53

[Jesus said to the crowds,] "I came to bring fire to the earth, and how I wish it were already kindled! I have a baptism with which to be baptized, and what stress I am under until it is completed! Do you think that I have come to bring peace to the earth? No, I tell you, but rather division!

From now on five in one household will be divided, three against two and two against three; they will be divided: father against son and son against father, mother against daughter and daughter against mother, mother-in-law against her daughter-in-law and daughter-in-law against mother-in-law."

- The gospel is a call to conversion, to becoming "a new creation" (2 Corinthians 5:17). It means shedding the skin of a former way of living. Does my Christian faith make a real difference to the kind of person I am and to the kind of life I lead?

- Lord, you disturb me, shake me out of complacency, and make my heart burn within me. Your message is not just about being nice. It means being angry at times, confronting injustice, making a stand.

Friday 23rd October
Luke 12:54–59

Jesus also said to the crowds, "When you see a cloud rising in the west, you immediately say, 'It is going to rain'; and so it happens. And when you see the south wind blowing, you say, 'There will be scorching heat'; and it happens. You hypocrites! You know how to interpret the appearance of earth and sky, but why do you not know how to interpret the present time? And why do you not judge for yourselves what is right? Thus, when you go with your accuser before a magistrate, on the way make an effort to settle the case, or you may be dragged before the judge, and the judge hand you over to the officer, and the officer throw you in prison. I tell you, you will never get out until you have paid the very last penny."

- A glance at the sky or a whiff of the wind, and you can have a good guess what the weather will be like. So, Jesus asks the crowds, why they are not perceptive enough to see what's going on around them? As humans created in God's image, we have the ability to perceive more than just the weather. I pray for help in cultivating wisdom and discernment.

- Weather forecasting has improved immensely. However, one's life is not so easy to predict. The ability to be honest with myself and to be in touch with the movements in my heart and mind provide a wonderful and solid foundation for interior growth. In my prayer I ask the Lord for the gift of sensitivity.

Saturday 24th October

Luke 13:1–9

At that very time there were some present who told him about the Galileans whose blood Pilate had mingled with their sacrifices. He asked them, "Do you think that because these Galileans suffered in this way they were worse sinners than all other Galileans? No, I tell you; but unless you repent, you will all perish as they did. Or those eighteen who were killed when the tower of Siloam fell on them—do you think that they were worse offenders than all the others living in Jerusalem? No, I tell you; but unless you repent, you will all perish just as they did." Then he told this parable: "A man had a fig tree planted in his vineyard; and he came looking for fruit on it and found none. So he said to the gardener, 'See here! For three years I have come looking for fruit on this fig tree, and still I find none. Cut it down! Why should it be wasting the soil?' He replied, 'Sir, let it alone for one more year, until I dig round it and put manure on it. If it bears fruit next year, well and good; but if not, you can cut it down.'"

- Jesus came to help us have a right relationship with God. If we listen to his word and try to correct our mistakes in our way of living, we are on the path to inner contentment. The time given for the fig tree to bear fruit testifies to God's patience with us.

- People of Jesus' day believed that whatever evil befell people was a punishment for sin. The more people had to suffer, the greater their sin must have been! Jesus rejects this simplistic notion. Instead he emphasizes repentance, which means a turning around toward God and one's neighbor. Cultivating and fertilizing the fig tree is a symbol of God's mercy in action. Lord, you know my strengths and my frailties better than I do. You are a patient and loving God, and you have planted the seeds of change in my heart. Now is the time for these seeds to bear fruit.

October 25—October 31

Something to think and pray about each day this week:

After much experimentation we eventually settled on a brief morning offering and then silent listening through spiritual reading or just being quiet, perhaps doing some journaling.

This type of prayer is most often how I seek to sort out the letter of the law from the spirit of the law. Fewer words make space for quiet listening. Some people pray through meditation, some say memorized prayers, some absorb the wonder of creation and see that "It is good." Some look at that same creation and are frightened by the power of wind, rain, and fire, wondering about the source of such a destructive force. Finding God in all things is the core of Ignatian spirituality but it can be a challenge and a mystery. Some things look very mundane and ordinary; hardly holy looking. Others look fearsome and confusing. It's both daunting and awesome. That's why we need to let go of cheap faith and deepen our faith for the long haul.

—Susan V. Vogt, *Blessed by Less*

The Presence of God

The more we call on God the more we can feel God's presence. Day by day we are drawn closer to the loving heart of God.

Freedom

I am free. When I look at these words in writing, they seem to create in me a feeling of awe. Yes, a wonderful feeling of freedom. Thank you, God.

Consciousness

Help me, Lord, become more conscious of your presence. Teach me to recognize your presence in others. Fill my heart with gratitude for the times your love has been shown to me through the care of others.

The Word

The word of God comes down to us through the Scriptures. May the Holy Spirit enlighten my mind and my heart to respond to the Gospel teachings. (Please turn to the Scripture on the following pages. Inspiration points are there, should you need them. When you are ready, return here to continue.)

Conversation

Conversation requires talking and listening.
As I talk to Jesus, may I also learn to pause and listen.
I picture the gentleness in his eyes and the love in his smile.
I can be totally honest with Jesus as I tell him my worries and cares.
I will open my heart to Jesus as I tell him my fears and doubts.
I will ask him to help me place myself fully in his care, knowing that he always desires good for me.

Conclusion

Glory be to the Father, and to the Son, and to the Holy Spirit,
As it was in the beginning, is now and ever shall be,
World without end. Amen.

Sunday 25th October
Thirtieth Sunday in Ordinary Time
Matthew 22:34–40

When the Pharisees heard that Jesus had silenced the Sadducees, they gathered together, and one of them, a lawyer, asked him a question to test him. "Teacher, which commandment in the law is the greatest?" He said to him, "'You shall love the Lord your God with all your heart, and with all your soul, and with all your mind.' This is the greatest and first commandment. And a second is like it: 'You shall love your neighbor as yourself.' On these two commandments hang all the law and the prophets."

• Isn't it possible for my heart, soul, and mind to want different things sometimes? Jesus calls me to integrity and to wholeness. As I am drawn into relationship with him, I come to love what he loves, to desire what he desires, and to think as he thinks.

• I can do nothing to make God love me more. God's love shines on me as the sun shines on Earth. Real prayer includes resting gratefully in that love. I have a treasure in my heart, which is the limitless love of God for me. But I must share it with my neighbor. I ask to be a true escort of God's love to others.

Monday 26th October
Luke 13:10–17

Now Jesus was teaching in one of the synagogues on the sabbath. And just then there appeared a woman with a spirit that had crippled her for eighteen years. She was bent over and was quite unable to stand up straight. When Jesus saw her, he called her over and said, "Woman, you are set free from your ailment." When he laid his hands on her, immediately she stood up straight and began praising God. But the leader of the synagogue, indignant because Jesus had cured on the sabbath, kept saying to the crowd, "There are six days on which work ought to be done; come on those days and be cured, and not on the sabbath day." But the Lord answered him and said, "You hypocrites! Does not each of you on the sabbath untie his ox or his donkey from the manger, and lead it away to give it water? And ought not this woman, a daughter of Abraham whom

Satan bound for eighteen long years, be set free from this bondage on the sabbath day?" When he said this, all his opponents were put to shame; and the entire crowd was rejoicing at all the wonderful things that he was doing.

- Notice the joy of this woman who, for the first time in eighteen years, can stand up straight. As a person of faith, she praised God who had healed her and given her freedom again. Yet, there is ongoing opposition between the Pharisees and Jesus. Why do I think Jesus' opponents are so insistent about the rules?

- I reflect on these questions: Can I care and heal through the listening skills I offer to others? And, am I also prone to the being hypocritical, and, if so, in what area of my life?

Tuesday 27th October
Luke 13:18–21

[Jesus said to the crowds,] "What is the kingdom of God like? And to what should I compare it? It is like a mustard seed that someone took and sowed in the garden; it grew and became a tree, and the birds of the air made nests in its branches." And again he said, "To what should I compare the kingdom of God? It is like yeast that a woman took and mixed in with three measures of flour until all of it was leavened."

- The kingdom of God is like a small seed that grew and became a large tree. The tree breathes in and out through its leaves and roots. Could I take a little time to breathe in and out, aware of the mysterious source of my life? I consider the second image of the kingdom of God: "It is like the yeast that a woman took and mixed in with three measures of flour until it was all leavened." How does that connect with me?

- Could it be that the simplest acts of kindness and service that I have experienced from others are truly the kingdom of God growing in the world? And that the simplest acts of kindness and service that I have offered to others are truly the kingdom of God growing in my heart? The growth is slow and undramatic. The source of kindness and service is like the source of nature's power: simple, humble, and mysterious.

Wednesday 28th October
Saints Simon and Jude, Apostles
Luke 6:12–16

Now during those days he went out to the mountain to pray; and he spent the night in prayer to God. And when day came, he called his disciples and chose twelve of them, whom he also named apostles: Simon, whom he named Peter, and his brother Andrew, and James, and John, and Philip, and Bartholomew, and Matthew, and Thomas, and James son of Alphaeus, and Simon, who was called the Zealot, and Judas son of James, and Judas Iscariot, who became a traitor.

• It seems that Jesus and his Father spent the whole night in conversation about the choosing of the twelve apostles. Can I imagine how the conversation went? Do I ever consult God about the decisions I have to make, especially those that would have a long-term effect?

• Whenever I see the names of the disciples listed, I dare to include mine among them as I acknowledge that Jesus calls me to be a disciple too. I am not being presumptuous or vain but ask again for the humility I need to be his follower. I thank God for people upon whom I have relied and from whom I have received blessings; their discipleship has built me up in faith, and I pray that I may do likewise for others.

Thursday 29th October
Luke 13:31–35

At that very hour some Pharisees came and said to him, "Get away from here, for Herod wants to kill you." He said to them, "Go and tell that fox for me, 'Listen, I am casting out demons and performing cures today and tomorrow, and on the third day I finish my work. Yet today, tomorrow, and the next day I must be on my way, because it is impossible for a prophet to be killed away from Jerusalem.' Jerusalem, Jerusalem, the city that kills the prophets and stones those who are sent to it! How often have I desired to gather your children together as a hen gathers her brood under her wings, and you were not willing! See, your house is left to you. And I tell you, you will not see me until the time comes when you say, 'Blessed is the one who comes in the name of the Lord.'"

- Despite the fact that his death was imminent, Jesus, because of his great love, continued to care for people who were suffering.
- I ask for this great grace: to persevere in doing good in the face of great difficulties.

Friday 30th October
Luke 14:1–6

On one occasion when Jesus was going to the house of a leader of the Pharisees to eat a meal on the sabbath, they were watching him closely. Just then, in front of him, there was a man who had dropsy. And Jesus asked the lawyers and Pharisees, "Is it lawful to cure people on the sabbath, or not?" But they were silent. So Jesus took him and healed him, and sent him away. Then he said to them, "If one of you has a child or an ox that has fallen into a well, will you not immediately pull it out on a sabbath day?" And they could not reply to this.

- Knowing that he was being watched by his critics, Jesus was able to act in freedom for the good of another. I ask God's help so that I don't hold back from what I know to be good, even at the risk of criticism.
- Even in Jesus' time, it seems that there were those who cared more for animals than they did for their brothers and sisters! Let us pray that our care for creation always begins with championing the rights of the poor and those most in need.

Saturday 31st October
Luke 14:1, 7–11

On one occasion when Jesus was going to the house of a leader of the Pharisees to eat a meal on the sabbath, they were watching him closely. . . . When he noticed how the guests chose the places of honor, he told them a parable. "When you are invited by someone to a wedding banquet, do not sit down at the place of honor, in case someone more distinguished than you has been invited by your host; and the host who invited both of you may come and say to you, 'Give this person your place,' and then in disgrace you would start to take the lowest place. But when you are invited, go and sit down at the lowest place, so that when your host comes, he may say to you, 'Friend, move up higher'; then you will be honored in the presence of all who sit at the table with you. For all who exalt themselves will be humbled, and those who humble themselves will be exalted."

- There is always someone more distinguished than me! Can I rely on the voice of God to assure me of my dignity and worth?

- It may appear that Jesus is talking about a false sort of humility that awaits promotion in the sight of others for its vindication. Then I remember that these words are not just for the Pharisees of Jesus' day. How does he speak to me?

Thirty-First Week in Ordinary Time
November 1—November 7

Something to think and pray about each day this week:

We begin and end with God. Sin is what gets in the way of grace and mercy. Unfortunately, when we think of the word *mercy*, we often think of someone groveling before an evil villain, crying out for his or her life to be spared. We do not have to beg for God's mercy; God offers it as a gift. *Mercy* is another word for compassion or kindness that is directed toward an offender. Mercy is what God always offers to us, despite our offenses. Sin is not the end of the story. Mercy is what awaits us. God's merciful love calls us out of sin and redeems us—saves us, delivers us—from every evil and restores us to grace. When we respond to God's mercy with repentance and contrition, we are restored to grace: our relationship with God is deepened. When we pray for God's mercy, we are praying for the grace we need to accept what God is always offering.

—Joe Paprocki, *Living the Sacraments*

The Presence of God

What is present to me is what has a hold on my becoming.
I reflect on the presence of God always there in love,
amidst the many things that have a hold on me.
I pause and pray that I may let God
affect my becoming in this precise moment.

Freedom

By God's grace I was born to live in freedom. Free to enjoy the pleasures
he created for me. Dear Lord, grant that I may live as you intended, with
complete confidence in your loving care.

Consciousness

To be conscious about something is to be aware of it.
Dear Lord, help me to remember that you gave me life.
Thank you for the gift of life.
Teach me to slow down, to be still and enjoy the pleasures created for me.
To be aware of the beauty that surrounds me: the marvel of mountains,
the calmness of lakes, the fragility of a flower petal. I need to remember
that all these things come from you.

The Word

God speaks to each of us individually. I listen attentively to hear what he
is saying to me. Read the text a few times, then listen. (Please turn to the
Scripture on the following pages. Inspiration points are there, should you
need them. When you are ready, return here to continue.)

Conversation

I begin to talk with Jesus about the Scripture I have just read. What part
of it strikes a chord in me? Perhaps the words of a friend—or some story
I have heard recently—will rise to the surface in my consciousness. If so,
does the story throw light on what the Scripture passage may be saying
to me?

Conclusion

Glory be to the Father, and to the Son, and to the Holy Spirit,
As it was in the beginning, is now and ever shall be,
World without end. Amen.

Sunday 1st November
All Saints

Matthew 5:1–12a

When Jesus saw the crowds, he went up the mountain; and after he sat down, his disciples came to him. Then he began to speak, and taught them, saying: "Blessed are the poor in spirit, for theirs is the kingdom of heaven. Blessed are those who mourn, for they will be comforted. Blessed are the meek, for they will inherit the earth. Blessed are those who hunger and thirst for righteousness, for they will be filled. Blessed are the merciful, for they will receive mercy. Blessed are the pure in heart, for they will see God. Blessed are the peacemakers, for they will be called children of God. Blessed are those who are persecuted for righteousness' sake, for theirs is the kingdom of heaven. Blessed are you when people revile you and persecute you and utter all kinds of evil against you falsely on my account. Rejoice and be glad, for your reward is great in heaven, for in the same way they persecuted the prophets who were before you."

- When Jesus has finished speaking, I sit with him and ask the question that has been lurking in my heart: "Lord, where do I fit in here?" He smiles at me and says, "Well, let's go over these beatitudes together!" So we do. He is wonderfully sensitive and helps me notice even small ways in which I live them out. I come away from our conversation determined to sit lightly to possessions, to be concerned for justice, to be merciful, to be a peacemaker, to be pure in heart. As he says to me, "This is a lifelong agenda, but we will work on it together!"

- Four times we are told that those who appear to be the most unfortunate in this world are actually the ones who are blessed by God. God will right the wrongs they suffer and bring them justice. This turns all worldly values upside down. Have I yet experienced the upturning of my worldly values?

Monday 2nd November
The Commemoration of All the Faithful Departed (All Souls' Day)

John 11:17–27

When Jesus arrived, he found that Lazarus had already been in the tomb for four days. Now Bethany was near Jerusalem, some two miles away, and many of the Jews had come to Martha and Mary to console them about their brother. When Martha heard that Jesus was coming, she went and met him, while Mary stayed at home. Martha said to Jesus, "Lord, if you had been here, my brother would not have died. But even now I know that God will give you whatever you ask of him." Jesus said to her, "Your brother will rise again." Martha said to him, "I know that he will rise again in the resurrection on the last day." Jesus said to her, "I am the resurrection and the life. Those who believe in me, even though they die, will live, and everyone who lives and believes in me will never die. Do you believe this?" She said to him, "Yes, Lord, I believe that you are the Messiah, the Son of God, the one coming into the world."

- As we celebrate our faithful departed, may we take to heart this conversation between Jesus and Martha. Martha is in fresh grief; she has just lost her brother. Yet she looks to Jesus and to her belief in the resurrection. In saying, "even now I know that God will give you whatever you ask," Martha seems to express faith that Jesus might undo even the damage of death. Whatever she thinks at this moment, her trust is in Jesus. May I turn to him when my grief is fresh or when it is years old but still brings much pain.

- Jesus must also feel grief because Martha's brother, Lazarus, was his friend. This friend suffered through illness and death—this is the current reality as Jesus talks with Martha. Hard days have been endured by this family. Jesus stands with Martha, there in that space of grief, and despite their mutual sorrow, he points to the greater reality: resurrection. Do I believe you, Lord? Can I entrust my departed loved ones to the power of your love and your victory over death? Please increase my faith.

Tuesday 3rd November
Luke 14:15–24

One of the dinner guests, on hearing this, said to him, "Blessed is anyone who will eat bread in the kingdom of God!" Then Jesus said to him, "Someone gave a great dinner and invited many. At the time for the dinner he sent his slave to say to those who had been invited, 'Come; for everything is ready now.' But they all alike began to make excuses. The first said to him, 'I have bought a piece of land, and I must go out and see it; please accept my apologies.' Another said, 'I have bought five yoke of oxen, and I am going to try them out; please accept my apologies.' Another said, 'I have just been married, and therefore I cannot come.' So the slave returned and reported this to his master. Then the owner of the house became angry and said to his slave, 'Go out at once into the streets and lanes of the town and bring in the poor, the crippled, the blind, and the lame.' And the slave said, 'Sir, what you ordered has been done, and there is still room.' Then the master said to the slave, 'Go out into the roads and lanes, and compel people to come in, so that my house may be filled. For I tell you, none of those who were invited will taste my dinner.'"

- Jesus' invitation to the banquet is for now. The time and place we meet Jesus and the mystery of God is now. Only the present is alive; the past is gone and the future yet to come. Prayer of any sort is entering into the "now" of God.

- It is easy to become familiar with comforts, to lose the savor of good things. I pray that I might have the generosity of the host who threw the banquet open. I think of how I embody the welcome and freedom that offer the goodness of God to all. Like the people invited to feast, I often resist God's invitation. I take time now just to be present with God, who loves my company.

Wednesday 4th November
Saint Charles Borromeo, Bishop
Luke 14:25–33

Now large crowds were traveling with him; and he turned and said to them, "Whoever comes to me and does not hate father and mother, wife and children, brothers and sisters, yes, and even life itself, cannot be my disciple. Whoever does not carry the cross and follow me cannot be my disciple. For which of you, intending to build a tower, does not first sit down and estimate the cost, to see whether he has enough to complete it? Otherwise, when he has laid a foundation and is not able to finish, all who see it will begin to ridicule him, saying, 'This fellow began to build and was not able to finish.' Or what king, going out to wage war against another king, will not sit down first and consider whether he is able with ten thousand to oppose the one who comes against him with twenty thousand? If he cannot, then, while the other is still far away, he sends a delegation and asks for the terms of peace. So therefore, none of you can become my disciple if you do not give up all your possessions."

• Large crowds were traveling with Jesus; perhaps that is why he spoke so strongly, to ensure that nobody was going along thoughtlessly or was being carried along by the mood of others. Discipleship is personal. Jesus wants to speak to me in particular. What do I hear him saying?

• Before all else, our minds and hearts belong to the Lord. We must do all in our power to seek him first, and all else will fall into place. Teach us to follow you faithfully, O Lord. Prepare our way and help us put our feet on the path that leads to freedom.

Thursday 5th November
Luke 15:1–10

Now all the tax collectors and sinners were coming near to listen to him. And the Pharisees and the scribes were grumbling and saying, "This fellow welcomes sinners and eats with them." So he told them this parable: "Which one of you, having a hundred sheep and losing one of them, does not leave the ninety-nine in the wilderness and go after the one that is lost until he finds it? When he has found it, he lays it on his shoulders and rejoices. And when he comes home, he calls together his friends and neighbors, saying to them, 'Rejoice with me, for I have found my sheep that was lost.' Just so, I tell you, there will be more joy in heaven over one sinner who repents than over ninety-nine righteous people who need no repentance. Or what woman having ten silver coins, if she loses one of them, does not light a lamp, sweep the house, and search carefully until she finds it? When she has found it, she calls together her friends and neighbors, saying, 'Rejoice with me, for I have found the coin that I had lost.' Just so, I tell you, there is joy in the presence of the angels of God over one sinner who repents."

• The parables of the lost sheep and the lost coin illustrate the constant, faithful, unrelenting love of God for each of us, but especially for sinners. God never gives up on anyone. Even apart from sin, there are many other ways in which we can become lost as we journey through life. Have you had such an experience? Do you feel lost now?

- While these parables can stand on their own, note the context in which Jesus tells them. He has drawn criticism from the Pharisees and scribes because he shares table fellowship with tax collectors and sinners. Are we ready to take abuse for our efforts to be inclusive?

Friday 6th November
Luke 16:1–8

Then Jesus said to the disciples, "There was a rich man who had a manager, and charges were brought to him that this man was squandering his property. So he summoned him and said to him, 'What is this that I hear about you? Give me an account of your management, because you cannot be my manager any longer.' Then the manager said to himself, 'What will I do, now that my master is taking the position away from me? I am not strong enough to dig, and I am ashamed to beg. I have decided what to do so that, when I am dismissed as manager, people may welcome me into their homes.' So, summoning his master's debtors one by one, he asked the first, 'How much do you owe my master?' He answered, 'A hundred jugs of olive oil.' He said to him, 'Take your bill, sit down quickly, and make it fifty.' Then he asked another, 'And how much do you owe?' He replied, 'A hundred containers of wheat.' He said to him, 'Take your bill and make it eighty.' And his master commended the dishonest manager because he had acted shrewdly; for the children of this age are more shrewd in dealing with their own generation than are the children of light."

- Jesus calls me to take care of the resources that are available to me. I consider the benefits that I have, such as intelligence, opportunities, and time, and I ask God how I might use them best for God's glory, for the service of others, and for my own growth.

- The manager made preparations for himself in the way that seemed best to him, even dealing dishonestly, possibly to get on the better side of his employer's debtors. Jesus finds value in this man's shrewdness. Lord, do I make an effort to handle what happens to me? Do I prepare myself for what is next? In what way might I be shrewd or wise?

Saturday 7th November

Luke 16:9–15

"And I tell you, make friends for yourselves by means of dishonest wealth so that when it is gone, they may welcome you into the eternal homes. Whoever is faithful in a very little is faithful also in much; and whoever is dishonest in a very little is dishonest also in much. If then you have not been faithful with the dishonest wealth, who will entrust to you the true riches? And if you have not been faithful with what belongs to another, who will give you what is your own? No slave can serve two masters; for a slave will either hate the one and love the other, or be devoted to the one and despise the other. You cannot serve God and wealth." The Pharisees, who were lovers of money, heard all this, and they ridiculed him. So he said to them, "You are those who justify yourselves in the sight of others; but God knows your hearts; for what is prized by human beings is an abomination in the sight of God."

- As I am here, giving time in prayer, my desire to serve God should be an encouragement to me just as it is valued by God. I pray that God may truly be the one I serve throughout this time even as I acknowledge how my heart is often drawn in other directions.

- Jesus is concerned with what is in the heart in the present; he is not preoccupied with the past. I ask for the forgiveness I need so that I may embrace the freedom to which Jesus invites me.

Thirty-Second Week in Ordinary Time
November 8—November 14

Something to think and pray about each day this week:

As a people redeemed, we recognize ourselves as once again having access to God. The role of the priest, then, is to remind people that God has rescued us from sin through Jesus Christ, that God is near to us through Jesus Christ and the Holy Spirit, and that each of us is, in turn, responsible to do the same for others. The priests in our midst are living reminders of the fact that we all "owe" God something—namely, the first fruits of our lives—for rescuing us from sin. This explains why, even at a subconscious level, many of us act differently in the presence of a priest; ultimately their role is symbolic, meaning that their presence reminds us of the presence of God, which, in turn, reminds us of God's wondrous deeds and the fact that we all "owe" God a worthy response.

—Joe Paprocki, *Living the Sacraments*

The Presence of God

"Be still, and know that I am God!" Lord, your words lead us to the calmness and greatness of your presence.

Freedom

God is not foreign to my freedom. The Spirit breathes life into my most intimate desires, gently nudging me toward all that is good. I ask for the grace to let myself be enfolded by the Spirit.

Consciousness

Where do I sense hope, encouragement, and growth in my life? By looking back over the past few months, I may be able to see which activities and occasions have produced rich fruit. If I do notice such areas, I will determine to give those areas both time and space in the future.

The Word

The word of God comes down to us through the Scriptures. May the Holy Spirit enlighten my mind and my heart to respond to the Gospel teachings. (Please turn to the Scripture on the following pages. Inspiration points are there, should you need them. When you are ready, return here to continue.)

Conversation

What is stirring in me as I pray? Am I consoled, troubled, left cold? I imagine Jesus standing or sitting at my side, and I share my feelings with him.

Conclusion

Glory be to the Father, and to the Son, and to the Holy Spirit,
As it was in the beginning, is now and ever shall be,
World without end. Amen.

Sunday 8th November
Thirty-Second Sunday in Ordinary Time
Matthew 25:1–13

"Then the kingdom of heaven will be like this. Ten bridesmaids took their lamps and went to meet the bridegroom. Five of them were foolish, and five were wise. When the foolish took their lamps, they took no oil with them; but the wise took flasks of oil with their lamps. As the bridegroom was delayed, all of them became drowsy and slept. But at midnight there was a shout, 'Look! Here is the bridegroom! Come out to meet him.' Then all those bridesmaids got up and trimmed their lamps. The foolish said to the wise, 'Give us some of your oil, for our lamps are going out.' But the wise replied, 'No! there will not be enough for you and for us; you had better go to the dealers and buy some for yourselves.' And while they went to buy it, the bridegroom came, and those who were ready went with him into the wedding banquet; and the door was shut. Later the other bridesmaids came also, saying, 'Lord, lord, open to us.' But he replied, 'Truly I tell you, I do not know you.' Keep awake therefore, for you know neither the day nor the hour."

- This is a story about being prepared. It's also a story about each person being responsible for herself. When have I relied too much on the spirituality or wisdom of others? In what area of my life does Jesus want me to take responsibility for my own lamp?

- "Keep awake": this is the invitation we meet so often in the Gospels. We are not to be afraid of the Lord's coming but to be awake so that we can welcome him when he arrives. I pray for the grace of a heart that is not distracted, fully alive to Jesus' presence in my world.

Monday 9th November
The Dedication of the Lateran Basilica
John 2:13–22

The Passover of the Jews was near, and Jesus went up to Jerusalem. In the temple he found people selling cattle, sheep, and doves, and the money changers seated at their tables. Making a whip of cords, he drove all of them out of the temple, both the sheep and the cattle. He also poured out the coins of the money changers and overturned their tables. He told those who were selling the doves, "Take these things out of here! Stop making my Father's house a marketplace!" His disciples remembered that it was written, "Zeal for your house will consume me." The Jews then said to him, "What sign can you show us for doing this?" Jesus answered them, "Destroy this temple, and in three days I will raise it up." The Jews then said, "This temple has been under construction for forty-six years, and will you raise it up in three days?" But he was speaking of the temple of his body. After he was raised from the dead, his disciples remembered that he had said this; and they believed the scripture and the word that Jesus had spoken.

- Jesus respected the holy place and time by going up to the temple at the Passover. The times, places, and people of our lives deserve to be honored and recognized for the part they play in helping us understand how God relates to us.

- Jesus cautions us against being careless or nonchalant. I think again about what I need to do to take him seriously. I review my life with the help of the Holy Spirit so that I can see how I honor what is really important.

Tuesday 10th November
Saint Leo the Great, Pope and Doctor of the Church
Luke 17:7–10

"Who among you would say to your slave who has just come in from ploughing or tending sheep in the field, 'Come here at once and take your place at the table'? Would you not rather say to him, 'Prepare supper for me, put on your apron and serve me while I eat and drink; later you may eat and drink'? Do you thank the slave for doing what was commanded? So you also, when you have done all that you were ordered to do, say, 'We are worthless slaves; we have done only what we ought to have done!'"

- Slavery was an accepted part of most ancient cultures, and Jesus' listeners would easily understand the point he is making here. In the modern world we see it as unjust. So, to apply this model, as Jesus does, to the relationship between God and ourselves is likely to make us uneasy. But can we at least accept that our obedience to God is required by the very nature of who God is? That it is not something to boast about or seek a reward for? Especially since our obedience is that of a son or daughter to a loving Father?

- Dear Lord, you didn't spend your time boasting about all you did and all you suffered. You were like a slave, serving us all, washing our feet, dying for us. Make me a bit more like you in your humility and self-forgetfulness.

Wednesday 11th November
Saint Martin of Tours, Bishop
Luke 17:11–19

On the way to Jerusalem Jesus was going through the region between Samaria and Galilee. As he entered a village, ten lepers approached him. Keeping their distance, they called out, saying, "Jesus, Master, have mercy on us!" When he saw them, he said to them, "Go and show yourselves to the priests." And as they went, they were made clean. Then one of them, when he saw that he was healed, turned back, praising God with a loud voice. He prostrated himself at Jesus' feet and thanked him. And he was a Samaritan. Then Jesus asked, "Were not ten made clean? But the other nine, where are they? Was none of them found to return and give praise to God except this foreigner?" Then he said to him, "Get up and go on your way; your faith has made you well."

- The lepers are regarded as unclean and forced to live outside of towns and villages. Even when approaching Jesus, they keep at a distance. Curing a leper restores that person to his or her community. How do poverty, depression, and other kinds of illness rob people of community today?

- I have done it myself, Lord. I go looking for something, advertising my need, seeking sympathy. And when somebody helps me, part of me is muttering, *He was only doing his job, or what you'd expect of a neighbor.* I take kindness for granted and do not bother to say thank you.

Thursday 12th November
Saint Josaphat, Bishop and Martyr
Luke 17:20–25

Once Jesus was asked by the Pharisees when the kingdom of God was coming, and he answered, "The kingdom of God is not coming with things that can be observed; nor will they say, 'Look, here it is!' or 'There it is!' For, in fact, the kingdom of God is among you." Then he said to the disciples, "The days are coming when you will long to see one of the days of the Son of Man, and you will not see it. They will say to you, 'Look there!' or 'Look here!' Do not go, do not set off in pursuit. For as the lightning flashes and lights up the sky from one side to the other, so will the Son of Man be in his day. But first he must endure much suffering and be rejected by this generation."

- Jesus encourages his disciples not to get worked up, or even overly curious, about the end times and the (second) coming of the Son of Man but to concentrate on the here and now and ponder Jesus' own teaching: that the Son of Man must first endure much suffering and be rejected by this generation. This they will soon see acted out in Jerusalem.

- The kingdom of God means the presence, love, and goodness of God. How have I experienced God in my life today? Am I allowing God to take me over more and more? It is thus that the kingdom of God comes to flower in my heart.

Friday 13th November
Saint Frances Xavier Cabrini, Virgin
Luke 17:26–37

"Just as it was in the days of Noah, so too it will be in the days of the Son of Man. They were eating and drinking, and marrying and being given in marriage, until the day Noah entered the ark, and the flood came and destroyed all of them. Likewise, just as it was in the days of Lot: they were eating and drinking, buying and selling, planting and building, but on the day that Lot left Sodom, it rained fire and sulfur from heaven and destroyed all of them—it will be like that on the day that the Son of Man is revealed. On that day, anyone on the housetop who has belongings in the house must not come down to take them away; and likewise anyone in the field must not turn back. Remember Lot's wife. Those who try to make their life secure will lose it, but those who lose their life will keep it. I tell you, on that night there will be two in one bed; one will be taken and the other left. There will be two women grinding meal together; one will be taken and the other left." Then they asked him, "Where, Lord?" He said to them, "Where the corpse is, there the vultures will gather."

- Jesus was himself criticized for eating and drinking, so we can see that he takes issue, not with the activity, but with the loss of attentiveness. I may recognize how I get carried away or distracted and ask God to help me remain aware of what I am doing and how God is with me.

- If I fast today, I ask that it remind me of how my truest and deepest appetites are fed; I may put something good aside so that something better may hold my attention.

Saturday 14th November

Luke 18:1–8

Then Jesus told them a parable about their need to pray always and not to lose heart. He said, "In a certain city there was a judge who neither feared God nor had respect for people. In that city there was a widow who kept coming to him and saying, 'Grant me justice against my opponent.' For a while he refused; but later he said to himself, 'Though I have no fear of God and no respect for anyone, yet because this widow keeps bothering me, I will grant her justice, so that she may not wear me out by continually coming.'" And the Lord said, "Listen to what the unjust judge says. And will not God grant justice to his chosen ones who cry to him day and night? Will he delay long in helping them? I tell you, he will quickly grant justice to them. And yet, when the Son of Man comes, will he find faith on earth?"

- Jesus is confident in God's vindication of those in need; I join him in praying for the resolution of unjust situations and consider how my efforts might be of help.

- The persistence of my prayer speaks of the depth of my need. Even if I find that my prayer has something for which I always ask, I take time to see how God may already be offering an answer.

November 15—November 21

Something to think and pray about each day this week:

We are on this journey to name and embrace sanctuaries—places of grace. Along this journey, some of us have named our sanctuaries. Some of us have discovered a place that has been there all along.

And some of us know how easy it is to forget or to allow the tide of life—busyness, obligations, misfortune, pain—to hide our sanctuary from us. In these times we need to help others create the sanctuary they need and offer help when they feel they cannot create or find it on their own.

Sanctuary is—after all the preaching is done—about liberation. And freedom. And grace. I know this now. Instead of preaching a sermon, many times it would have been more appropriate if I had dismissed the service and told the congregation to run out into the crowds of their day and hug everybody.

—Terry Hershey, *Sanctuary*

The Presence of God

"Come to me, all you who are weary and are carrying heavy burdens, and I will give you rest." Here I am, Lord. I come to seek your presence. I long for your healing power.

Freedom

God is not foreign to my freedom. The Spirit breathes life into my most intimate desires, gently nudging me toward all that is good. I ask for the grace to let myself be enfolded by the Spirit.

Consciousness

I remind myself that I am in the presence of the Lord. I will take refuge in his loving heart. He is my strength in times of weakness. He is my comforter in times of sorrow.

The Word

I take my time to read the word of God slowly, a few times, allowing myself to dwell on anything that strikes me. (Please turn to the Scripture on the following pages. Inspiration points are there, should you need them. When you are ready, return here to continue.)

Conversation

Jesus, you always welcomed little children when you walked on this earth. Teach me to have a childlike trust in you. Teach me to live in the knowledge that you will never abandon me.

Conclusion

Glory be to the Father, and to the Son, and to the Holy Spirit,
As it was in the beginning, is now and ever shall be,
World without end. Amen.

Sunday 15th November
Thirty-Third Sunday in Ordinary Time
Matthew 25:14–30

"For it is as if a man, going on a journey, summoned his slaves and en-trusted his property to them; to one he gave five talents, to another two, to another one, to each according to his ability. Then he went away. The one who had received the five talents went off at once and traded with them, and made five more talents. In the same way, the one who had the two talents made two more talents. But the one who had received the one talent went off and dug a hole in the ground and hid his master's money. After a long time the master of those slaves came and settled accounts with them. Then the one who had received the five talents came forward, bringing five more talents, saying, 'Master, you handed over to me five talents; see, I have made five more talents.' His master said to him, 'Well done, good and trustworthy slave; you have been trustworthy in a few things, I will put you in charge of many things; enter into the joy of your master.' And the one with the two talents also came forward, saying, 'Master, you handed over to me two talents; see, I have made two more talents.' His master said to him, 'Well done, good and trustworthy slave; you have been trustworthy in a few things, I will put you in charge of many things; enter into the joy of your master.' Then the one who had re-ceived the one talent also came forward, saying, 'Master, I knew that you were a harsh man, reaping where you did not sow, and gathering where you did not scatter seed; so I was afraid, and I went and hid your talent in the ground. Here you have what is yours.' But his master replied, 'You wicked and lazy slave! You knew, did you, that I reap where I did not sow, and gather where I did not scatter? Then you ought to have invested my money with the bankers, and on my return I would have received what was my own with interest. So take the talent from him, and give it to the one with the ten talents. For to all those who have, more will be given, and they will have an abundance; but from those who have nothing, even what they have will be taken away. As for this worthless slave, throw him into the outer darkness, where there will be weeping and gnashing of teeth.'"

- This is a parable of wasted opportunities! We are each gifted uniquely by God, and we must use our giftedness as God wishes. What matters isn't what we are given but what we do with our gift. Do not be afraid to use your talents. Stop comparing your gifts with the gifts of others. Share what you have received. To bury your giftedness leads only to sorrow and regret—the "gnashing of teeth."

- The parable can remind us of the beautiful hymn attributed to Saint Teresa of Avila: "Christ has no body now but yours. No hands, no feet on earth but yours. Yours are the eyes through which he looks compassion on this world, Yours are the feet with which he walks to do good."

Monday 16th November
Luke 18:35–43

As [Jesus] approached Jericho, a blind man was sitting by the roadside begging. When he heard a crowd going by, he asked what was happening. They told him, "Jesus of Nazareth is passing by." Then he shouted, "Jesus, Son of David, have mercy on me!" Those who were in front sternly ordered him to be quiet; but he shouted even more loudly, "Son of David, have mercy on me!" Jesus stood still and ordered the man to be brought to him; and when he came near, he asked him, "What do you want me to do for you?" He said, "Lord, let me see again." Jesus said to him, "Receive your sight; your faith has saved you." Immediately he regained his sight and followed him, glorifying God; and all the people, when they saw it, praised God.

- I take some time to allow Jesus to ask me, "What do you want me to do for you?" I hear the patience and love with which I am addressed and take time in answering with what is in my heart.
- The poor can be a nuisance because they disturb our comfortable lives. I talk with Jesus about my attitude toward the needy. I see that Jesus reverses human values and puts this blind beggar first. I ask for grace to do the same.

Tuesday 17th November
Saint Elizabeth of Hungary, Religious
Luke 19:1–10

He entered Jericho and was passing through it. A man was there named Zacchaeus; he was a chief tax collector and was rich. He was trying to see who Jesus was, but on account of the crowd he could not, because he was short in stature. So he ran ahead and climbed a sycamore tree to see him, because he was going to pass that way. When Jesus came to the place, he looked up and said to him, "Zacchaeus, hurry and come down; for I must stay at your house today." So he hurried down and was happy to welcome him. All who saw it began to grumble and said, "He has gone to be the guest of one who is a sinner." Zacchaeus stood there and said to the Lord, "Look, half of my possessions, Lord, I will give to the poor; and if I have defrauded anyone of anything, I will pay back four times as much." Then Jesus said to him, "Today salvation has come to this house, because he too is a son of Abraham. For the Son of Man came to seek out and to save the lost."

- Jesus has come to seek out and to save the lost. This final verse is the lens through which we are asked to contemplate this entire story. Zacchaeus is a high-ranking tax collector in the pay of the Roman occupiers. To his fellow Jews he is a traitor and, in their words, a sinner. Yet he is the man whom Jesus chooses to be his host during his stay in Jericho. What does this say about Jesus? About his ministry? About his priorities? Do I share these, or am I among the naysayers and critics?

- How do you imagine Zacchaeus relating this story to his friends weeks or months from now?

Wednesday 18th November
Matthew 14:22–33

Immediately he made the disciples get into the boat and go on ahead to the other side, while he dismissed the crowds. And after he had dismissed the crowds, he went up the mountain by himself to pray. When evening came, he was there alone, but by this time the boat, battered by the waves, was far from the land, for the wind was against them. And early in the morning he came walking toward them on the sea. But when the disciples saw him walking on the sea, they were terrified, saying, "It is a ghost!" And they cried out in fear. But immediately Jesus spoke to them and said, "Take heart, it is I; do not be afraid." Peter answered him, "Lord, if it is you, command me to come to you on the water." He said, "Come." So Peter got out of the boat, started walking on the water, and came toward

Jesus. But when he noticed the strong wind, he became frightened, and beginning to sink, he cried out, "Lord, save me!" Jesus immediately reached out his hand and caught him, saying to him, "You of little faith, why did you doubt?" When they got into the boat, the wind ceased. And those in the boat worshiped him, saying, "Truly you are the Son of God."

- Identify with the feelings of Jesus as he prays, having heard of the death of John the Baptist. What are his thoughts? What is the content of his prayer? Compose a prayer that you think Jesus might have made. Imagine yourself in the boat with the disciples and listen to what they say as the storm develops.

- Listen to the disciples as they observe the figure coming across the water! Note how Peter's trust slips when he turns his focus from Jesus to himself. Reflect on your own life and draw some conclusion.

Thursday 19th November
Luke 19:41–44

As he came near and saw the city, he wept over it, saying, "If you, even you, had only recognized on this day the things that make for peace! But now they are hidden from your eyes. Indeed, the days will come upon you, when your enemies will set up ramparts around you and surround you, and hem you in on every side. They will crush you to the ground, you and your children within you, and they will not leave within you one stone upon another; because you did not recognize the time of your visitation from God."

- We often see Jesus filled with longing for the people he meets; as the sick and sinners come before him, he invites them to see their wholeness before God. Here, he looks at the city of Jerusalem and prays for its populace, wishing that it might receive what God is offering. If I consider how Jesus looks at me, I realize that he longs for my growth, for me to embrace all the possibilities God offers to me each day.

- Images of threat and destruction can haunt and immobilize us if we neglect to see that there is always an alternative, an offer of life. If these words of Jesus appear to be grim, I listen again to notice what he is longing for.

Friday 20th November
Luke 19:45–48

Then he entered the temple and began to drive out those who were selling things there; and he said, "It is written, 'My house shall be a house of
prayer'; but you have made it a den of robbers." Every day he was teaching
in the temple. The chief priests, the scribes, and the leaders of the people
kept looking for a way to kill him; but they did not find anything they
could do, for all the people were spellbound by what they heard.

- My poor heart is a "house of prayer." God is active there, transforming me, even though I notice the changes only later. In praying with
  Scripture, am I ever spellbound by what I read?

- In listening to Jesus, the minds of the people are opening as the minds
  of the officials are closing. I think of my habitual reactions and ask
  Jesus to shape them. Jesus calls me to the clarity with which he saw
  the world.

Saturday 21st November
The Presentation of the Blessed Virgin Mary
Luke 20:27–40

Some Sadducees, those who say there is no resurrection, came to him and
asked him a question, "Teacher, Moses wrote for us that if a man's brother
dies, leaving a wife but no children, the man shall marry the widow and
raise up children for his brother. Now there were seven brothers; the first
married, and died childless; then the second and the third married her,
and so in the same way all seven died childless. Finally the woman also
died. In the resurrection, therefore, whose wife will the woman be? For
the seven had married her." Jesus said to them, "Those who belong to
this age marry and are given in marriage; but those who are considered
worthy of a place in that age and in the resurrection from the dead neither
marry nor are given in marriage. Indeed they cannot die anymore, because they are like angels and are children of God, being children of the
resurrection. And the fact that the dead are raised Moses himself showed,
in the story about the bush, where he speaks of the Lord as the God of
Abraham, the God of Isaac, and the God of Jacob. Now he is God not of
the dead, but of the living; for to him all of them are alive." Then some of

the scribes answered, "Teacher, you have spoken well." For they no longer dared to ask him another question.

- The Sadducees scorned the idea of rising from the dead. Jesus lifts them from the tangles in which their theology has trapped them. "He is God not of the dead but of the living, for to him all are alive." We are part of that cosmos that transcends space and time and embraces not merely Abraham, Isaac, and Jacob but our parents and all our ancestors to the beginning of creation. In the resurrection we will share the eternal *Now* of God.

- I watch as Jesus tries to raise the minds of his questioners to a higher level. I ask him to share his vision, so that I may see something of the wonderful plans God has for us all.

November 22—November 28

Something to think and pray about each day this week:

Since spiritual wellness is all about being aligned with the Spirit, we should ask, What is God fired up about? I think he is most fired up by selfless love. Mercy. Compassion. Justice. God's great imagination envisions a world in which the hungry are fed, the thirsty are given drink, the sick are tended to, the homeless are sheltered, the imprisoned are visited, the naked are clothed, and the estranged are welcomed. A healthy spirituality compels us to be present to people in need, offering them the possibility of seeing the presence of God, which is obstructed by the pain in their lives. Dorothy Day insisted that everything a baptized person should do every day should be directly or indirectly related to the corporal and spiritual works of mercy. She knew that God's fire could be found there. If you are looking for God—the goal of spirituality—these are the places to look. As the traditional Christian hymn *Ubi Caritas* reminds us: "Where charity and love prevail, there God is ever found."

The God we seek is on fire, has a mission, and invites you and me to be a part of it.

Imagine that.

—Joe Paprocki, *7 Keys to Spiritual Wellness*

The Presence of God

"I am standing at the door, knocking" says the Lord. What a wonderful privilege that the Lord of all creation desires to come to me. I welcome his presence.

Freedom

I will ask God's help
to be free from my own preoccupations,
to be open to God in this time of prayer,
to come to know, love, and serve God more.

Consciousness

In God's loving presence I unwind the past day,
starting from now and looking back, moment by moment.
I gather in all the goodness and light, in gratitude.
I attend to the shadows and what they say to me,
seeking healing, courage, forgiveness.

The Word

Now I turn to the Scripture set out for me this day. I read slowly over the words and see if any sentence or sentiment appeals to me. (Please turn to the Scripture on the following pages. Inspiration points are there, should you need them. When you are ready, return here to continue.)

Conversation

Sometimes I wonder what I might say if I were to meet you in person, Lord.
I think I might say, "Thank you" because you are always there for me.

Conclusion

I thank God for these moments we have spent together and for any insights I have been given concerning the text.

Sunday 22nd November
Our Lord Jesus Christ, King of the Universe
Matthew 25:31–46

"When the Son of Man comes in his glory, and all the angels with him, then he will sit on the throne of his glory. All the nations will be gathered before him, and he will separate people one from another as a shepherd separates the sheep from the goats, and he will put the sheep at his right hand and the goats at the left. Then the king will say to those at his right hand, 'Come, you that are blessed by my Father, inherit the kingdom prepared for you from the foundation of the world; for I was hungry and you gave me food, I was thirsty and you gave me something to drink, I was a stranger and you welcomed me, I was naked and you gave me clothing, I was sick and you took care of me, I was in prison and you visited me.' Then the righteous will answer him, 'Lord, when was it that we saw you hungry and gave you food, or thirsty and gave you something to drink? And when was it that we saw you a stranger and welcomed you, or naked and gave you clothing? And when was it that we saw you sick or in prison and visited you?' And the king will answer them, 'Truly I tell you, just as you did it to one of the least of these who are members of my family, you did it to me.' Then he will say to those at his left hand, 'You that are accursed, depart from me into the eternal fire prepared for the devil and his angels; for I was hungry and you gave me no food, I was thirsty and you gave me nothing to drink, I was a stranger and you did not welcome me, naked and you did not give me clothing, sick and in prison and you did not visit me.' Then they also will answer, 'Lord, when was it that we saw you hungry or thirsty or a stranger or naked or sick or in prison, and did not take care of you?' Then he will answer them, 'Truly I tell you, just as you did not do it to one of the least of these, you did not do it to me.' And these will go away into eternal punishment, but the righteous into eternal life."

- This long and exciting parable has a simple message: "Minister to the needy around you, or else you are missing the whole point of living!" Saint Matthew's hearers had difficulty with what would happen to non-Jews, since they themselves were the Chosen People. Jesus says that with his coming into the world, everyone is a "chosen person." Everyone is to be treated with limitless respect. This is the way to get ready for God's final community of love. Jesus is already present but in disguise, in every person. Only at the end will he and they be revealed "in glory."

- What do I see when I see the needy? Do I focus on the hidden glory of others? How would I fare if human history were to be terminated today?

Monday 23rd November
Luke 21:1–4

He looked up and saw rich people putting their gifts into the treasury; he also saw a poor widow put in two small copper coins. He said, "Truly I tell you, this poor widow has put in more than all of them; for all of them have contributed out of their abundance, but she out of her poverty has put in all she had to live on."

- A simple act inspired Jesus to appreciation, to see the woman's action as an invitation to live with trust. I ask God to help me observe what is going on around me and to appreciate even small actions of love and care.
- I ask for God's help to see the best in the small and impoverished everyday gestures that I might notice. I bring these moments before God for blessing. Talk of recession makes us cautious. Generosity can be a sign of the goodness of God. In a time of constraint, it may be all the more necessary.

Tuesday 24th November
Saint Andrew Dūng-Lạc, Priest, and Companions, Martyrs
Luke 21:5–11

When some were speaking about the temple, how it was adorned with beautiful stones and gifts dedicated to God, he said, "As for these things that you see, the days will come when not one stone will be left upon another; all will be thrown down." They asked him, "Teacher, when will this be, and what will be the sign that this is about to take place?" And he said, "Beware that you are not led astray; for many will come in my name and say, 'I am he!' and, 'The time is near!' Do not go after them. When you hear of wars and insurrections, do not be terrified; for these things must take place first, but the end will not follow immediately." Then he said to them, "Nation will rise against nation, and kingdom against kingdom; there will be great earthquakes, and in various places famines and plagues; and there will be dreadful portents and great signs from heaven."

- The temple was built to honor God and as a place of prayer, but there were those who didn't see beyond its surface. When our cathedrals and holy places become tourist sites, they risk becoming, in the eyes of Jesus, empty of their true meaning. Let us pray that we may appreciate the reverence and intentions of those who have gone before us, even as we value the beauty of their self-expression.

- Given the significance of the temple for Jewish religion and culture, Jesus' words could be seen as symbolizing the end of their messianic hopes. Nothing could ever be the same again. Did I have to deal with painful endings during the past few years? Deaths of loved ones, failed relationships, illness, job loss? Where was God for me during these crises? Did any of these endings bring me freedom or open up new opportunities?

Wednesday 25th November
Luke 21:12–19

"But before all this occurs, they will arrest you and persecute you; they will hand you over to synagogues and prisons, and you will be brought before kings and governors because of my name. This will give you an opportunity to testify. So make up your minds not to prepare your defense in advance; for I will give you words and a wisdom that none of your opponents will be able to withstand or contradict. You will be betrayed even by parents and brothers, by relatives and friends; and they will put some of you to death. You will be hated by all because of my name. But not a hair of your head will perish. By your endurance you will gain your souls."

- It is easy for people to measure their self-worth by the number of "likes" and "followers" they accumulate on social media. Jesus asks us not to confuse popularity with happiness. In fact, living by kingdom values will require endurance and faith.

- Sporadic persecution of Christians had already begun when Luke was writing his Gospel. Similar persecution is also happening in many parts of the world today. Are those of us living in more tolerant countries sensitive to the sufferings of our fellow Christians who find themselves hated by all because of Jesus' name? Are we in effective solidarity with them? Do we pray for them? Engage in advocacy on their behalf?

Thursday 26th November
Luke 21:20–28

[Jesus said to his disciples,] "When you see Jerusalem surrounded by armies, then know that its desolation has come near. Then those in Judea must flee to the mountains, and those inside the city must leave it, and those out in the country must not enter it; for these are days of vengeance, as a fulfillment of all that is written. Woe to those who are pregnant and to those who are nursing infants in those days! For there will be great distress on the earth and wrath against this people; they will fall by the edge of the sword and be taken away as captives among all nations; and Jerusalem will be trampled on by the Gentiles, until the times of the Gentiles are fulfilled. There will be signs in the sun, the moon, and the stars, and on the earth distress among nations confused by the roaring of the sea and the waves. People will faint from fear and foreboding of what is coming upon the world, for the powers of the heavens will be shaken. Then they will see 'the Son of Man coming in a cloud' with power and great glory. Now when these things begin to take place, stand up and raise your heads, because your redemption is drawing near."

- Here we see the convergence of two events: the destruction of Jerusalem and the coming of the Son of Man. One happens within history, and the other marks the end of history. Notice how aware Jesus is of the horrors of war, especially how the innocent and vulnerable suffer. I pray for all who are living right now through war, disease, and famine.

- The Second Coming will be announced by strange cosmic happenings. These will cause terror and confusion among all earth's peoples. But believers need have no fear. Indeed, they are to stand up and raise their heads because Christ's coming is the final stage of their redemption (or liberation). "The one who testifies to these things says, 'Surely

I am coming soon.' Amen. Come, Lord Jesus!" (Revelation 22:20). Is this my desire today? Do I long to be with him?

Friday 27th November
Luke 21:29–33

Then [Jesus] told them a parable: "Look at the fig tree and all the trees; as soon as they sprout leaves you can see for yourselves and know that summer is already near. So also, when you see these things taking place, you know that the kingdom of God is near. Truly I tell you, this generation will not pass away until all things have taken place. Heaven and earth will pass away, but my words will not pass away."

• What signs of God working do I see today? In my own life? In the world around me?

• The universe is ancient; its millions of years of age boggle the mind. And yet it is passing—an ephemeral thing compared to the word of God, which will not pass away. I say a prayer of thanks that in this vast universe I am important to God, and loved.

Saturday 28th November
Luke 21:34–36

[Jesus said to the disciples,] "Be on guard so that your hearts are not weighed down with dissipation and drunkenness and the worries of this life, and that day catch you unexpectedly, like a trap. For it will come upon all who live on the face of the whole earth. Be alert at all times, praying that you may have the strength to escape all these things that will take place, and to stand before the Son of Man."

• Supervision is important when we have responsibilities to meet. A good supervisor helps keep us up to the mark. God is the ultimate supervisor who wants only what is best for us. Let us stay awake to welcome him when he comes.

• Prayer can be difficult. Remember that the strength we need to pray, as for every aspect of our lives, comes from God. We just need to hang in there.

Sacred Space
YOUR DAILY PRAYER ONLINE

Make a 'Sacred Space' in *your* day

www.sacredspace.ie

Visit our **online prayer space** and join the 15,000 daily participants in our global prayer community as you go through your day.

Create your own quiet time anywhere, any time with our daily prayer, scripture, reflections and suggested readings.

ihs *the* JESUITS *in* IRELAND

Inspired by the Ignatian practice of 'finding God in all things', Sacred Space is brought to you by the Irish Jesuits.

THE IRISH JESUITS ⁂ Sacred Space

A Little Book
of
Encouragement

SACRED
SPACE

From the website www.sacredspace.ie

148pp

€9.95

available from all good bookshops,
or from www.messenger.ie